Roman Britain

Blackwell Classic Histories of England

This series comprises new editions of seminal histories of England. Written by the leading scholars of their generation, the books represent both major works of historical analysis and interpretation and clear, authoritative overviews of the major periods of English history. All the volumes have been revised for inclusion within the series and include updated material to aid further study. *Blackwell Classic Histories of England* provide a forum in which these key works can continue to be enjoyed by scholars, students and general readers alike.

Published

Roman Britain
Third Edition
Malcolm Todd

England and Its Rulers: 1066–1272
Second Edition
M. T. Clanchy

Church and People: England 1450–1660
Second Edition
Claire Cross

Politics and Nation: England 1450–1660
Fifth Edition
David Loades

Forthcoming

Crown and Nobility: England 1272–1485
Second Edition
Anthony Tuck

ROMAN BRITAIN

Third Edition

Malcolm Todd

BLACKWELL
Publishers

First published by Fontana Press 1981
Second edition published 1997
Third edition published by Blackwell Publishers Ltd 1999

2 4 6 8 10 9 7 5 3 1

Blackwell Publishers Ltd
108 Cowley Road
Oxford OX4 1JF
UK

Blackwell Publishers Inc.
350 Main Street
Malden, Massachusetts 02148
USA

British Library Cataloguing in Publication Data

A CIP catalogue record for this book is available from the British Library.

Library of Congress Cataloging-in-Publication Data

Todd, Malcolm, FSA.
Roman Britain / Malcolm Todd. – 3rd ed.
p. cm. – (Blackwell classic histories of England)
Rev. ed. of: Roman Britain, 55 BC–AD 400. 1981.
Includes bibliographical references and index.
ISBN 0–631–21463–1 (hbk: alk. paper). – ISBN 0–631–21464–X (pbk: alk. paper)
1. Great Britain – History – Roman period, 55 BC–AD 449.
2. Romans – Great Britain – History. I. Todd, Malcolm, FSA. Roman Britain, 55 BC–AD 400. II. Title. III. Series.
DA145.T63 1999
936.2'04–dc21 98–51845
CIP

Typeset in 10.5 pt on 12.5 pt Sabon by PureTech India Ltd, Pondicherry
http://www.puretech.com
Printed in Great Britain by TJ International, Padstow, Cornwall

This book is printed on acid-free paper

Contents

Figures

Plates

Preface to the Third Edition

A new edition of a book which has been continuously in print for nearly two decades calls for some kind of apologia, or at least explanation. The pace of discovery and publication has scarcely slackened since the first appearance of this volume and it is no exaggeration to say that some of the most significant accessions to our knowledge of Roman Britain have been made in these same years. Assessment of wider themes has been made in a number of major monographs, enabling a fuller understanding of what we may call the cultural history of Britain under Rome. Perspectives also change and need constant scrutiny. Some of those currently being applied are salutary and stimulating: others are more suspect. This book is a *history* and I have tried to portray Roman Britain as part of an Empire, not merely as an island with its own idiosyncratic structures and traditions, important as these are. It does not require wide knowledge of other parts of the Roman world to make one realize how different Britannia was.

I am very grateful to Blackwell Publishers for the opportunity to revise parts of this book and to present it in a new format. I have been encouraged to hear in many communications that readers have found earlier editions so useful.

Malcolm Todd
Trevelyan College, Durham
September 1998

Preface to the Second Edition

The past fifteen years have witnessed an immense outpouring of general studies and detailed monographs on the Roman province of Britannia. I have tried to take account of the most significant of these in this second edition, though there is much that has been omitted for lack of space. Roman Britain continues to surprise us by the range of historical as well as purely archaeological material which it yields. The Vindolanda texts stand out among any of the new documentary sources revealed anywhere in the Roman world, but there is much else. The focus of the book remains the history of Roman Britain. The wealth and diversity of the archaeological sources can only be displayed and assessed in other volumes. I am very grateful to Fontana Press for the opportunity to update this text after the lapse of several years and to innumerable friends and colleagues who have, consciously or otherwise, contributed to the work.

Malcolm Todd
Durham, November 1996

Preface

In this volume I have attempted a brief history of the Roman province of Britain, with the needs of students very much in mind. Remarkably, despite the flood of books on Roman Britain over the past twenty years, only one history of the province has so far appeared, the excellent and indispensable *Britannia* of Professor S. S. Frere. There is thus ample space for other historical treatments of the subject, not least because every year brings new and important evidence to light. In few periods of British history can new discoveries have such immediate impact. The planning of the book is simple. I have eschewed the practice of providing separate discussions of such themes as the cities and towns, the countryside and industry, prefering a consecutive narrative in which these strands, so far as is possible, are woven together.

I owe a debt of thanks to many friends and colleagues who have supplied me with information or discussed matters with me. Three in particular have generously allowed me to read important works before publication: Professors E. A. Thompson, A. C. Thomas and K. Cameron. I am further indebted to my colleagues, Professor A. C. Thomas, Dr V. A. Maxfield and Professor C. J. Holdsworth for their comments on parts of the manuscript of this book and to Professor G. R. Elton for helpful criticism of a final draft. The remaining defects are the author's alone.

I

Discovery and the First Invasions

The discovery of Britain

Knowledge of Britain among the peoples of the Mediterranean down to the first century BC was neither extensive nor detailed. To Greek geographers it was a land of unknown size, wrapped in mists beyond an uncertain sea. Direct contact was sporadic and largely inspired by commercial interest, especially in mineral resources. The fame of Britain rested principally upon her deposits of tin in the south-western peninsula of *Belerion*, and the earliest accounts of the island and its inhabitants were circulated in Mediterranean ports by explorer-traders. The earliest voyage of which any report survives is that of the merchant-adventurer Pytheas of Massilia at a date in the later fourth century BC, perhaps about 325.[1] He not only visited the tin deposits of Cornwall and the tin depot of St Michael's Mount, but circumnavigated the island and passed on to Northern Germany and the Baltic islands. What should have been one of the most celebrated feats of ancient navigation and one of the most invaluable early accounts of North-western Europe is known to us only in fragments, for most later commentators rejected Pytheas' account of the lands and peoples he saw. But there were Mediterranean sailors who could have offered corroboration of some of what Pytheas described. From at least the sixth century BC, South-western Britain and the peninsula of Brittany were linked by commerce, and Brittany was perhaps visited by Carthaginian and Tartessian traders. Archaeological traces of such contacts are meagre indeed and they may never be otherwise. The Greek pottery vessels of the fourth century from Teignmouth (Devon) are not above suspicion, but there can be no doubt about the Sicilian bronze axe found in the sea off Hengistbury Head (Dorset), and from later periods the evidence for direct contact between Britain and the Western Mediterranean is steadily accumulating.[2] Little is known as yet of the social and economic impact of this trade on the peoples of southern Britain. There may have been only limited effects before 100 BC. The occurrence of Hellenistic silver and bronze coins in Dorset and Devon is particularly striking, especially as many of these pieces are of types which were circulating in Mediterranean ports in the third to first centuries BC but are unlikely to have remained current later. They may, then, be fairly regarded as indicating the areas of the Mediterranean from which the trade with Britain was promoted. Southern Italy, Sicily, Cisalpine Gaul and Provence are prominently to the fore.[3]

Britain thus lay at the north-western margin of a network of commerce which stretched from the western Mediterranean, over Spain, southern Gaul and the Atlantic and Channel shores. After Pytheas, the literary record is virtually blank for a century and a half, but the archaeological evidence for contact, though still sporadic, clearly indicates exchange linkages between South-western Britain and the Roman West. South-eastern Britain had long-established connections with northern Europe, especially with northern Gaul and the regions about the lower Rhine. Commercial exchange no doubt played some part here, but a more powerful connection was forged by the movement of elites from the Continent into Britain, not necessarily in numbers, but sufficient to transmit the Celtic language (about the middle of the first millennium BC), a material technology derived from the Iron Age cultures of Hallstatt and La Tène, and a social structure which was embedded in the tribal polities between the Rhine and the Channel. From the late second century BC onward, political links between the peoples of Gaul and some of the southern British tribes were developing apace, a process which was to accelerate as Roman power was extended across Gaul.

In the second century BC, trade was regularly conducted between the Mediterranean and South-western Britain along a route which combined an overland journey to the Atlantic coast of Gaul with a sea-passage around Brittany to Cornwall, with Gaulish merchants, especially the Veneti, taking an active role in these transactions. By this date Cornish tin was being transported to the port of *Corbilo* on the estuary of the Loire and thence to Massilia for distribution in the Mediterranean lands. Publius Licinius Crassus, when governor of Hispania Ulterior in 96–93 BC, opened up the western sea-route to the Tin Islands (Cassiterides) to anyone who wished to try his luck.[4] The shallow mines and peaceable natives visited by Crassus were probably in North-western Spain. Direct contact by sea with Britain had not yet been made, though it followed shortly. Gaulish entrepreneurs and others already knew South-western Britain well. Not only could copies of Massiliote silver coins reach Cornwall and Gallic gold

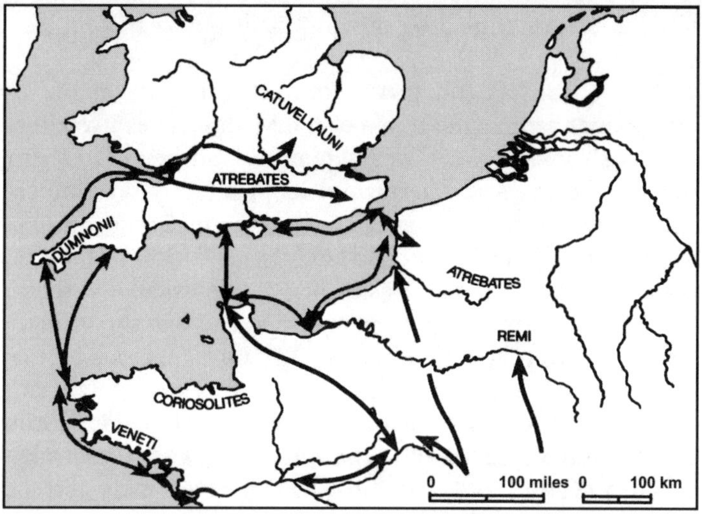

Figure 1 Trade connections between later prehistoric Britain and the Continent.

be hoarded there: the south-western pottery tradition also plainly reveals the impress of Armorican decorative styles. In the decades after 100 BC, there began the importation of Mediterranean wine borne in amphorae into certain parts of Southern Britain. Hengistbury Head, on the Dorset coast adjacent to Christchurch harbour, was apparently the major British point of entry for traded goods from the western Mediterranean and Gaul in the first century BC, and a distribution point for British commodities to the Continent.[5] The former included wine carried in amphorae, pottery, glass and coinage. The exports from Britain included a variety of metals, silver, lead, copper, possibly some gold, cattle products, probably corn and no doubt slaves, as Strabo reports. Further to the west, at Mount Batten on Plymouth Sound, another port was both receiving and exporting goods, probably mainly metals from south-western deposits. There will have been other trading places. There is evidence for Gaulish imports in the late Iron Age at Portland Bill in Dorset, and the long estuaries of Devon and Cornwall offered easy points of entry for navigators and safe anchorages close to relatively rich deposits of metal. In the later first century BC, contacts had less to do with commerce than with diplomacy, especially so far as south-eastern Britain was concerned. Rich gifts of silver drinking-sets, fine bronzes, glass, pottery and wine amphorae passed into the hands of British elites and were in due course consigned to their graves. The closest concentration of these rich burials lies in Hertfordshire and Essex, precisely the area occupied by the dominant power-bloc in late Iron Age Britain.

Apart from traders' and prospectors' descriptions of the island, Britain remained largely unknown to the Mediterranean world before Julius Caesar's invasions; it was a remote land beyond Ocean and thus outside the true *orbis terrarum*. Its geography was imperfectly understood, even in crude outline, before the mid-first century BC.[6] Ptolemy, writing in the mid-second century AD, seems to have had no astronomical data for the islands of Britain: he calculated their position by reference to the latitude of Massilia. It is not surprising, then, that before the conquest by Claudius Britain could not be mapped with any certitude. The notion that Britain was a roughly triangular island, the three points of which were the capes *Belerium* (Cornwall), *Orcas* (Northern Scotland) and *Cantium* (Kent), goes back to Pytheas in the fourth century and was subsequently given wide currency by Eratosthenes of Cyrene before 200 BC. From Eratosthenes, too, may have been ultimately derived the long-held error that Scotland bent away to the north-east from the rest of the island, a conceit perpetuated by Marinus of Tyre and thus reaching Ptolemy. From Pytheas to Caesar there was little progress in the definition of British geography. Caesar himself added nothing to the corpus of knowledge except for the south-eastern corner of England. For the rest, his information on the land and its inhabitants is largely derived from the writings of Posidonius and partly perhaps from the erudite Timaeus, whose work takes us back again to Pytheas. There was nothing to dispel the idea that Britain belonged almost to another world. Hence the extraordinary clamour raised by Caesar's first expedition. Even a century after that, the troops of Claudius felt that they were being led out of the known world.

The first invasions

divus Iulius . . . potest videri ostendisse posteris, non tradidisse

Caesar's two expeditions to Britain are among the least important, and certainly the least successful, of that conqueror's career. In the course of early British history, too, they were scarcely of great significance. Brilliantly lit for us by Caesar's own account, the two excursions did little or nothing to alter the relationship between the Britons and Rome. That was to come later and as a result of diplomacy, not invasion. Commercial and cultural contacts across the

Channel in later days were to do far more than Caesar's campaigns to bring Britain within the Roman orbit. Even the passage of Caesar's army through South-eastern Britain has left no certain trace for the modern observer.[7]

After only two seasons of campaigning, Caesar had overrun almost all of Gaul and received the submission of the major tribes. His claim that this vast land was completely pacified was premature, but in 56 Caesar could go to the conference of Lucca with the easy confidence that a further command in the Transalpine province would be his. Britain, of course, was not included in his mandate, and there is no good reason for thinking that a campaign in Britain was in anybody's mind except Caesar's in the summer of 56. It may not yet have even entered Caesar's thoughts. The completion of the conquest of Gaul was still the immediate task.

In the spring of 56, the Veneti of Brittany had risen in revolt against Caesar. They were a powerful tribe whose skilled seamen held a virtual monopoly of the trade with South-western Britain. Their neighbours were drawn into the revolt, along with the Menapii and Morini of the coast of Belgium, immediately opposite Kent. Auxiliaries from Britain also joined the rebels, from which tribes is unknown. Their participation gave Caesar what he needed, a plausible pretext for an expedition to Britain which might be both punitive and exploratory. But that attractive scheme had to wait until the serious revolt of the maritime peoples was quelled. The task proved no easy one. The Veneti and their allies showed unusual resource in a campaign of attrition, concentrating their limited supplies of grain in their numerous promontory forts on the rocky coast and relying on their fleet to hinder the transport of Roman supplies. Caesar's task thus involved the breaking of Venetic sea-power, either in a battle or by depriving their fleet of its shore-bases. Either course was difficult. The Venetic fleet was numerically superior to the Roman and, one might guess, the captains more skilful in dealing with the Channel tides and weather conditions, while the potential bases on the broken Breton coastline were numberless and difficult of access.

After storming a number of the cliff strongholds, Caesar decided that the issue could only be settled by a naval engagement. The Veneti played into his hands by taking up station in front of the Roman fleet. The manoeuvrable oared Roman vessels were able to dart into the midst of the Gaulish fleet, destroy their sails and rigging and open the way to boarding-parties. The Roman victory was total. The Venetic fleet was destroyed, their nobles liquidated and many of humbler rank sold into slavery. The commercial connection between

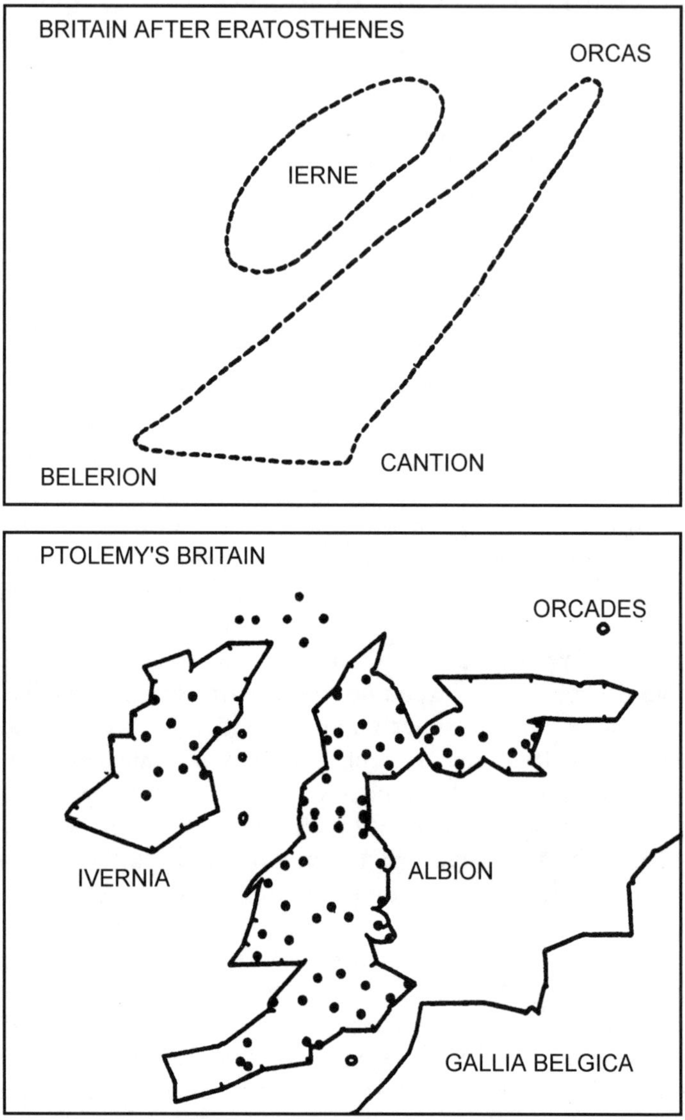

Figure 2 Britain according to the early geographers.

Brittany and Southern Britain was broken and the succeeding pattern of trade took another form. A further brief campaign was necessary in the early autumn to deal with the Menapii and Morini. When the notorious Flanders rain brought fighting to an end, the advantage lay with Caesar. He could now plan enterprises which were to take Roman arms into fabulous realms.

The early months of 55 were devoted to securing the north-eastern frontier of Gaul against incursions from the peoples across the Rhine, an operation which involved the crossing of that river for the first time by a Roman commander. It was not until late in August that an expeditionary force could be hastily mustered and equipped for an invasion of Britain, and there are clear signs that the planning of the venture was sketchy as well as hurried. Advance food supplies were not taken: they would be found *en route* in Kent. Barely enough transport vessels could be released from other duties. No intelligence about good harbours or anchorages in *Cantium* had been gathered, though the tribune C. Volusenus had carried out a five-day reconnaissance. This failure was to dog the entire campaign and it almost led to disaster.

Before the expeditionary force – the seventh and tenth legions and their cavalry – sailed from its bases at *Portus Itius* (Boulogne) and Ambleteuse, eight miles to the north, Caesar received intimations from several British tribes (we do not know their names) that they were prepared to surrender to him. Most probably these offers came from lesser peoples who were under pressure from their neighbours. Caesar sent on ahead of the expedition his friend Commius, a leading member of the Gaulish Atrebates who was thought to enjoy considerable influence in Southern Britain. The intention was, no doubt, to bring other tribes over to Caesar and thus ensure supplies from, or safe passage through, several areas. But Commius' influence was not all-pervasive. As soon as he landed in Britain he was taken captive and played no further part in the affair until its close.

The two legions in eighty transports stood out to sea at midnight on 25 August and by 9 a.m. next morning the bulk of the force rode at anchor off the cliffs of Kent. The eighteen vessels carrying the cavalry were kept in port at Ambleteuse, missed the tide and were again confined to port on the following day. Most probably Caesar lay off Dover or very close by and, seeing the British forces drawn up above the near-vertical cliffs, decided to seek some other landfall. He waited until mid-afternoon for the remainder of his fleet to assemble and then sailed northward along the coast to a point where open, shelving beaches gave the legionaries the chance of effecting a landing. This must have been in the stretch between Kingsdown and Deal, possibly on the beach later commanded by Walmer castle. After the celebrated engagement in which the nameless *signifer* of the tenth legion so distinguished himself, a beach-head was won and a concerted charge scattered the Britons. Had Caesar's cavalry been with him, he would have had the opportunity of pursuing and breaking the Britons and he might have taken immediate possession of the entire south-eastern corner of the island. Even as it was, British morale was severely dented. The tribes of Kent offered surrender, handed over hostages and returned Commius to Caesar. Shortly, chiefs from other southern tribes began to sue for peace. Thus far, things had gone well for Caesar, but without cavalry and adequate supplies he could not move far from the beaches. Four days later the transports ferrying over the cavalry finally appeared, but a storm straightaway dispersed them and they limped back to Gaul.

That storm and the accompanying high tide also wrought havoc with Caesar's galleys, which were somewhat casually disposed on the beach, and with the transports riding offshore. Several vessels were lost and virtually the entire fleet was crippled. Rarely in his career was Caesar found so negligent. Had he been opposed by a better organized foe, the disaster for him would have been much graver. As it turned out, he was allowed enough time to repair the majority of his ships, using material from a dozen shattered vessels. An attack by British cavalry and chariots on the tenth legion foraging some way from the coast was beaten off by reinforcements from the base-camp, Caesar again demonstrating the ease with which British forces could be repulsed by well organized infantry. The breathing-space thus gained was more than welcome. Caesar had had enough for the moment and in the following night he took his army back to Gaul. Only two of the British tribes which had offered hostages subsequently sent them to Caesar's winter quarters among the Belgae.

Napoleon thought the campaign of 55 a second-class operation and, if pressed, Caesar would probably have agreed with that judgment. Ill luck played its part, but Caesar displayed an uncharacteristic lack of foresight in so risky an undertaking. This was *celeritas Caesariana* at its most foolhardy. What had he hoped to achieve and were any of his hopes realized? One hope certainly was: that no one should question the very legality of the operation. Britain did not lie within the province of Transalpine Gaul and Caesar was no doubt relieved that events in Britain gave none of his opponents any grounds for a prosecution. But it was a near thing. Had there been any mishap, it might well have jeopardized Caesar's command in Gaul. In the event, the reaction in Rome was most gratifying. The campaign beyond the limits of Ocean was on everyone's lips, and the period of thanksgiving voted by the Senate, twenty days, was longer than that which had celebrated the conquest of Gaul. Caesar's personal triumph was immense and the venture was counted one of his most notable achievements.

In reality Caesar had achieved nothing by this reconnaissance in force. The punitive intention of the invasion, stressed by Caesar as the main objective, was hardly satisfied. There was no tangible military gain, no loot and virtually no hostages. Nothing was learnt about the coast of Britain that any Channel trader did not already know, and the failure to gain information about harbours is surprising in one whose intelligence service was normally so efficient. The interior of Britain and its mineral resources remained as dark as before and, as events in 54 were to prove, Caesar had not yet encountered the most powerful of the southern British tribes. Much had been risked for very little. But Caesar was in no doubt about a return to the island in the following year.

Before he departed for Italy, Caesar left orders that the old fleet was to be repaired and as many new vessels built as was possible during the winter. The new ships were to be of a design more suitable for rapid loading and beaching, lower and wider than usual, and all were to be equipped with both oars and sail and supplied with improved rigging and other tackle. The materials for the new vessels were to come from Spain. These preparations were unusually detailed and they provide a measure both of the difficulties of campaigning across the Channel and of the seriousness with which Caesar viewed the coming enterprise. This was to be no mere reconnaissance. Six hundred transports of the new design, together with nearly two hundred of the vessels used in 55, and twenty-eight war galleys were ready on his return to Gaul in the spring of 54. There were delays before the great fleet, assembled at *Portus Itius*, was able to sail, due to machinations against Caesar by Treveran nobles with support from Germanic as well as other Gaulish chieftains. But by early July, Caesar felt able to entrust the defence of Gaul to Labienus. At dusk on or about 6 July, the great fleet set sail.

Five legions and some two thousand cavalry made for Britain, the largest army hitherto sent outside the bounds of Roman territory. Unfortunately, we are told nothing of the way in which this armada was marshalled and organized in the dark. We hear nothing of ships fouling one another or of later confusion on the British beaches. If such problems were avoided, it was a proof of superb navigational skills on the part of their captains. At dawn, the British coast was visible to port as the fleet drifted northwards on the Channel tide. When the tide turned, the fleet was rowed ashore at a point chosen the previous summer, and thus to be located in the neighbourhood of Deal and Worth. There was no sign of the Britons, who, as Caesar later learnt from captives, had been so terrified by the size of the fleet that they had fled to the protection of higher ground inland. By midday, the entire army had disembarked and a camp was constructed. The ships were left riding at anchor off an open beach, protected by ten legionary cohorts and three hundred cavalry under the charge of Quintus Atrius. No time was to be spent in beaching them. The mistake of 55 was repeated in 54.

Caesar was eager to take the initiative and engage the Britons as soon as possible. They had retired to a river some twelve miles away, almost certainly the Stour in the Canterbury area. After a night's march Caesar's legions attacked them at a crossing and pushed them back. The Britons then retired to a fortified place north of the river, quite probably the hill-fort at Bigbury, a mile and a half from the Stour crossing. The seventh legion took the position without great difficulty and the army rested overnight in a camp constructed nearby. Next day, the Roman forces were split into three columns so as to pursue the Britons more effectively. The operation was going well, but again Caesar's advance was halted by a Channel storm. Most of the fleet had been driven on to the beaches, with the destruction of forty ships and severe damage to many others. The flying columns were hastily recalled and a general retreat to the coast was ordered. The position was serious, though not as dangerous as in the previous year. The main loss was in time. The repairs would take weeks and skilled craftsmen had to be brought from Gaul. Ten days were consumed in rescuing the stores, in ensuring that everything was safely away from the water's edge and in building a beach-head fortification. That work must have been massive to accommodate nearly eight hundred ships, and of all Caesar's vanished works in Britain it is surely the one most likely to reveal itself some day.

The most important result of the storm-damage was the respite it gave to the Britons. It was now clear to them that not only Kent was threatened by the invaders. Tribes living north of the Thames realized that they too would have to defend their territory. At a council of war of all the interested tribes, it was decided to entrust the supreme command to one Cassivellaunus, a warrior whose previous status is unknown. All that we know for certain about him is that he came from north of the Thames. There is no justification for the assumption that he was a hereditary *rex*, much less that he was *rex Catuvellaunorum*, a tribe not named by Caesar. It is also clear that Cassivellaunus was to prove himself one of the most redoubtable barbarian opponents whom Caesar had to face anywhere.

The first clash with the enlarged British forces came at the same river-crossing to which Caesar had earlier penetrated. There followed a series of running skirmishes in which the British cavalry and charioteers made little impression on the Roman horsemen. It was the first time that Caesar had faced chariots in considerable numbers, and he quickly discovered that by keeping his own horsemen in close contact with the legions, when the clash with the charioteers came, the heavy Roman infantry could move in quickly and engage in hand-to-hand fighting with a foe ill-equipped with body armour and thrusting weapons. Once this had been grasped, the only advantage of the British war-chariot lay in the initial confusion it could cause in the battle-line. It nevertheless remained in use for centuries after Caesar's invasions.

British strategy in the face of the five legions was to attack detachments as they operated away from the main army. On the day after the fighting in the Stour valley, the Britons attacked a force on forage duties. They seem to have miscalculated the size of the detachment, for it comprised three legions and all the cavalry. The Britons broke and fled. This was a major setback for Cassivellaunus, whether or not he was present at this engagement. This was warfare of a kind the Britons had not experienced before. There could be no plunder, no herds of cattle to drive home. They were fighting to retain a hold on their lands. When this realization sank in, within days the confederacy brought together by Cassivellaunus began to fall apart.

The way was open for Caesar to push on to the Thames. He does not record his route. If he attempted the shortest route, he would have faced an awkward crossing of the Medway between Chatham and Rochester. A more likely route lay to the south-west, following in part the prehistoric trackway known as the Pilgrim's Way, which would bring him to the Medway near Maidstone. From here, the Thames was two days' march away and Caesar hastened to it. The river was forded with some difficulty, the crossing being impeded by timber stakes. The enemy had massed on the far bank, but the combined onrush of legionaries and cavalry was too much for them and again they fled without offering a battle. The site of this ford lay in the region of London, probably not further upstream than Fulham or Hammersmith, where there appear to have been Iron Age crossings. More probably the passage was forced some miles downstream from these, in the area of the later city of *Londinium*. The British failure to offer any serious resistance at the Thames may at first seem surprising, but it is possible that Cassivellaunus had already determined upon the next phase of his strategy. Being master of the ground, he resorted to a kind of warfare which technically inferior forces have often waged with success against highly organized armies acting in unfamiliar terrain. Using his chariot-force (4000 strong, we are told) to nag at the flanks of Caesar's columns, the countryside in front of the Roman advance was emptied of people, cattle and supplies, the intention being to compel the Romans to split up on forage expeditions. The policy was the right one in the

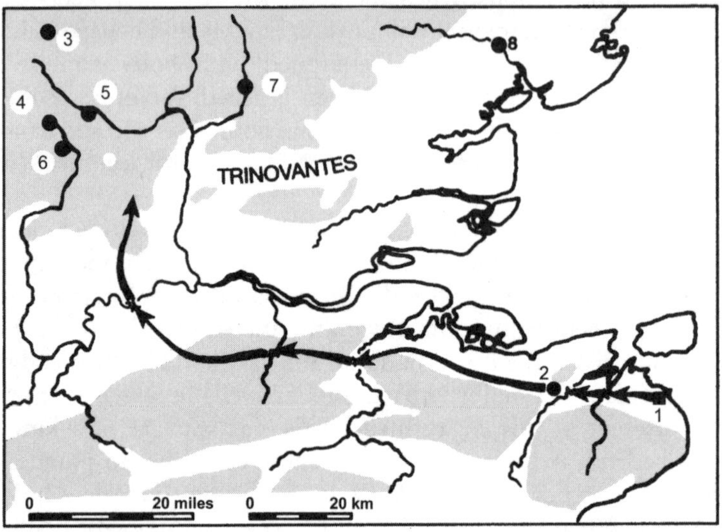

1. Beach-head camp. 2. Bigbury. 3. Ravensburgh. 4. The Aubreys.
5. Wheathampstead. 6. Verulamium. 7. Wallbury. 8. Camulodunum.

Figure 3 Caesar's march through south-eastern Britain.

circumstances, but it failed, ironically because of Cassivellaunus' earlier activities.

Some time before this, Cassivellaunus had killed a king of the Trinovantes, and Mandubracius, the son of that ruler, had fled to Caesar's protection in Gaul. The Trinovantes now approached Caesar asking that Mandubracius be sent back to them as king, offering surrender terms, hostages and supplies of grain. In return they were promised Roman protection against Cassivellaunus, as well as immunity from Roman depredations. This lead was followed by other peoples, the Cenimagni, Segontiaci, Ancalites, Bibroci and Cassi (names only to us, though the Cenimagni might later appear as the Iceni). Among, no doubt, much else, Caesar discovered from these tribes that the stronghold of Cassivellaunus lay quite close to his present position. He resolved to take the strongly defended site and did so without much difficulty. Many prisoners were taken, along with a large herd of cattle concentrated there out of the legions' way.

The location of the stronghold is unknown, and we are not helped by having no real indication of where Caesar was when the Trinovantian surrender was made. It has been argued that a substantial earthwork at Wheathampstead, lying by the River Lea six miles north-east of St Albans, is the best candidate, but the case is not impressive.[8] It is not absolutely certain that this work was entirely surrounded by defences (which seem to be required by Caesar's account), nor can it be proved on present evidence that it was occupied as early as Caesar's day. We may then reasonably look elsewhere, even though a confident identification cannot be made. The absence of any reference by Caesar to a lengthy march, coupled with the fact that it was the Trinovantes of Essex who had suffered most from Cassivellaunus, should indicate that Middlesex and Hertfordshire were the places where the guerrilla campaign was fought out. The stronghold seems unlikely to have been a hill-fort, nor need it have been very extensive, though large enough to house many head of cattle. The Prae Wood earthworks in the Ver valley would suit the case admirably in terms of position, but they are not known to have been in existence as early as this. The site at Braughing in western Essex, apart from being too far to the east, has no known earthworks and may also have developed later. Wallbury, too, by the River Stort, probably lies well to the east of the centre of operations, although it does lie in the right kind of lowland position close to meadow-land. Another possible site is the fort at The Aubreys, near Redbourn in the upper valley of the Ver. This lies on the lower slopes of a hill and resembles a strongly guarded corral rather than a powerful military stronghold. Both Wallbury and The Aubreys are unexcavated so that it is unknown whether or not they were occupied in the mid-first century BC.[9] To illustrate the range of possibilities is one thing; it is another to prefer one to the next. None has more claim than the others at present, and only excavation can help us further.

Even now, when most barbarian leaders would have conceded defeat, Cassivellaunus attempted to strike where Caesar was most vulnerable, at his fleet on the Kent coast. Word was sent to four rulers in kent, ordering them to attack the naval base, and it is a remarkable testimony to the authority of the war-lord that they did so. Their force, however, was beaten off and defeated. Cassivellaunus accepted that the time had come to end resistance and, employing Commius as a mediator, he formally surrendered. The fact that Commius figured in the affair suggests that Caesar may have made the first move towards arranging terms, but this is not certain. The terms included hostages, an annual tribute to Rome and an agreement not to attack or encroach on the Trinovantes. We hear of no booty, only of hostages and prisoners being taken back to Gaul, and Caesar seems to have left Britain no wiser about the resources of Britain than he had been in 55. There had been no chance of discovering more about the geography of the island or the disposition of its inhabitants. Enquiries to that end might have been made had Caesar wintered in Britain, which he hints was his original intention, but some of the Gaulish tribes were growing restive once more, encouraged perhaps by Caesar's absence. He had paid an unexplained visit to the Kent coast about 5 August, perhaps to receive intelligence about the state of Gaul. On 29 August, he wrote to M. Cicero from Britain, by which date the fighting was over and negotiations probably already completed. He was then on the point of ferrying the army back to Gaul, but uncertain weather was to make two trips necessary. The remainder of the army and their prisoners were crammed into the available vessels and got back to Gaul before the September equinox. It was to be ninety-seven years before a Roman general set foot again in Britain.

Both Caesar the politician and Caesar the general intended that Britain should be a Roman island. The reconnaissance in strength of 55 was followed by a major expedition intended to subdue as much of Britain as possible. Caesar's motives in pursuing conquest in Britain were no different from his motives in invading Gaul in 58. Roman rule over the provinces had to be reinforced and secured afresh by vigorous action. This was the assumption behind Caesar's own brief explanation of his crossing of the Rhine and of the Channel. But this was not all. Caesar's own ambitions were not satisfied by the conquest of Gaul; a remote and glittering prize of war was offered beyond Ocean. There was no economic motive to match that of personal glory, though booty was always welcome. The British adventure thus cannot be separated from Caesar's other exploits in Western Europe. It was one more opportunity for conquest and profit. Neither conquest nor profit, however, was achieved. The first step towards the direct administration of Southern Britain was indeed taken, but Britain could not be taxed without being governed and Caesar could not leave an army in the island. There was no conquest and no new province,[10] but henceforward Britain could not be ignored by the ruler of Rome when he turned his eyes to the west.

2

Britain and the Britons

Britain and Belgic Gaul

As Caesar himself observed, the prevailing culture of South-eastern Britain had much in common with that of Northern Gaul, and he was also well aware that contacts of various kinds had existed for some time between the two regions. Although his name is the only one to have reached the ears of Caesar, Divitiacus of the Suessiones is unlikely to have been the only leader to claim lordship over territory on both sides of the Channel, though he was apparently the last. Divitiacus' rule may be dated very approximately to about 80–60 BC, a period for which there is important numismatic evidence bearing on the question of contact between Britain and Belgic Gaul.[1] The earliest series of Gallo-Belgic gold coins to enter Britain (Gallo-Belgic A) appeared in the island around or shortly before 100 BC. Beginning slightly later and originating in the west of Belgic Gaul were Gallo-Belgic B coins, their British distribution centring on the lower Thames basin, Essex and north Kent. A major influence on development of the earliest British coinages was the Gallo-Belgic C series, usually attributed to the Ambiani of the lower Somme valley, which occurs most commonly in Kent. Its date of import probably lay in the period 75–60 BC and there are obvious temptations towards linking it with the rule of Divitiacus, though there is nothing more substantial than a general congruence of date. A somewhat later series, Gallo-Belgic E, also assigned to the Ambiani, was widely distributed in South-eastern Britain and can now be firmly dated to the middle years of the first century BC. Dr S. Scheers[2] has argued plausibly that this was the coinage of the Belgic confederation which opposed Caesar in the 50s. If this is so, we have to explain what it was doing in Britain. The coins can hardly have been imported in bulk by the refugee chieftains of the Bellovaci in 57. Nor indeed does any kind of migration from Gaul seem a reasonable occasion for their appearance in Britain.

They are better interpreted as payment to British leaders by Gauls, for troops, for grain and other supplies during the years of warfare into which Belgic Gaul was now plunged. The areas in which the Gallo-Belgic E coins occur in Britain are precisely those in which supplies were most readily available: Kent, the Thames valley and the lands of the Trinovantes.

Following the magisterial studies of D. F. Allen, the evidence of the Gallo-Belgic and the later British coinages has (until recently) been regarded as proof of successive migrations from Northern Gaul into Southern Britain, each movement of population leaving its mark by the import of a major coinage. This simplistic view has for some time involved serious difficulties which have increased as study of the Gaulish coinages has steadily gained a securer footing. No straightforward equation between any of the imported coinages already mentioned and an influx of population can be demonstrated. Indeed, such an hypothesis is unnecessary. South-eastern Britain and Northern Gaul were so close in cultural, economic and, at times, political terms that there existed a rich variety of circumstances in which Gaulish currency (as well as other material) might be transferred to Britain.[3] The recorded flight of the chiefs of the Bellovaci in 57, and of Commius later in the decade, are on the whole less likely occasions for the introduction of Gaulish coinage in *quantity* than relatively mundane transactions between Gauls and Britons in the Celtic *koiné* about the Channel, as the wealth of Southern Britain began to assume greater significance for Gauls now facing the advance of Rome.

If, then, the Gallo-Belgic coin evidence offers no real support for movements of population into Britain in the first century BC, what of the contemporary equipment such as metalwork and pottery? The material from the classic cemeteries of Aylesford and Swarling does represent a clear break with the earlier traditions of the south-east, notably in the wheel-made pottery vessels, but very little of this material dates from before the time of Caesar.[4] As with the coinages, there are few grounds for thinking that the new elements in the Aylesford-Swarling culture were brought to Britain by immigrants who came to settle, rather than by processes of trade and exchange. The pottery aside, among the metal vessels at Aylesford, for example, there were a bronze jug of Kelheim type and a *patella*, both being items among the finest goods traded to other parts of barbarian Europe in the first century BC. No folk-movement need be invoked to explain the appearance in Britain of objects such as these. Rather, one is impressed by the prevalence of features of material culture which were patently not imported, but were firmly rooted in a cultural amalgam which can be traced back well before the introduction of iron. Those features range from the stable, mixed farming characteristic of sites of the Little Woodbury type (*page 22*) to the persistence of individual pieces of equipment like the ring-headed pin and the weaving comb, or of a major tradition like the construction of round houses. So vigorous and pervasive were such traditions that it is reasonable to ask whether the immigrants attested by the literary sources were numerous enough or powerful enough to have had much influence over the cultural development of Southern Britain. There may never be a clear answer to the question, but for the present the direct impact of immigrants from Belgic Gaul on the Britons should not be overstated. That there were contacts with the Belgae of Gaul is not to be doubted. Caesar is not the only writer to link the Belgae with Britain. When Propertius, writing before 20 BC, sought to describe a British-style cosmetic used by fashionable Roman ladies, he referred to its *Belgicus color*, without believing that his readers needed any further explanation.[5] There are, moreover, certain place-names in Southern Britain, including a group with the element *duro*, which find their nearest analogues in Belgic Gaul.

In its sum, this evidence cannot prove a large-scale migration from Gaul into Britain. Those tribal names which Caesar noted as occurring on both sides of the Channel do little to strengthen the case. Certain names (e.g. Cornovii, Brigantes) recur in several parts of Celtic Europe, and folk-movement cannot adequately explain their distribution. Such names as Atrebates, Parisi and Belgae could have been introduced into Britain by individual chieftains and their retinues: when this occurred cannot be determined, but it may have been long before the first century BC.

Augustus and Britain

Caesar had indeed revealed Britain to his successors without handing it on to them, as Tacitus' famous judgment has it. Whether or not anyone considered that Britain had been conquered in 54 BC, there is no doubt that Caesar's adopted heir and eventual successor did feel himself obliged to take Britain into account when contemplating the security of the north-western provinces. On several occasions between 31 and 16 BC these deliberations included the possibility of mounting an expedition against the island. C. E. Stevens argued firmly that 'contemporaries realized that Caesar's settlement meant a conquest of Britain...' and, 'It only remained to implement his action by "walking in" and taking over.'[6] Later opinion has tended to follow this line, though with caution. It is in truth by no means clear that contemporaries recognized Caesar's actions as amounting to a conquest of Britain. When Virgil wrote of Britain in 41 BC, he clearly conceived of the island as outside Roman dominion, along with such regions as Scythia and India. A few years later, Horace saw the Britons as independent, though still liable to provide a triumph. In 34 BC, Octavian arrived in Gaul with the intention of 'emulating' Caesar and invading Britain. Nothing came of the project, as a revolt in Dalmatia turned Octavian's attention back to the Mediterranean.

After 31 BC there seems to have been further speculation at the Augustan court about a British expedition, especially in 27–26. In 27, Augustus again came to Gaul but did not go ahead with an invasion of Britain as the Britons seemed to be prepared to accept terms, and matters in Gaul itself needed attention. This sounds very much as though diplomatic contact had been enough to settle whatever was at issue in Southern Britain. In the following year the invasion plan was revived but then dropped again in the face of trouble in the Alps and in Spain.

How prominently Britain figured in Augustus' policy towards the North-west after 31 cannot be clearly determined. Consistent planning towards an invasion seems not to have been undertaken. Augustan treatment of the British tribes was flexible and seemingly expressed through diplomatic channels, with the backing of the threat of military intervention on occasion. But there was never real need of more drastic action, and after about 25 BC Augustus' attitude towards Britain seems to have shifted away from annexation towards a cautious watch on the dynasts of the south-east and a measure of control exercised through treaty relations. The closure of the Temple of Janus in 25 implies that no campaigns were envisaged for the immediate future, and two years later the sixth book of Virgil's *Aeneid* was laying open a vista of conquest in the east without any mention of Britain. By 15, Horace – who had earlier prophesied conquest in Britain – was sounding the same note. The Britons were still remote beyond Ocean, and Britain now gave place to that preoccupation with the Germanic peoples which was to endure through most of the reign. From now until after the death of Tiberius in AD 37, Rome's dealings with Britain rested mainly on the basis of diplomacy and not on military threat.

Amid the turbulent politics of tribal barbarism, however, there were bound to be setbacks and sudden shifts of fortune. The flight of Tincommius and Dubnovellaunus to Rome before AD 7 must represent a major reverse for the Augustan system.[7] However, the arrangement was quickly replaced by something similar or even by something more formal, as both Eppillus and Verica call themselves *rex* on their coinages which should mean that they had been formally recognized as client rulers. Towards the end of Augustus' reign, probably shortly before AD 10, the main power bloc in Southern Britain came under the control of Cunobelin, who quickly became the most powerful of all the British dynasts. He has been generally seen as standing outside the Augustan arrangement, pursuing an independent, or even an anti-Roman, line, though without pressing it to open hostility. There is no justification for this view of Cunobelin. The long period of relatively stable relations between barbarian Britain and the Rome of Tiberius strongly suggests that the British ruler had accepted a working arrangement backed by a treaty. For a time his bronze coinage proclaimed him a *rex*, and it may be significant that during his long reign the quantity of Roman imports into *Camulodunum* greatly increased and British exports were beginning to make an impact on continental markets. It may have been he who returned several of Germanicus' ships and their occupants when they were driven on to the British coast in AD 16. Cunobelin's wealth, as reflected in the size of his gold coinage,[8] was immense by comparison with earlier British kings and although it may simply indicate an increased tribute from a greater dominion, it may legitimately be asked whether he did not also benefit from a Roman subsidy, like that which Tiberius issued to Vannius beyond the upper Danube. His coinage was not only large: it was also of good weight and purity. It was rarely hoarded (an indication of the prevailing monetary stability within his domains), and his currency as a whole came closest to the Roman trimetallic model, although his silver was coined in relatively small quantities.

With Cunobelin's death, a year or two after that of Tiberius in AD 37, there came a radical change in the relations between Britain and Rome. The equipoise which had lasted for over fifty years came to an abrupt end.

Celtic society in Britain

Barbarian society in Britain before the Roman conquest had as its fundamental territorial unit the tribe, the *tuath* of the later Irish laws. The *tuath* embraced a small unit of population ruled by a petty king, the *ri*. Below the *ri* came the two main orders of society: the nobles, who comprised the warriors (the *equites* of Julius Caesar's account), Druids and skilled craftsmen, and the free men, the peasants and rank-and-file of Celtic hosts. There were slaves, too, but slavery was a relatively minor element in Celtic society. Between the three major social divisions there existed a close-knit complex of graded obligations, prescribed loyalties owing to persons, clans and leaders, a system of clientship well understood by classical writers. This system was the basis of a king's power and a noble's prosperity. This tripartite social order, kings, nobles, free men, can be detected in several areas of the Indo-European world, most clearly among the continental Celts and the early Germans, peoples who shared much else in common. Although it is not clear how far back the distinction may be traced, in the later law tracts there appear two grades of clientship: base and free. Under the terms of the former the lord enjoyed additional rights over his followers, as well as increased financial responsibilities.

In those parts of Britain most exposed to influence from the continental Celts, the primitive order outlined in Irish sources was fast disappearing by the time of Caesar. The southern British tribes in the middle of the first century BC were not small population groups on the lines of the *tuath*. That kind of organization had enjoyed its heyday in earlier centuries, when local chieftains had lorded it from hill-top strongholds. In Northern Britain and in Wales the old order still survived, but in the south, by the second half of the first century BC, there had been radical change. The kings who now signed issues of coins and, in some cases, entertained embassies from Rome were no mere tribal monarchs. The old tribal units had been built up into a superstructure of larger monarchies, some of them approaching in size the great tribes of Gaul and Germany. There are glimpses of the process in our sources. Of five tribes which sent legations to Caesar in 54, four are never heard of again: Segontiaci, Ancalites, Bibroci and Cassi. The fifth, the Cenimagni, may be known to later history as the Iceni. The others were presumably merged in larger groupings. In the north, some of the septs of the huge tribe of the Brigantes (Setantii, Gavranticii, Carvetii) may be seen as older units drawn under the power of an over-king or -queen.

We learn nothing about any of the tribal kings of Wales from our sources. Their opposition to Rome in the first century AD found its leader not in a western king but in the easterner Caratacus – a war-leader and not a hereditary king. In Northern Britain, we hear little about hereditary kings. Among the Brigantes it was Venutius, the consort of the pro-Roman queen Cartimandua, who took charge of the hosts which faced Rome. Later still, the Caledonian armies were led by a warrior whose status is nowhere precisely defined, but who is never called a *rex*. Virtually nothing is known about Caledonian kingship at this date, but it seems probable that Calgacus ('the swordsman') was a war-leader, chosen for his prowess in battle rather than for his kingly origins. This does not mean that hereditary kingship was of no account in Northern and Western Britain. Most probably it was the normal form of tribal leadership. But there was a marked readiness among the British tribes to entrust the conduct of major campaigns to distinguished warriors, elected presumably by their peers. This had long been so among the continental Celts and Germans, as the careers of Vercingetorix and Ariovistus prove. Cassivellaunus was also of this company. He is not styled *rex Catuvellaunorum* or even *rex* by Caesar, nor is his tribal origin specified. What we are told is that he was chosen to lead the British forces against Caesar by a council of leading warriors, presumably from several tribes. There is no doubt that, whether or not Cassivellaunus had been a tribal monarch before 54, his election as supreme commander was due to his military qualities. Unfortunately, his status and career after 54 are unknown. Certainly there is no proof that he was the founder of the dynasty to which Tasciovanus and Cunobelin were heirs.

Nothing, then, in Caesar indicates the existence of a powerful centralized monarchy in Southern Britain by the mid-first century BC. The evidence of later Roman sources and of settlement-history points clearly to the presence of several vigorous tribal monarchies in the south-eastern part of the island, in which respect Britain differed sharply from Gaul. There, the power of kings had begun to wane in many regions by Caesar's day, to be replaced by councils of *nobiles* and by colleges of magistrates. There is no sign of this in Britain, and the policies of Augustus and Tiberius towards the British leaders may have done much to strengthen the power-base of the barbarian kings. When the word *rex* appears on the coinage of a British ruler, it is expressive of a Roman idea, that of client kingship, and its very usage may have been inspired by Rome. The position of a Celtic king was never inviolate, but it might be made much stronger by recognition from the Roman emperor, particularly if that recognition was attended by a subsidy of some kind.

The dominant force in Celtic society was its aristocracy, the influence of which was felt in everything from agriculture to art. The life of the chieftain and his *clientes* was a full-blooded, roistering affair, a mingling of ferocity and geniality, of warfare and feasting. In the brief classical references and in the later vernacular sources, we catch a glimpse of a world close to that described by Homer, a world in which personal valour and the power to amass treasure were the prime qualities of a leader. There are indications in the coinage that by the later first century BC merchants had become an influential group among the clients of southern British aristocrats. Certainly the spread of bronze and potin coinage suggests a more widespread commercial activity, stimulated no doubt by Gaulish and Gallo-Roman enterprise.

The place of women in Celtic society at this date is illuminated only at the highest level. No female rulers are recorded in Gaul, nor were women prominent in the political sphere. The position of authority occupied by Cartimandua and Boudicca in Britain of the first century AD, however, is a pointer to the influence noble women may have exercised in the later Iron Age, even though not a single pre-Roman queen or consort is named by any of our sources. Some of the richly furnished graves of La Tène Europe may have been of noble women and thus their occupants may in life have been accounted the possessors of their own property, but it would be dangerous to assume that the same kinds of social structure existed in Britain and all over the western Celtic lands. The ties of marriage were not exclusive. A man might take other wives in addition to his principal consort, a custom which may help to explain the accounts in some classical writers of an unbridled polygamy. Divorce seems to have been freely allowed and the ending of marriage by mutual consent may have been frequent. The evidence for matriarchy and matrilineal succession among Celtic peoples is very dubious and is best consigned to the large corpus of myths surrounding Celtic society.

Settlement on the land

The accepted view of the economic basis of Iron Age settlement in Southern Britain has for long been based upon the excavation by Professor G. Bersu of the site at Little Woodbury in Wiltshire, and even now any examination of the essentials of later Iron Age agricultural settlement must begin with a summary of what that excavation revealed.[9] The settlement, covering four acres bounded by first a palisade and later by a bank and ditch, had been occupied from the late fourth to the first century BC. The whole complex was interpreted as a single farmstead with one main dwelling, a large roundhouse, one smaller house and several subsidiary buildings, granaries and racks. Large numbers of pits, an estimated 360 in all, were dotted about the settlement, these being identified as storage-pits for grain. As well as arable farming, the rearing of stock, particularly sheep and cattle, was practised. The evidence provided by Little Woodbury seemed to be supported at certain points by allusions made by classical writers, and its internal cohesion carried general conviction. But while many of the conclusions drawn by Bersu on the farming economy of Little Woodbury still seem well founded, the notion that the *Einzelhof* type of settlement which he outlined here was the norm in the southern British Iron Age must be modified. Large-scale survey and extensive excavation of a small number of sites in Lowland Britain indicate that the pattern of settlement was much more complex and varied than Bersu and later commentators believed. Further, outstanding excavation though it was, the examination of Little Woodbury was not total. A little over a third of the settlement was excavated, so that there can be no certainty that this was no more than a single farmstead. Even if it was, it cannot be assumed that more nucleated forms of settlement-pattern of dispersed farms will not readily reveal the degree of community life which literate societies often show to have been a characteristic feature of such settlements.

There is abundant, if poorly defined, evidence for variety in the size and character of social units over most of Southern and Midland England.[10] As yet, regional differences are not clearly evident but we can see that they exist. Single-family steadings seem to be represented everywhere, but usually alongside nucleated settlements of varying size. Even in areas such as the great river valleys of the Thames, Trent and Severn, where single homesteads within their own enclosures seem to have been the norm, those homesteads probably did not exist in isolation from each other. Their inhabitants may well have combined for certain social and religious purposes as well as for major agricultural tasks. Such communal labour undertaken by apparently scattered groups is familiar from later days, but it is very doubtful whether it can ever be proved for Iron Age Britain.

If one generalization may be permitted, it seems as though the larger communities did not come into existence before the first century BC and many did not develop until the later decades of that century. But the sum of cogent evidence available at present is not impressive and there will be little real advance in knowledge until more total excavation of settlements has been carried out. Nucleated settlements are now attested in several regions of Southern Britain, especially in the Eastern Midlands – an area where large hill-forts were conspicuously rare. Some of those in Lincolnshire may begin as early as the third century BC, though their most significant period of growth was probably after 100 BC. So far as is known, these were open settlements without elaborate planning, usually lying on low ground. The majority remained in use into the Roman period, generally as minor townships, though some, such as Leicester, formed the basis for more considerable communities.

The place in later Iron Age society of that heterogeneous array of strongholds and fortified settlements known as hill-forts is only now beginning to be clarified in the wake of the large-scale excavation of the interior of a small number of sites. Study of such works long dominated Iron Age studies, but attention was usually focussed upon the development and chronology of their defences and gates. Extensive examination of the interior at sites like South Cadbury (Somerset), Croft Ambrey (Herefordshire), Crickley Hill (Gloucestershire), Danebury (Hampshire) and Pilsden Pen (Dorset) has done much to illumine the place of hill-forts in the social and economic scene.

In Britain, as in the continental *Hohensiedlungen*, certain hill-top settlements were being surrounded by defences as early as the seventh century BC, and not only in the south. Radiocarbon dates indicate that certain Scottish hill-forts – e.g. Finavon (Angus) and Dun Lagaidh (Wester Ross) – were first occupied in the seventh century or even somewhat earlier, and there are similar indications from sites in North Wales and the Marches. The heyday of hill-forts was the period from the fifth century to the later second, though others were built *de novo* after that. The purely military aspects of hill-forts, understandably enough, long dominated thinking about their functions, but though they could serve as strongholds against raiders and neighbours casting envious eyes on herds of animals, the very nature of Celtic warfare makes it less than likely that prolonged sieges of hill-forts were the norm. It is equally uncertain that hill-forts contained the residences of tribal leaders. The distribution of fine objects and indices of wealth and prestige suggests that chieftains and their followings lived elsewhere, the hill-forts being used as repositories of food and other commodities, and possibly as places of assembly for social and religious purposes. Whether the larger forts served as tribal centres is unclear. In the first instance they represent the power and prestige of individual chiefs and their leading *clientes*. If one man's power proved to be durable, the site might become to some extent a centre for tribal or sub-tribal organization, a meeting-place for councils, religious ceremonies, markets and festivals. Some of these gatherings might continue to take place at a hill-fort long after it had ceased to be a stronghold. That certain sites *began* as ritual centres and only later developed other functions has been suggested, but on slight evidence.

It is now clear that the interiors of some hill-forts were fairly densely built up and the internal buildings disposed in a planned layout, in certain cases at a remarkably early date, as at Moel y Gaer (Clwyd), Crickley Hill (Gloucestershire) and Danebury

(Hampshire). The plans of these sites reveal them to be highly developed settlements with an evidently coherent social structure. Their buildings include large aisled halls (at Crickley Hill), long rectangular buildings at Pilsden Pen, small square buildings at Danebury and Moel y Gaer, and circular houses almost everywhere. It is quite possible that other quite sophisticated houses existed within hill-forts, and in other kinds of settlement, of which virtually no archaeological traces are likely to be discovered as they were not firmly founded in the subsoil.

Stable, orderly communities like these, emerging early in the first millennium BC, were obviously the focal points of sizeable units of land with a resident population principally dependent on agriculture and stock-rearing, but also probably able to produce goods over and above their own needs. They were sufficiently well organized not only for communal agricultural tasks, but also for the construction of defensive works and large timber buildings. We cannot say whether that degree of organization was normally imposed by a single prominent figure or was the result of decisions taken by a group of equals, such as the heads of families. Of greater importance is the fact that the most fundamental features of community life were already present many centuries before the time of Caesar. These settlements were not towns in the senses comprehended by classical observers, even though many of the characteristic functions of the smaller classical town were shared by these barbarian communities. Though not themselves urban, these settlements do represent an important stage in the emergence of those primitive urban communities which came into being in the century before the Roman conquest.

In the same period in which many hill-forts went out of use – the first century BC and early in the first century AD – sizeable settlements were beginning to develop in valley-ward positions; sites such as Dyke Hills, Dorchester (Oxfordshire), Salmonsbury (Gloucestershire), The Aubreys (Hertfordshire), Loose and Canterbury (Kent). In many cases, the commanding hill-top was abandoned in favour of a strategic lowland position protected by a bend of a river, a marsh or a belt of woodland, and in some instances further strengthened by systems of dykes. Some dyke systems cordoned off huge territories, as in the case of the North Oxfordshire Grim's Ditch, the Beech Bottom Dyke of Hertfordshire, or the dykes surrounding the great *oppidum* of *Camulodunum*. Enormous areas like these could not be protected against all inroads, but the defenders presumably depended as much on natural defences of forest and marsh as on lengths of earthwork. Counter-strikes of cavalry and chariots against intruders in this kind of terrain could have been devastating, and increased use of these forces no doubt accounts for the new mode of fortification. The extensive areas so enclosed included both pasturage and arable land, so that herds could be brought into safe areas in times of unrest. Sites of settled habitation within the dykes seem to have been rather scattered, though some degree of nucleation within a great stronghold like *Camulodunum* or *Calleva* is to be expected.

The dates at which these great dyke systems were constructed cannot yet be fixed within close limits. The *Camulodunum* dykes were not built before the end of the first century BC and a date about AD 10–20 is more probable. The Grim's Ditch in Oxfordshire also dates to the earlier first century AD, perhaps to AD 20–40. The earthworks surrounding the Atrebatic centre at *Calleva* (Silchester, Berkshire) belong to the beginning of the first century AD, replacing a smaller settlement to the north-west and others in the vicinity. The Prae Wood site near *Verulamium* has so far produced no evidence for a foundation before the end of the first century BC and the same is true of the dykes north-west of Chichester. The works at Bagendon (Gloucestershire) may well be later still.

Most of these *oppida* were well sited to take advantage of fertile river valleys, to control communications and trade-routes over a wide area. But they represent more than a response to simple economic forces. Their growth must be linked with major advances in social organization within the southern British tribes. The move to valley positions and the large area occupied or enclosed within dykes implies lordship over a much larger block of territory than had been ruled from a hill-fort. That some of the *oppida* were seats of political control is evident from the siting of coin-mints at places like *Camulodunum*, *Verulamium*, *Calleva* and Bagendon, while the presence of rich imported goods at the same centres tells its own story. Whether these *oppida* were in any sense *tribal* centres rather than simply the residences of tribal leaders is not clear but this is probable in the case of *Camulodunum*, *Verulamium* and *Calleva*. There is as yet little known of the internal arrangement of the large *oppida*, but it may not be assumed that only scatters of huts lay in the interior. If they resembled in any way the great *oppida* of continental Europe, they may well have included well planned settlement areas on some scale. There does appear to have been a marked increase in the number of homestead sites accompanying the rise of the British *oppida*, suggesting both an increase in population and a more intensive exploitation of the cultivable land. All in all, the rise of these huge sites seems to mark a decisive stage in the development of late Iron Age society. A break was made with the clannish, familiar past and an era of centralized tribal monarchy began. At Camulodunum, within a rich late Iron Age cemetery lay a large earthen mound covering a burial with unusually wealthy grave-goods, laid within an iron-bound timber structure. Roman imported bronzes, wine amphorae, chain mail, richly ornamented cloth and several silver objects indicate the high status of the occupant of the grave, but what marks out the Lexden interment above all else is a silver portrait medallion of Augustus, struck in 17 BC, set in a bronze mount. This can only have been a diplomatic gift from the emperor or his representative to a British leader. Unfortunately it is not certain who the recipient was. The date of the burial cannot be precisely fixed, though it is likely to date to the end of the first century BC. Addedomarus might thus appear to be a strong candidate.

Agricultural resources

The animals principally bred in Britain were cattle, sheep, pigs and horses, in most regions in that order of importance. The cattle were small, being mostly of the Celtic shorthorn strain (*bos longifrons*) introduced into the island in the later Bronze Age and subsequently not improved by cross-breeding. The sheep too were small, the common breed being that which still survives on the island of Soay (after which the breed is named), the Hebrides, Orkneys and Shetlands. Probably both cattle and sheep were milked as well as eaten but wool may have been the principal product of the sheep. Weaving on the upright loom was practised in all parts of Iron Age Britain, as is evidenced by loom-weights of clay and stone, spindle-whorls, weaving-combs and, in the south at least, settings for the loom-frame itself. Cattle hides provided leather, and their bones could be used for a variety of tools and ornaments. Pigs were commonly kept in Southern Britain, the choicer joints of their meat being the chieftain's portion and thus well represented in rich graves. In the uplands of the north and west pigs were relatively rare. Horse-rearing was certainly carried on, as among other things the size of Cassivellaunus' chariot-force makes clear, but it may have been practised more intensively in certain areas than in others. The animals again were very small, indicating that cross-breeding with imported stock was unknown or rare. These British ponies would have been of more use in warfare and transport than in the work of farming. For draught-animals cattle are more likely to have been used.

Hunting may have added to the range of Iron Age diet, though archaeology records little of hunting weapons or of the remains of deer, hares and wild fowl. But hunting is reported by Caesar and both

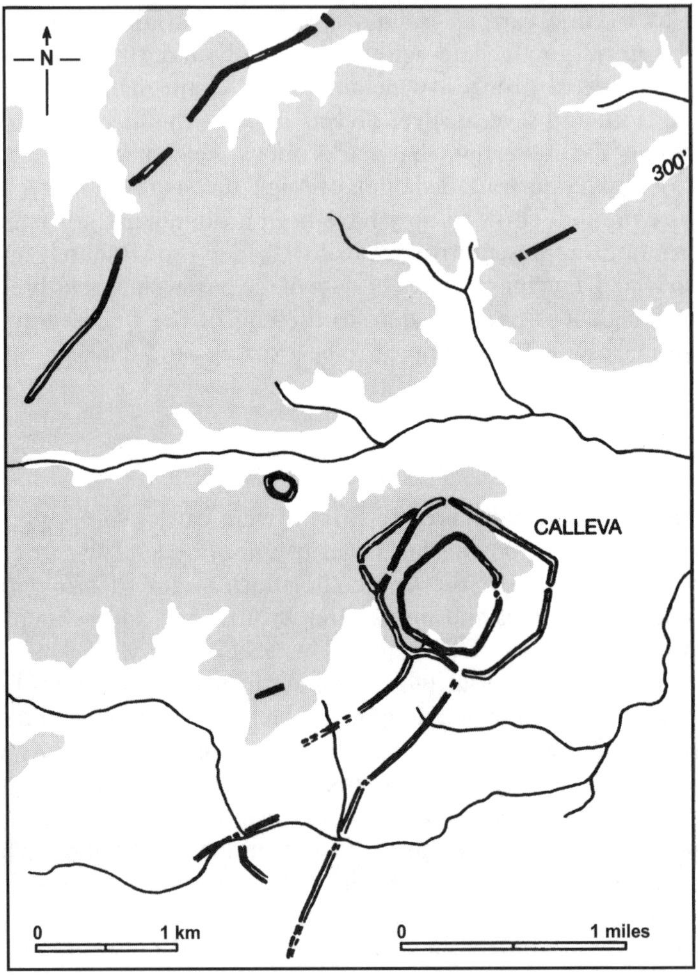

Figure 4 The *oppidum* at *Calleva* (Silchester).

Britain, and later Ireland, were noted for their hunting dogs. Several breeds of dog are later recorded from Britain, including large hounds, terriers and perhaps the bulldog, all of these probably with Iron Age antecedents.

Few parts of Europe outside the Mediterranean zone of the vine and olive were better provided for by nature than Southern Britain. The common grain crops were wheat and barley, with emmer wheat as the principal variety, though the hardy spelt had spread widely by the first century BC. In certain regions, barley appears to have been prominent. Rye was grown in small quantities; oats apparently not at all. Wild grains and weeds seem to have been harvested with the cultivated crops, as elsewhere in Northern Europe. Considerable care was taken over the storage of the harvested grain. Large storage-pits for corn are a notable feature of many Iron Age settlements in Southern Britain (though not a universal one). The roofed structures implied by Diodorus[11] may be in evidence in the form of square and rectangular timber buildings raised above the ground on four or six stout posts. These structures are also well attested in continental Europe, but the storage pits so far appear to be confined to Britain. Their distribution is uneven, being commoner in the south and south-west, rare in the Midlands and virtually unknown in the east. Hay and straw were no doubt used as animal-fodder, while flax was grown for use in fine textiles perhaps, but principally for its oil-bearing seeds.

Tribes and dynasties

The Atrebates

The flight of Commius from Gaul shortly after 51 BC so graphically related by Frontinus, resulted in the formation of a major British kingdom with its heartland around the middle Thames and extending southwards to the sea. It is not certain that Commius fled to a tribal grouping which already called itself Atrebates, having earlier split away from the Atrebates of Gaul, though that remains most likely. In any case, it is notable that Commius was able to establish himself with evident ease as a monarch in Britain, which may have been due either to his reputation in the island, so overrated by Caesar in 55 BC, or to the weakness of the British Atrebates at the time of his arrival. Commius' renown in Britain may have been enhanced as a result of his support for the Gallic rebellion against Caesar in 53, and his cause may have been furthered by Gaulish forces arriving in Britain after his celebrated flight. He may well have been able to use his prestige to unite several tribal units into a major confederacy. The Regni, or Regini, of Sussex, who later emerged into history as a Roman *civitas*, were probably one such group.

The coins issued by Commius, inscribed COMMIOS and with a triple-tailed horse on the reverse, are almost certainly the earliest inscribed British coins. They are found in the area of South Berkshire, Hampshire and Sussex, the area also covered by their uninscribed prototypes (British Q). It is possible that these prototypes were also struck at the behest of Commius, though this cannot be demonstrated. How long Commius ruled after 50 BC is not known, but it is likely that he survived until well after 30 and perhaps to about 25 or 20 BC. His domain thereupon passed to his son Tincommius. (The recent find of a coin bearing the name Tincomaros or Tincomarios may add a complication. This ruler may be identical with Tincommius or a close contemporary. In either event, the family link with Commius is placed in some doubt, but there would be some easing in the chronology.) So close are the early coins of this ruler to those of his father that a period of joint rule may be suspected. Such an arrangement would not be unusual in Celtic tribalism, and in the latter stages of his reign Commius must have been of advanced years. The coinage of Tincommius covers the same broad territory as that of his father and reveals in most details a clear continuity with it. Then, shortly after about 15 BC, a striking Roman issue was put out by the Atrebatic moneyers. This had a plain obverse with the legend TINC in fine Roman lettering inside a recessed panel and, on the reverse, a galloping horse and rider executed in a thoroughly Roman style. The hand of a Roman die-cutter was almost certainly responsible for this issue and for certain later coins, though the quality of the later workmanship was not so high. Perhaps a Roman mission to Tincommius' court about 15 was responsible for the best dies, while native craftsmen later did their best to continue the tradition. In any event, the Roman elements in the coinage are to be ascribed to the concluding of some treaty arrangement between Tincommius and Augustus (*page 18*), and it is interesting that precisely from this date onward the threat of aggressive expeditions against the Britons faded in the literature of the day.

It was during the reign of Tincommius that the *oppidum* of *Calleva* (Silchester) developed in size and importance to become the main centre of the Atrebates. Planned streets and rectangular timber buildings appeared about 20 BC and imported goods from the Roman world began to reach *Calleva* at the same time: pottery, wine and possible other luxury items.[12] By AD 7, Tincommius had been compelled to flee from Britain to Rome, apparently as a result of some family intrigue since he was replaced by a brother, Eppillus. The connection with Rome, however, was maintained and the coins make the position of Eppillus quite clear. On a small issue he is designated REX, which must be taken to mean a client king in the eyes of Rome and not simply a tribal monarch to those Britons who handled his currency. Eppillus was not long in residence at *Calleva*, being replaced by someone else who claimed to be a son of Commius, Verica. Eppillus seems to have established a domain in Kent for a time. Verica's rule at *Calleva* was long, perhaps from about AD 15 to

1. Bagendon. 2. Calleva. 3. Chichester. 4. Camulodunum. 5. Verulamium. 6. Canterbury.

Figure 5 The tribes of southern Britain.

42, when he too was expelled and forced to flee to the emperor Claudius (under the light disguise of Berikos in Dio's text). This had been a turbulent dynasty. All three sons of Commius had been impelled to relinquish their rule at *Calleva* and two of them had been forced to do what their father had sworn never to do again, namely look upon the face of a Roman, though both Tincommius and Verica were able to repair to the protection of the leading Roman of the day..

The Catuvellauni

North of the Thames and centred on the Chilterns and the areas to the north and north-west lay the tribal kingdom which had fallen to Cassivellaunus and which later sources name as the *Catuvellauni* or

Catualani. Of the origins of the kingdom, nothing is known for certain. It is usually assumed that it was already in existence before 54 BC, but even this is not beyond doubt. It is worth note that Caesar, contrary to his usual practice, does not give the name of the tribe which provided him with the strongest opposition in 54, nor does he say from which tribe Cassivellaunus came. One possible explanation for this is that the tribal grouping was not yet in existence by that date, and it may be that it was due to Cassivellaunus' actions that it came into being, presumably as an amalgam of smaller peoples north of the Thames valley. The subsequent career of Cassivellaunus is unchronicled. No inscribed coinage of his is known and no uninscribed series can be reasonably assigned to him.

The next identifiable ruler in the Catuvellaunian area is Tasciovanus (known only from his inscribed coinage) who began to reign about or shortly after 20 BC. His gold coins were derived from the uninscribed Whaddon Chase type, which had first appeared some thirty years before. On some of the later gold issues the mint-name VER (*ulamium*) appears for the first time; it occurs frequently on later coinages in gold, silver and bronze, including those on which the king's name is omitted. A very rare gold issue bears the monogram which may be expanded to CAMV (*lodunum*). This dates to between 15 and 10 BC and has usually been interpreted as reflecting a short-lived occupation of *Camulodunum* by the Catuvellaunian ruling house. But it could also have resulted from a client relationship between the Trinovantes and Tasciovanus. The later coins of Tasciovanus are enormously varied and reveal a strong Roman character, as do those of his contemporary Tincommius (*page 34*).

The later coinage of this ruler includes a fascinating assembly of types and legends, giving us several names, some occurring with that of Tasciovanus, others on their own. The issues inscribed TASCIO/RIGON have a somewhat wider distribution than the others and may have been coined at several centres. The meaning of RIGON or RICON is not certain but is probably equivalent to the Latin REX. Other combinations are TASC and DIAS, TASCIO and SEGO, TAS and ANDO, while ANDO and RVES also appear alone. Coins inscribed ANDOCO appear to overlap with the issues of Tasciovanus in the later stages of the latter's reign, the distribution suggesting that Andocos or Andocoveros ruled over a territory on the western flank of the Catuvellauni. Although these tribal princelings are no more than names, they do give support to the idea that the Catuvellauni were a confederacy of several groupings, not firmly welded into a single tribe until late in the first century BC.

Tasciovanus' capital was clearly the *oppidum* of *Verulamium* sited on a plateau above the river Ver. The earthworks on that plateau are probably of several phases and have not yet been fully studied so that it is not known when the place was first settled. By the late first century BC, occupation had extended into the valley floor at several points and the minting of coins was also going on there. No other Iron Age centres of comparable size are yet known on the tribal territory, though there were sizeable fortified sites at The Aubreys, near Redbourn, at Wheathampstead and at Ravensburgh (Bedfordshire).

A few miles north of *Verulamium*, a group of richly furnished burials dating from the period 20 BC to AD 40 indicates the residence there of aristocratic families. The graves are all cremations, the remains being placed among the grave-goods in a deep pit, not apparently covered by a mound. The best known examples occur in the area of Hertford and Welwyn, at Hertford Heath, Welwyn and Welwyn Garden City. Others lie to the east and north and are more likely to be the graves of Trinovantian nobles. There is a marked homogeneity among the grave-goods, common items being Italian amphorae and bronze vessels, high quality Roman and Gallo-Belgic pottery along with excellent native metalwork. The most costly objects are Graeco-Roman silver drinking cups at Welwyn and Welwyn Garden City, probably of Augustan date. Together with the fine bronze vessels, these will have made drinking sets which were fit company for the imported wine in large amphorae. The relatively limited distribution of these burials is notable. Nothing so rich occurs in Kent or to the west of *Verulamium*. In the territory north of the lower Thames there have been recorded most of the Italian wine amphorae of Augustan and Tiberian date yet known from Britain. The inference is clear. Roman traders were active here as at the court of Maroboduus in Bohemia, with the connivance and perhaps the active support of the British rulers.

Near the end of the first century BC, an entirely new element enters the British coinages, beginning on coins of Tasciovanus and continuing on those of Andoco. – The reverses of the coins were taken over by an astonishing range of classicizing types, several of which were executed with so assured a skill that the die-cutters must surely have come from Italy or Gaul.[13] First registered on the issues of Catuvellaunian rulers, these types later appear on Atrebatic and Trinovantian issues as well. The whole representational manner evident on the coins is foreign to the Celtic world, and the craftsmen responsible for the dies possessed an intimate knowledge of Greek and Roman religious and mythological themes, Graeco-Roman symbolism and contemporary portraiture in miniature. The widest range of classical themes appears on the coinage of Tasciovanus, but the best executed and the closest to Roman tradition are certain issues of Tincommius and Verica of the Atrebates. Most catholic of all in their allusion to Roman myth and personifications are the coins of Cunobelin, though their execution was frequently inferior to that of earlier issues.

Almost all the rulers who issued classicizing coins went to some lengths to present their obverse portrait-busts (for so they are to be interpreted) as close in style as possible to those of their Imperial contemporaries, and the die-cutters of three of them, Tasciovanus, Verica and Cunobelin, occasionally succeeded in achieving a virtual assimilation with the coin-portraits of emperors. Nothing could be less like the heads of Celts as portrayed by Roman artists or by Celts at a later date. Yet not all sense of reality was lost. On one bronze issue, for example, Tasciovanus was shown (against Roman fashion) wearing a peaked helmet, while Andoco once added a Celtic pigtail to his otherwise Roman hairstyle. These are glimpses into a Celtic milieu in some cases through the eyes of a Roman artist, in others perhaps of a British craftsman who had learnt from an immigrant master. This taste for Roman motifs on the coinage of the south-eastern rulers is revealing in two respects. First, the coins give us virtually our only knowledge of a cultural tradition in which Roman elements were mingled with Celtic. These were not superficial versions of Roman types; rather, Roman figures, scenes and symbols were adapted to a Celtic milieu. Secondly, we see something of the artistic and, to an extent, the political aspirations of the southern British kings as we do in no other source. On these coins the British dynasts state their claim to be considered seriously by the greater power and demonstrate to the world that that power acknowledged more than their mere presence.

The Cantii

The reference of Caesar to four kings in *Cantium* suggests that the *civitas Cantiorum* was also made up of several smaller groups settled in Surrey and Eastern Kent. This was never the seat of a powerful barbarian kingdom, and chieftains like Dubnovellaunus and Eppillus were always liable to be dominated by their northern and western neighbours. Large settlements in valleys began to be established from the first century BC at Rochester, Canterbury and Loose; of these, Canterbury in due course formed the basis for the

Roman city. For the rest, the common settlement type was the familiar single homestead. Caesar regarded *Cantium* as the most civilized part of Britain, perhaps impressed by the extent of cereal-growing on the productive land of Eastern Kent as well as by its proximity to Gaul. This was the best of the tribal land. To the west lay the vast forest of the Weald, sparsely settled but productive of iron.

The Trinovantes

North of the lower Thames lay the most powerful tribe of Southern Britain in the mid-first century BC, the Trinovantes. Caesar had left Mandubracius ruling them in 54. Nothing is subsequently heard of him so that we have no idea of the duration of his reign or how it ended. The next identifiable ruler in this region is Addedomarus, whose reign began about 20–15 BC and lasted for a decade or so. His place was taken by Dubnovellaunus, before he was compelled to seek safety in the Roman world. Like Tincommius, he fled Britain before AD 7. He was supplanted at *Camulodunum* by the greatest of the British monarchs and the only one to earn the style *rex Britannorum*, Cunobelin. His coins proclaim him to be the son of Tasciovanus and thus of Catuvellaunian stock, which raises the question how he came to be ruling at *Camulodunum*. Whether or not there had been armed conflict between the two tribes will probably never be known for certain. The coinage, our only guide, indicates that Cunobelin's earliest gold issues bear the mint signature of *Camulodunum* and circulated mainly within the Trinovantian area. His next series, bearing the famous barley ear on the obverse, was a much larger coinage and was more widely distributed, notably towards the upper Thames and into Hertfordshire and Cambridgeshire. The distribution of the contemporary bronze coinage was similarly wide. The most reasonable interpretation of these major coinages is that they are a palpable result of the unification of the two tribes under the rule of Cunobelin, probably between AD 10 and 20. That rivalry between the two tribal blocs north of the Thames should come to a head is entirely credible, though the details of the union are not recoverable.

Henceforward, almost to the Claudian invasion, Cunobelin dominated the stage from his base at *Camulodunum*. He had at least one brother, Epaticcus, who carved out a territory immediately south of the middle Thames, presumably at the expense of Verica, but he was a minor figure and may have owed his position to his brother. It is often assumed that the Trinovantes tended to suffer from the expansionist drive of their Catuvellaunian neighbours. There is little to commend the view, to which the Roman treatment of the two tribes gives no support. The site of *Camulodunum* was alienated from native possession first by a legionary fortress, later by a *colonia* of veterans, whereas *Verulamium* became in due course a *municipium*. Too much should not be read into this, but it remains true that Rome always had a clear sense of who her opponents were and how they should be treated.

The Iceni

To the north of the Trinovantes in Norfolk and Northern Suffolk lay the Iceni, a tribe frequently dismissed as minor and backward by modern writers, but one which seemed significant enough to Rome to merit recognition as an independent kingdom after AD 43, and which twice thereafter pitted its strength against Roman armies. The pre-Roman rulers of the Iceni are no more than names to us: in sequence, CAN DVRO, ANTED, AESV ED and SAENV. Probably all these rulers belong to the four decades immediately before the Roman conquest. Their coinages reveal scarcely any influence of the southern dynasties and it is remarkable that the southern coinages themselves, including that of Cunobelin, are sparsely represented on Icenian territory. The earliest uninscribed coins were derived from Kentish prototypes, but they were quickly adapted into an unimaginative local pattern. No Roman types were used or imitated; taken all in all, the Icenian coinage follows its own path. Neither it nor the fine metalwork from Snettisham and Ipswich offers any support for the view that southern aristocrats had lodged themselves among the Iceni and taken over direction of their affairs. Equipment of such quality was at the command of any chieftain with the means to employ suitably skilled craftsmen. Numerous enclosed settlements are known on the territory of the Iceni, some with substantial defences. Among larger settlements the most striking is an obviously high-status site with substantial timber structures near Thetford. This was occupied in the first half of the first century AD and probably down to the great revolt of AD 60/1 (see below, p. 70). This was clearly a major centre of power, quite probably a residence of Icenian rulers, a possibility strengthened by the burial of several major hoards in the vicinity.

The Dobunni, Cornovii and Corieltauvi

The Dobunni of the lower Severn valley and the Cotswolds were a large tribe, probably an association of several septs. An uninscribed coinage in gold began shortly after the middle of the first century BC, and before the end of the century the first named rulers appear: ANTED, EISV, CATTI, COMVX and INAM. The obverses of the gold bear a distinctive branched emblem, the reverses the triple-tailed horse of the Atrebates. The silver coinage is more varied and betrays no close links with other issues. Much has been made of the presence of imported Roman and south-eastern British pottery and other goods at the stronghold at Bagendon, near Cirencester, but on its own this cannot be regarded as evidence of political dependence on the Catuvellauni rather than commercial relations with their region. Moreover the date of most of the material recovered from Bagendon is closer to the Roman conquest than was suggested by its first interpreters.[14] We are informed by Dio (when his text is suitably emended) that in AD 43 a part of the Dobunni was subject to the Catuvellauni. This is important evidence for the westward extension of Catuvellaunian influence, but it may not be assumed that this influence had been exercised for decades before the Roman arrival.

The latest rulers of the tribe, probably in the period AD 20–40, were CORIO and BODVOC. It has been argued that these were contemporaries, that Corio ruled over the southern part of the tribal territory and Bodvoc the northern, and finally that Bodvoc was firmly under the influence of the Catuvellauni, as his coins often bear Roman-style lettering of good quality. None of these propositions can be demonstrated. There is no firm evidence that the two rulers held sway over separate parts of the tribe or that they were contemporaries. Nor does the romanity of Bodvoc's coinage necessarily mean that he was under the wing of Cunobelin. It may mean only that he had acquired a skilled moneyer.

North of the Dobunni, inhabiting the upper Severn valley and the Cheshire plain, lay the poorly known tribe of the Cornovii. Numerous large and powerfully defended hill-forts existed on both sides of the Severn and in the hills further west, but it is not known how many of these were still occupied in the later Iron Age. As with the Dumnonii, it is significant that the Roman city of Wroxeter developed over the site of a legionary fortress and seemingly had no immediate native predecessor. No coinage was issued in the region and the prevailing material culture, as expressed in pottery and metalwork, compares unfavourably even with that of the Iron Age population of Herefordshire and South Wales.

The broad territory from the Trent basin to the valleys of the Welland and Nene was occupied by the Coritani (or Corieltauvi). Several areas of their territory were densely settled, especially the alluvial land of the Trent and Welland valleys. The uplands of Leicestershire and Lincolnshire, too, probably maintained a larger population than is often assumed and the heavier clay lands of the Midland plain had also been opened up long before the coming of Rome. The characteristic larger settlement type is a lowland site without defences, the best known instances being at Leicester, Old Sleaford, Ancaster, Dragonby and, a recent discovery, Lincoln. The later Iron Age culture of the region had much in common with that of South-east England. The earliest coin issues were derived from Gallo-Belgic gold staters which arrived in Britain early in the first century BC. Silver coins first appeared after the middle of that century and the first inscribed issues half a century later. The sequence of the inscribed issues is not yet clear, though AVN AST (or AVN COST) and ESVP ASV seem to be the earliest. The pairing of names continued to be a feature of the coinage, to an extent unmatched among other British issues. Paired magistrates on the Gaulish model may have been responsible for these coins, though joint rulers are a distinct possibility. The later inscribed issues are dominated by the name VOLISIOS, in conjunction with DVMNOCOVEROS, DVMNOVELLAV (NOS) and CARTIVEL (IOS or LAVNOS). Most specimens of the VOLISIOS coinage have been found well north of the tribal heartland, notably in two hoards from West Yorkshire dating from well after AD 43. These may be seen as the coinage of a refugee chieftain after the conquest of the Corieltauvi had been completed, but it is worth note that the distribution of individual finds of VOLISIOS coins points to South-west Yorkshire, with an extension into South Lancashire and Cheshire, as their area of circulation. It may be, then, that here was a distinct sept, neither Coritanian nor Brigantian, which continued to issue coins until the Roman occupation of the Pennines after AD 71.

The Belgae

In Hampshire and extending north-westwards were the Belgae, of whom the literary and numismatic sources have little to report. Their centre in the Roman period lay at Winchester (*Venta Belgarum*), though, as Bath is also assigned to them by Ptolemy, their lands must have reached far to the west, between the Dobunni and the Durotriges. It is often assumed that the *civitas Belgarum* was entirely a Roman creation, but for this there is no warrant. The tribal name can be as convincingly interpreted as an introduction from Belgic Gaul by migrants who had earlier passed to Britain as an arbitrary imposition by Rome upon a heterogeneous population. Unless these people were calling themselves Belgae, there seems to be no particular reason why a Roman administrator should apply that name. No Iron Age coinage has yet been attributed to chieftains of the Belgae, though the coinage inscribed CORIO and usually assigned to the Dobunni should be seriously considered in this connection. The tribe, or a part of it, may have been one of those which passed under the rule of Cogidubnus at some date after AD 43 (*page 53*).

The Durotriges (or Durotrages)

To the south, in Dorset and Wiltshire, lay the Durotriges. This tribe had been cut off from their profitable external markets in North-western Gaul by the campaigns of Julius Caesar and in particular by his destruction of the Venetic fleet. There is virtually no evidence available on individual personalities, which may be connected with the fact that the complete unification of the tribe may not have been achieved until the Roman conquest. The continued existence of a large number of strongly defended hill-forts down to the Roman conquest, and the absence of any one obvious political centre, point firmly in this direction. The coinage offers little further guidance. From its origin, shortly before the mid-first century BC, it was in silver only. No clear links with the south-eastern coinages are evident. Despite the presence of the Mendip silver-lead deposits on their northern borders, the Durotrigian issues degenerated into base silver and bronze, many of the later coins being cast, not struck. Upon the material culture of the Durotriges there is very little impress either of Rome or of the south-eastern British tribes. But certain crafts were highly developed. Wheel-made pottery of excellent quality was produced, and shale from Kimmeridge was lathe-turned into elegant urns which found a market further east. The relative isolation of the tribe from its eastern neighbours may have helped to foster that independent spirit which the Roman army was to encounter on its westward drive shortly after AD 43. The Durotriges may have had rather more to do with their neighbours to the west, the Dumnonii.

The Dumnonii

The south-western peninsula of Devon and Cornwall was the territory of the Dumnonii, probably a grouping of several septs. In the west of the canton, the ancient hundreds of Cornwall may reflect divisions of people much older than those of medieval days. The ancient sources make only sparse reference to the tribe. No site with claims to be regarded as the tribal *chef-lieu* has yet emerged and it is thus significant that the Roman centre developed out of the *canabae* of a legionary fortress at *Isca* (Exeter). Even large hill-forts are rare in the region, among the more notable being those, like Hembury and Dumpdon, that lie east of the Exe. Much commoner are multivallate forts sited on the slopes of hills, such as Clovelly Dykes and Milber Down, a settlement type probably adapted to the keeping of large herds of stock. Well known features of the Cornish landscape are large numbers of small, embanked enclosures or 'rounds', probably representing family settlements. Recent observation suggests that these also existed in Devon. A distinctive feature of the late Iron Age in the Lands' End peninsula are stone courtyard-houses, occurring both in groups, as at Chysauster and Porthmeor, and singly amid terraced fields. Numbers of the impressive cliff-castles, occupying coastal promontories and analogous to cliff-forts in Brittany, also appear to have remained in use down to the Roman period and in some cases for longer.

It seems highly unlikely that a tribe which covered this immense and varied region was ever a united force. The eastern area shared many characteristics with Durotrigian territory. To the west of Dartmoor, material culture followed a more independent line, though certain finds of exotic objects, like the Paul hoard of *drachmae* or the Carn Brea deposit of Gallo-Belgic gold coins, give occasional glimpses of contacts from far afield.

The Brigantes

The Brigantes, the most numerous people of Britain in the first century AD according to Tacitus, held much of the Pennines and the broad plains to east and west. Iron Age settlement in Northern Britain is still poorly recorded, except in the region between the Tyne and the Forth, the territory of the Votadini. Little extensive excavation has been carried out in the Pennines, Cumbria and south-western Scotland, though the first indications are that settlements in these regions have much in common with those between the Tyne and the Forth. The predominant settlement-type is a roughly circular or sub-rectangular enclosure surrounded by a timber palisade. The enclosures were generally small, measuring no more than two acres at most and often considerably less. Within lay a small number of dwellings, rarely more than four at one time and frequently only one or two. Settlements of this type can now be traced back to at least the sixth century BC and they survived with little change down to the Roman period. The dwellings were of timber and invariably circular in plan. In scale the larger examples were broadly similar to those of the south. In the settlements on the Northumbrian hills, the dwellings were usually stone-walled and were set inside walled enclosures which frequently developed over the sites of earlier palisaded settlements. Some steadings were sited on artificial terraces scooped out of the hill-side, thus finding greater protection from the weather as well as easing the problem of building on a slope. Pastoralism was no doubt prominent in the economy of these sites, but earlier emphasis upon this has been too extreme.[15] Pastoral nomadism was of much less significance than a settled pastoralism supported by limited arable cultivation. Large community settlements within hill-forts were rare in the north, sites like Traprain Law, Ingleborough and Almondbury standing out among the others. At the time of the Roman conquest, or shortly after it, the Brigantes were ruled by a queen, Cartimandua, who quickly recognized the changed political realities and entered into a treaty relationship with Rome. This created serious strains within the tribe and these were to lead in due course to a full-scale Roman assault on northern Britain (*page 82*).

The tribes of Wales

The uplands and valleys of Wales were held by four major tribes and by a variety of smaller septs. The Silures of south-east Wales gave the Romans most trouble, so that we hear most about them. Their territory was the broken country between the Towey and the Wye, and the fertile coastal plain. No major centres are known, the population being scattered over this mixed terrain. To the north of them lay the Ordovices in central and north Wales, perhaps including Anglesey. They, too, were opponents of Rome, but unlike the Silures they were not to form a *civitas* under Roman rule. Their population was also scattered across hill-country and no single focus is known. In the borderland of Powys lay the Deceangli, their chief claim to fame their wealth in silver, lead and copper. South-west Wales was occupied by the Demetae, another people whose population was scattered in homesteads and small enclosures. No major Iron Age centre is known; in the Roman order their *caput* was at Carmarthen.

3

The Claudian Triumph

gentes b(arbaras trans Oceanum) primus in dici (onem populi Romani redegerit)

In AD 37 the aged and embittered Tiberius died, followed within a year or two by Cunobelin. With them perished the Augustan relationship between Britain and Rome. Tiberius was succeeded by the capricious and headstrong Gaius, for whose mercifully brief reign we have little to throw into the balance against the weight of abuse and ridicule heaped up by the surviving sources. In attempting to make any sense of Gaius' activities in Germany and Northern Gaul, it is important to recall that he was the son of Germanicus and a descendant of Julius Caesar, both of whom he admired above the other members of the Julio-Claudian house. Yet both these generals had failed to achieve a desired and publicized conquest; Caesar in Britain, Germanicus in Germany. The prospect of out-doing both of his ancestors must have been heady for a young man whose resistance to the intoxication of power was so weak.[1] The need to restore Roman fortunes on the Rhine was clear even before Gaius' accession. Discipline was lax owing to the incapacity of the legates of both the German armies, and German bands were raiding across the Rhine. The reputation of Rome was lower than it had been since the debacle of AD 9.

Gaius left Rome for Germany in August of 39. Before he could turn his attention to the Germans, there was a conspiracy to deal with, hatched by the legate of Upper Germany, Cn Cornelius Lentulus Gaetulicus. That was swiftly quashed, and the only point of immediate significance in the affair is that Gaetulicus had planned to dedicate to the emperor a poem which treated of the conquest of Britain, an interesting sign of what was thought at that moment most flattering to Gaius. It is impossible to reconstruct even an outline of the subsequent campaign against the Germans. Suetonius and Cassius

Dio present it as an inglorious farce. Eutropius is a little kinder: *nihil strenue fecit*. There is no real evidence that Gaius mounted a major expedition against the trans-rhenan peoples. More probably he was intent on clearing marauders out of the districts on the west bank of the Rhine, and perhaps on a punitive raid across the river. Anything more than this seems unlikely, particularly because of the recent poor showing of both the armies in Germany. The army on the lower Rhine was still below standard eight years later when Corbulo assumed command. That the Upper German legions needed a dose of strenuous discipline is evident from Gaius' choice of a successor to Gaetulicus, the stern, no-nonsense Ser. Sulpicius Galba, later briefly emperor after the death of Nero.

Before Gaius retired for the winter to *Lugdunum*, a British prince and son of Cunobelin, Adminius, fled to the protection of the emperor, either having been ejected by his father or anticipating a worse fate. Gaius' reception of Adminius was warm: indeed he rejoiced as if the entire island of Britain had been surrendered to him. The news was duly announced in Rome near the end of the year and the emperor is even reported to have gone so far as to be hailed *Britannicus*. These extravagances may mean no more than that the exile had represented the present circumstances as offering an excellent opportunity for a Roman invasion. But Adminius may have gone further and sought Roman support for a coup d'état in the south-eastern kingdom, fearing that otherwise there could be no place for him in a Britain which also contained Caratacus and Togodumnus. This episode might lie behind the anger felt in Britain over certain fugitives whom the Romans failed to return to the island, though the later flight of Verica provides another occasion. One can imagine the volatile mind of Gaius turning with delight from the fruitless pursuit of Germans to a project which the deified Julius had failed to perfect. Britain was the target for the next year.

A force of unknown size and composition assembled at Boulogne in the spring of 40. Work had probably already begun on a lighthouse overlooking the harbour there, a fine work which survived until the seventeenth century.[2] There can be no doubt that this was installed as an improvement to the military base and not out of some paternalist interest in the welfare of Channel traders. The army was drawn up as if for embarkation. The emperor himself set sail – and then quickly turned back. The troops had not moved. Gaius' behaviour following the incident, giving the signal for battle and then bidding the soldiers pick up shells and take their fortunes away with them, if it has not been unrecognizably distorted by Suetonius and Xiphilinus, is strange enough, but perhaps not unfathomable. The frustration of the planned expedition could be due either to a change in Gaius' own intentions, a view expressed by Tacitus, or to a change in the temper of the army, the explanation favoured by recent historians. Guesses that the situation in Britain had drastically altered so that Adminius' assessment was no longer valid, or that matters had deteriorated in Rome, remain quite without support. Just as likely as a change in Gaius' intentions (and perhaps contributing to such a change) is a further manifestation of serious indiscipline among his legions, such as had required correction in the previous year. Troops which had served with a lack of distinction on the Rhine are not likely to have been enthusiastic for an invasion of Britain. Even in better days for the legions, Claudius was to face a similar difficulty. Whether a mutiny actually broke out in 40 will never be known. Matters need not have gone so far. But even Gaius was unlikely to embark on such a venture with an army of dubious mettle. Having reviewed them at Boulogne and taken the advice of his senior commanders, he may have been compelled to put off the invasion. His antidote to disappointment was the unveiled contempt expressed in the command to collect shells and, more telling, the miserable donative of 400 sesterces. So far as anything can be grasped of Gaius' aims in 40, then, there are grounds for thinking that he seriously intended to take an expedition to Britain and that the plan was foiled by the indiscipline or unpreparedness of the army. Attempts to dismiss his operations on the Gaulish coast as military manoeuvres do not adequately explain his scornful reactions when the plan had to be abandoned.[3] He had his *casus belli* in the flight of Adminius, and his dispatch to the Senate late in 39 shows the way his mind was working. Moreover, the building of the Boulogne lighthouse, no less than the earlier appointment of Galba, reveals an intelligent grasp of what was needed to further the project. The raising of two new legions, *XV Primigenia* and *XXII Primigenia*, the first additions to legionary strength since the Augustan reforms, points to planned offensive action in some theatre of war, and after the German provinces were quieted Britain was the obvious aim. The failure was not of the emperor, but of his army. Britain could no longer be ignored, and the events of 39–40 oddly presage those which were shortly to make the island a Roman possession.[4]

Claudius was fifty-one at his accession, the unlikely son of Drusus and brother of Germanicus.[5] In infancy and youth he was the victim of an illness which rendered him an invalid and retarded his mental growth for a time. By the time he reached manhood, he had lived not so much a sheltered existence as one of near isolation, the effects of which never left him. He received none of the minor offices which would lead to the normal *cursus honorum* of an Imperial prince. Claudius turned to scholarship, especially to history, and asked searching questions about the nature and legitimacy of the Principate. To his elder kinsmen this was sufficient proof that he was incurable. This was a seemingly impossible apprenticeship for an emperor; few in Rome, and fewer in the Senate, can have approved the actions of the Praetorians who gave him the throne.

It has often been asserted, and rightly, that the new regime needed the prestige which military success alone could bestow. It might be argued further that not only Claudius himself stood in need of some outstanding success in his early days. The Principate needed the restoration of some of the dignity lost during the long stagnation of the later reign of Tiberius and the frenzy of the Gaian *triennium*. The man who, in youth, had shocked the Julio-Claudian house by questioning the very basis of the Principate would, in maturity, ensure its survival. Two military enterprises offered themselves to the new *princeps*, both inherited from Gaius: Mauretania and Britain. Mauretania was the lesser problem, promptly resolved by C. Suetonius Paullinus and, later, by Gn. Hosidius Geta. Britain, too, formed part of the tarnished legacy of Gaius and offered greater material rewards as well as greater glory.

But there was more. Claudius came to power with little experience of public life, but with a mind steeped in the history and politics of the previous century. His attempts to enter politics had been all but fruitless before he became consul, with Gaius, in 37. But he was much more than a scholarly recluse and his judgment of his predecessors was based on careful analysis of their policies and achievements. Gaius and Tiberius seemed neglectful. Towards Augustus he was respectful but cool. It was, above all, to the administration of Julius Caesar that he looked for a model and an inspiration. This is evident in his attitude to the extension of *civitas*, to the revival of provincial colonization (in abeyance for some thirty years) and to public works. Behind all this lay an emulation of those qualities of Caesar which the Romans of the early Principate summarized as *clementia*. Britain, the land which Caesar had failed to subdue, could thus hold a special place in Claudius' mind. Its conquest meant more than a brilliant military success: it made a true Caesar of the man who had no other claim to the name.[6]

Once again, as in 39, a plausible reason for intervention in Britain was provided by the flight of a British leader to the protection of Rome. This time it was the Atrebatic king, Verica (Berikos in Cassius Dio's narrative), ejected it may be surmised by the sons of Cunobelin.[7] Even without the timely arrival of this exile, however, the expedition would have gone forward. The legionary army was drawn mainly from the German provinces: *Legio II Augusta* from Strasbourg, *Legio XIV Gemina* from Mainz and *Legio XX* from Neuss. The force was completed by *Legio IX Hispana* which came from Pannonia with the expedition commander, Aulus Plautius. The two legions newly raised by Gaius were used to strengthen the depleted garrison of the Rhine frontier. There was plainly no place in Britain for untried units. Little is known about the composition of the auxiliary forces which accompanied the four legions, but the majority were probably drawn from the Rhine armies and from Gallia Belgica, and there may have been a particular emphasis upon the cavalry arm. In all, the invasion army from the Rhine and Northern Gaul necessitated many changes in the garrisoning of those regions. These are little known as yet and it is not always clear whether recognizable changes are to be referred to Claudius rather than Gaius. In the period 40–3 forts were established at Tournai and Courtrai and at Valkenburg and Velsen near the mouth of the old Rhine, which could all date to the reign of Gaius or the beginning of that of Claudius. In 41, the Chauki broke into the region between the Rhine and the Ems, and the forts on the Rhine may owe their foundation to that occasion rather than to the invasion of Britain. The main springboard for the assault was in any case the Pas de Calais, though the Rhine mouth would have provided an excellent assembly point for supplies.

The commander of the expedition, Aulus Plautius, belonged to a family which had enjoyed high regard with the Julio-Claudian house since the reign of Augustus. A cousin of Claudius' ex-wife Urgulanilla, his only recorded consular command before this was as legate in Pannonia, where he is not likely to have seen much action. Although his appointment may have seemed less likely than that of Sulpicius Galba or Domitius Corbulo, he was to prove himself a tenacious and capable general. The conquest of Britain was far from being treated as a walk-over, and the quality of the high-ranking officers on the staff of Plautius and in the retinue of the emperor shows that difficulties were fully expected.[8]

Among the senior *viri militares* were Sulpicius Galba from Upper Germany, Hosidius Geta, fresh from successes in Mauretania, A. Didius Gallus, later governor of Britain, and T. Flavius Sabinus, the elder and hitherto more successful brother of Vespasian. P. Ostorius Scapula, later to return as governor, may also have come to notice in the expedition. Among lesser luminaries were T. Flavius Vespasianus, legate of *Legio II Augusta*, P. Graecinius Laco, the procurator of Gaul, Rufrius Pollio, commander of the Praetorians, and C. Stertinius Xenophon and Ti. Claudius Balbillus, both *praefecti fabrum*. The presence of Graecinius Laco is presumably to be explained in connection with the mineral wealth of Britain, in addition to other problems of finance which annexation would bring. When Claudius himself joined the expedition some time later, his entourage was a mixture of distinguished consulars chosen for their merit and experience and others who could not safely be left behind in Rome. In the latter category, D. Valerius Asiaticus had made a bid for power when Gaius was assassinated. Gn Sentius Saturninus had pressed for the restoration of the Republic on the same occasion. M. Vinicius, too, had had ambitions far beyond those of decent senatorial *quies*. Claudius was not forgetful of those two days in January 41 when Republican feeling, or at least distaste for the Principate, was so strongly expressed. Nor would he have forgotten the moves of certain senators in 42, aimed at deposing him with the aid of the Dalmatian legions. Vinicius and Asiaticus never convinced Claudius that they had repented of their earlier opinions. Although both received second consulates, in 45 and 46 respectively, both were removed from the scene shortly after holding office. The entourage included relatives too: Ti. Plautius Silvanus Aelianus, a brother of Urgulanilla, L. Junius Silanus Torquatus, engaged to his daughter Octavia, Cn Pompeius Magnus, husband of another daughter, and his father M. Licinius Crassus Frugi, later executed. Even on members of this family party, *ornamenta triumphalia* were later bestowed with absurd generosity, despite their lack of rank and experience. Back in Rome, affairs of state were entrusted to L. Vitellius, formerly a legate of Syria and a 'safe' man. Also left behind, to add weight to military counsels, was Domitius Corbulo, one of the best generals of the day.

The opening of the great enterprise was far from auspicious: it may indeed have recalled the fiasco of AD 40. Overcome by the prospect of sailing beyond the bounds of the world, the army refused to embark. Their fears of what awaited them in a still largely mysterious island were real enough, and that mood of indiscipline which had haunted the north-western armies for some years may not yet have been entirely dispelled. It took the appearance of one of Claudius' closest confidants, the freedman Narcissus, to change their minds. Whatever message Narcissus had intended to deliver went unread. It was enough for the freedman to mount the tribunal for the soldiery to feel ashamed and cover the emotion with raucous humour. Embarkation followed immediately.

Cassius Dio reports that the expedition sailed in three separate squadrons in order to obviate any difficulties which might arise in landing so large a force. Some have argued that a commander would not have so readily split the main body of his troops. But even a third of approximately 40,000 men was a very considerable army in antiquity, and such doubts about Dio's veracity are not justified. So large a sea-borne force might well have met difficulty if it had attempted to come ashore in one place. Separate land-falls on the coast of Kent may not be out of the question, and there were suitable commanders for three divisions in Aulus Plautius, Hosidius Geta and Flavius Sabinus. The Britons had not mustered, their fears of an invasion perhaps allayed by reports of the mutiny, and there was no opposition to the Roman landings. From the start, British strategy was based upon the guerrilla warfare which Cassivellaunus had used so successfully. But much had changed since 54 BC. The Romans were now invading from a secure Gaul and their knowledge of the south-eastern coasts was evidently much better than in Caesar's day.

The harbours where the Claudian army disembarked are to be sought in Eastern Kent. The best candidate is Richborough, on the River Stour, as it crosses mud flats on its path to Pegwell Bay.[9] Subsequent marsh formation has robbed the site of any vestige of its ancient anchorage so that it is impossible to be certain that the entire fleet was accommodated here. It seems less than likely that it was, in view of the three divisions. Of the other Kentish harbours, Dover stands out as worthy of consideration, but there is no clear evidence for a Claudian force here.[10] More probably, havens were sought on the north coast of Kent and thus Reculver comes into the reckoning. Here traces of Claudian occupation have been found, though little is known of the character of the earliest site and much has been irrevocably lost to sea-erosion. If the Wantsum Channel was navigable at this date, the harbours of Richborough and Reculver eight miles apart could easily have been linked behind the Isle of Thanet, thus avoiding navigation around the North Foreland.

Plautius began operations circumspectly, perhaps at first incredulous that the Britons had not marshalled a major force to oppose him. Early skirmishing against forces led by Caratacus, and later against others headed by Togodumnus, posed no difficulties for the invaders and the Britons were driven back to a river, surely the Medway, where they regrouped. At this point the Romans gained a useful diplomatic success. A part of the 'Bodunni', by which Dio clearly meant the Dobunni of the Severn basin, surrendered to Plautius. They had read the signs quickly and accurately. The Romans must have been looking to other tribes to follow this lead, but there is no other mention of defection or fission in Dio's account. Within the regions dominated by Caratacus and Togodumnus, on the contrary, strong resistance was to be encountered.

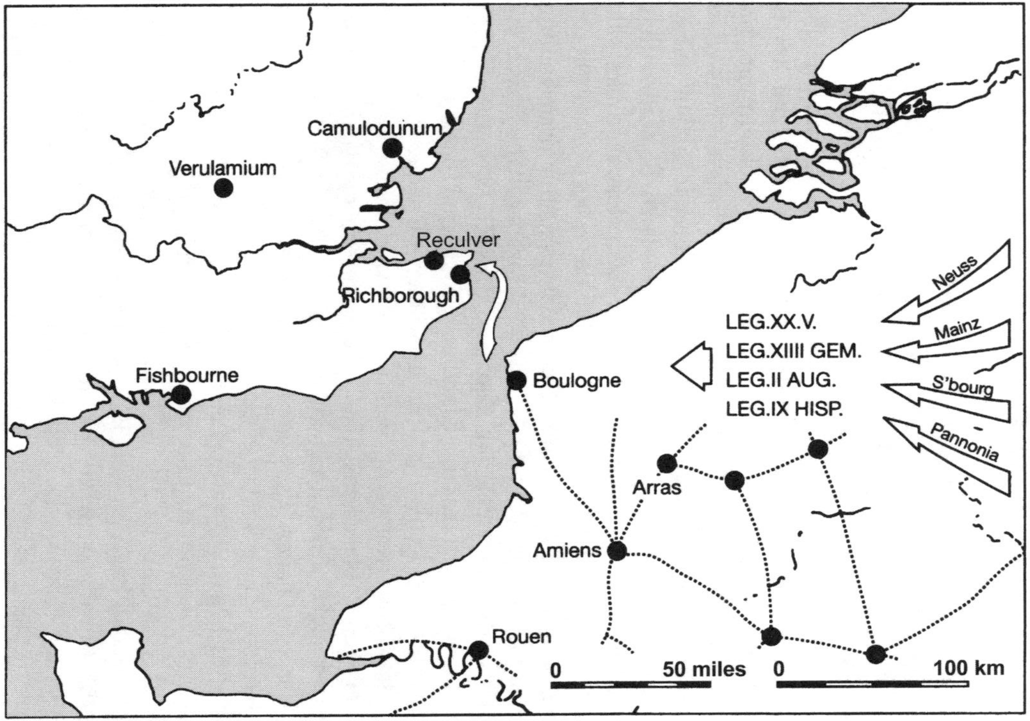

Figure 6 The invasion of AD 43.

The sons of Cunobelin massed their forces on the Medway, perhaps immediately upstream of Rochester. If the hoard of *aurei* buried about this time at Bredgar[11] (near Sittingbourne) is accepted as an indicator of Plautius' route, then he was following the line later taken by Watling Street. Information provided by traders about possible routes and obstacles in the terrain must by now have been extensive, and there is no need to believe that Caesar's *Commentaries* were Plautius' main guide to the topography of Kent. The Medway will thus have come as no surprise to the general, and he may have hoped to bring his enemy to battle east of it rather than on its banks.

The battle on the Medway was probably the most difficult engagement of the initial campaign, lasting for two days. The Britons were drawn up on the west bank. Rather than consume time in building boats or rafts, Plautius sent across auxiliaries, probably Batavi, swimming in full battle gear. They set about the British chariotry and created great confusion among the horses. Meantime, a force spearheaded by *Legio II Augusta*, its legate Vespasian acting under his elder brother Flavius Sabinus, had got across some distance away and managed to make some ground, though without driving off the Britons. Night fell with the issue undecided. Next morning a fresh attack was led by Hosidius Geta, one would imagine with troops held in reserve on the previous day. This new onslaught swung the battle to the Romans, Geta distinguishing himself in the action. The primary roles taken by Flavius Sabinus and Hosidius Geta on successive days are interesting, raising the possibility that the Roman forces were operating in at least two battle groups and perhaps in the original three brigades.

The Britons had no choice but to fall back on the Thames, making their crossing 'near where the river enters the sea and forms a large pool at high tide' evidently in the vicinity of London Bridge. Plautius lost no time in following them, but the river-crossings posed problems before a group of auxiliaries managed to swim across and engage the Britons on the further bank. Others got across over a bridge some distance upstream, not necessarily a native bridge carelessly left open. Legionaries would be well able to construct a timber bridge in a few days. The British levies were now caught in a vice and suffered heavy losses. The main obstacle to the Roman advance was now the marshy ground of Southern Essex. There was no further set battle before the capture of the next target, the British strong-hold at *Camulodunum*, only skirmishes. During these, Togodumnus lost his life and British resistance thereafter centred upon Caratacus.

Chronological details are denied us, but by now it must have been June or July. Roman advance columns were within fifty miles of

Camulodunum and there was every prospect of that prize falling to the invaders in this same summer. The campaign had gone well, a reward for sound planning, careful intelligence work and sensible generalship. Plautius and his commanders had seen hard fighting, but there had been no insurmountable obstacles. The opposition possessed no greater military unity than it had a century before, despite the growth of a centralized power based on *Camulodunum*. The heirs of Cunobelin could hardly have done more than they did with the forces at their disposal, but the Roman advance was inexorable. When the Thames was crossed, Caratacus probably already realized that there was nothing more he could do in the south-east. He retired westwards with kinsmen and brothers to continue the struggle on ground of his own choosing for another eight years.

For a time, the onward sweep of Roman arms was halted on the Thames. The summoning of Claudius to lead his army against the remaining opposition before *Camulodunum* is an extraordinary episode, without parallel in the Principate hitherto, leaving aside the jaunts of Gaius in 39–40. Dio's version of events has it that the legate had received prior instructions to bring in the emperor should there be any untoward turn in the campaign. Preparations had already been made for such an eventuality and troops were assembling. It seems most unlikely that Plautius and his commanders felt that they could not complete the task they had set themselves for that year, or that the arrival of Claudius would change anything on the military side. The emperor had surely intended to come to Britain himself if at all possible. The predetermined plan had worked well. It may indeed have worked too quickly, which is perhaps why Claudius was still at Rome and not closer to the scene of operations, and why some weeks were wasted in waiting for him to arrive. The unlikely scion of the Julio-Claudian house thus won his triumph and could justify it by further fighting between the Thames and *Camulodunum* in the late summer. His sixteen days in Britain saw the capture of the sprawling native stronghold, time enough to savour his emulation of the Dictator. Claudius could then return to Rome, taking six months over the journey, to a formal triumph in 44. Aulus Plautius was left with instructions to proceed to conquer 'the rest'.[12]

Roman successes in the opening campaign had repercussive effects on the peoples adjacent to those already overrun. The earlier surrender by a sept of the Dobunni was followed by others in the late summer. The Iceni on the northern flank of the Trinovantes were almost certainly one of these tribes. Their status allowed the retention of their own king, a privilege which was not finally removed until about AD 60. Other surrendering tribes are more difficult to identify. Those bordering the old dominion of Cunobelin or absorbed within it are the obvious candidates: the remainder of the Dobunni, the Coritani, the tribes of Kent and of Hampshire apart from the Atrebates. Even the Brigantes of the Pennines, or at least the head of their leading dynasty at the time, the queen Cartimandua, may at this early date have decided that here was a power better recognized as a neighbour than opposed as a foe. These diplomatic successes, whether they came in 43 or immediately afterwards, were as satisfying as the success of the military expedition and go far towards explaining the rapid advance of Roman armies in the next few years. Plautius, retained as legate of the inchoate province, could now take stock of the military position with some confidence, and Claudius could reflect, with justice, that his army had achieved more than that of the deified Julius. Beyond question he was 'the first to subject the barbarian peoples beyond Ocean to the power of the Roman State'.[13] Claudius was not tacitly ignoring Caesar's conquest: he was obliterating it.

It was a long time since so large a provincial area had been overrun so convincingly. The expanse of territory now subject to Rome could be adequately policed by the expeditionary army, but there was still much fighting to be done, especially in Western Britain. There were, then, powerful inducements to accept aid from native rulers when their assistance could reduce the number of troops needed for routine garrison purposes. Hence the accommodation with the ruling house of the Iceni. Within the Atrebatic realm a more novel solution was arrived at. The territory, or a part of it, over which Verica had ruled before his flight to the Romans together with other tribal lands, remained under separate authority, rule being entrusted to a native king, Ti. Claudius Cogidubnus. It is not known for certain that Cogidubnus had held a position of authority in Britain before 43, nor that his rule dated from shortly after the conquest. The famous inscription from Chichester, on which he boasts the title *rex magnus*,[14] is not intrinsically dated and there is no other evidence offering clarity on this man's career. We thus know nothing about his rise to prominence. Had he fled from Britain before 43, entering the emperor's *clientela* and earning a *viritim* grant of citizenship well before the position of *rex* was accorded? This might recall in outline the career of Arminius forty years before. What, if any, was the relationship of Cogidubnus with the house of Verica? Was he regarded as the heir to Verica's kingdom or was he simply a trusted Briton who could be relied on to administer the territory of several tribes in the Roman interest? Recognition as a native monarch, and the assigning of other

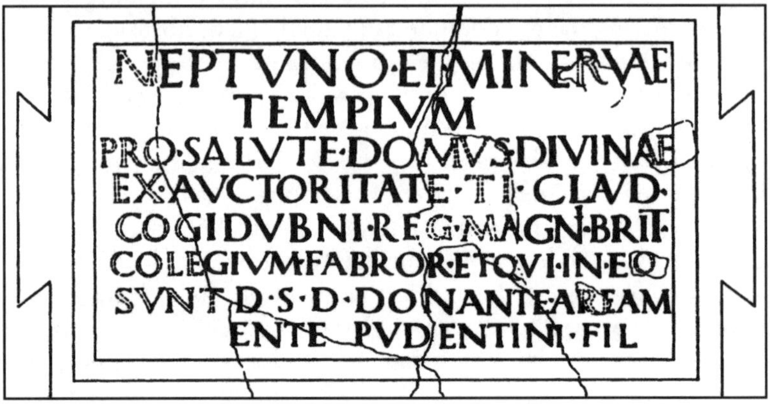

Figure 7 The Cogidubnus inscription from Chichester. Reconstruction after J. E. Bogaers.

peoples to his rule, is more appropriate to the very early days of the province, probably very shortly after 43. It is not known how long Cogidubnus survived. Tacitus' sole mention of him, however, implies that he was still alive in the early Flavian period. His exceptional powers are to be regarded as a convenient interim arrangement between outright military occupation and municipal authority.

4

The Conquest of Lowland Britain

The surviving literary sources give us little help in charting the progress of Roman armies across Southern Britain in the years immediately following the invasion. In the absence of Tacitus' narrative, archaeology and its indispensable ancillary air photography provide the bulk of our information, not only on points of detail, but also in the aggregate of these on overall strategy as this unfolded in the face of changing circumstances. Most of this archaeological information has been gained in the past twenty years and there can be no doubt that there is still much to learn. Although the outline of the Roman advance towards upland Britain is becoming clearer, there are limits to what the evidence, by its very nature, can tell us.[1] It is difficult, and often impossible, to distinguish between fort sites established in the governorship of Aulus Plautius and those established under his successor Ostorius Scapula. The same problem recurs in later periods of the Roman advance and must be firmly borne in mind, particularly when the discussion centres on forts from which very little stratified pottery has been recovered.

A second limitation is the lack of large-scale excavation of forts of the Julio-Claudian period. Most are known from air photography and limited examination of their defences, whereas only extensive excavation of the interior, and particularly of the barracks, can provide the detail necessary to reconstruct the history of the site. As yet, only a handful of Claudian and Neronian forts have been studied in such detail and few indeed belong to the very earliest years of the province. Finally, it must be remembered that the earliest operations in Midland and Southern England should be represented by marching camps, not by the establishment of forts, and few such camps are yet known in these regions, where subsequent agricultural processes have often removed all traces which might be detectable on the ground.

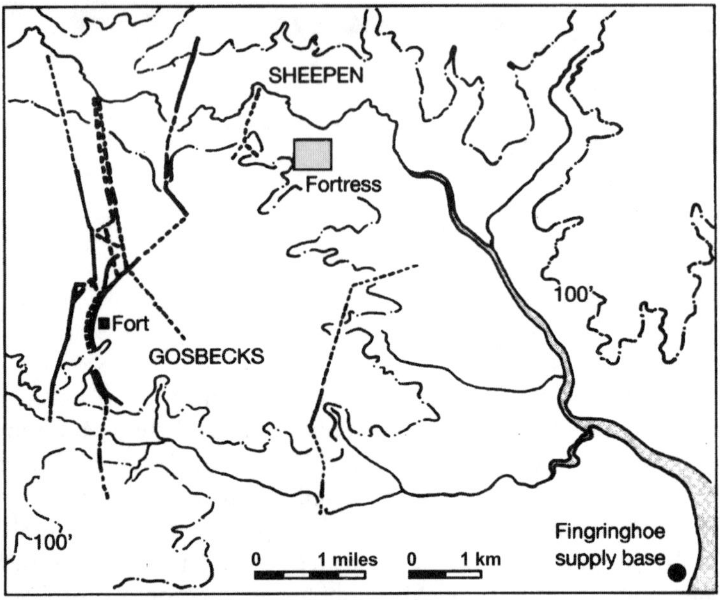

Figure 8 Early Roman *Camulodunum*.

There are few guidelines in the archaeological evidence to the legionary dispositions immediately after 43. It is likely that troops were quickly dispatched to the territories newly won by terms of surrender as well as those overrun in war, but detail is lacking. A fortress for a single legion was established at *Camulodunum* on the western side of the site later to be occupied by the *colonia*. This may not have been the earliest military work at *Camulodunum*. A large base may have been required to house a substantial part of the expeditionary army in 43, though if such a base existed it is yet to be sought, perhaps on Sheepen Hill where an early Roman fortification is known.[2] A small fort was placed at Stanway on the western side of the Iron Age *oppidum*, overlooking the important native site at Gosbecks, its defences incorporating a length of Iron Age dyke. A unit which seems to have remained in station at *Camulodunum* for some time is *Legio XX*, from which regiment a centurion was buried in the military cemetery here. Another tombstone from the cemetery, erected for a trooper in *Ala I Thracum*, may indicate that auxiliaries were in occupation nearby (perhaps at Stanway), as they not infrequently were in the legionary establishments on the lower Rhine. Also linked with the fortress was a naval base at Fingringhoe Wick on the Colne estuary, its main purpose being to receive supplies direct from Lower Germany rather than from the Channel ports via Kent.

The fields of operations taken by the different legions appear to have been determined early in at least two cases, and the arrangement was long maintained. *Legio II Augusta* under its legate Vespasian struck westwards through the Atrebatic kingdom towards the Belgae and Durotriges. *Legio IX Hispana* is later attested among the eastern tribes; from the beginning it probably policed the northern Catuvellauni, the Iceni and Coritani. This left the broad midland plain to *Legio XIV Gemina* and *Legio XX*.

The operations spearheaded by *Legio II* alone receive mention in the surviving literature.[3] Suetonius' sentence on the exploits of its legate offers only one location, the Isle of Wight, but there is no doubt about the sphere in which Vespasian's thirty battles were fought and twenty-odd native strongholds taken. The Durotriges were one of the two powerful tribes he subdued, the other being probably the Belgae.

Evidence for the attack on native hill-forts has been claimed at Maiden Castle and Hod Hill, both in Dorset.[4] There was certainly a struggle between Roman troops and natives at Maiden Castle, though it is not certain that this occurred in AD 44/5.[5] Roman military occupation seems to have continued within this great fortress down to the 60s and the 'war-cemetery' at the east gate could be the result of a fracas well after AD 45. Something similar may have occurred at South Cadbury (Somerset), where Roman troops may also have been stationed, and there are further signs of conflict at Spettisbury Rings (Dorset), in the form of human remains and Iron Age weapons in the hill-fort ditch. At Hod Hill, after the capture of the hill-fort, a Roman fort was established in one corner of the native work, suggesting that the surrounding area was not yet wholly pacified. A Roman garrison was also established within the largest of the southern hill-forts at Ham Hill (Somerset), as is shown by abundant coins and military metalwork, and later also at Hembury (Devon). The large strongholds of the region were thus used as nodal points in the early garrisoning of Durotrigian territory, taking full advantage of existing networks of supply and communication. But although the reduction of the Durotriges may have been a tedious business for Vespasian's troops, the issue cannot long have been in doubt. If the Britons retreated to their strongholds, they were virtually imprisoned within their own earthworks. To fight in the open meant equal disaster. The legate seems to have been able to visit Rome late in 44 to receive his triumphal *ornamenta*, possibly rejoining his legion for mopping-up operations in 45.

The operations of the southern army were supplied and supported from a number of coastal bases of which two, possibly three, are now known. That at Fishbourne, just west of Chichester, lies at the head of a navigable creek, where harbour installations are to be expected. The timber buildings of the base included both barracks and store-buildings dating from the 40s.[6] Further west, a large site at Hamworthy looked out over the anchorages of Poole harbour, and there are several other likely harbours between the Isle of Purbeck and Portland Bill. The westward push may well have been greatly facilitated by the movement of troops by sea, taking advantage of the excellent harbours on the coast of Hampshire and Dorset. This will help to explain the speed with which forts could be set up in Dorset, and also account for the total lack of temporary camps in Wessex. Elsewhere in the West Country there is striking evidence of rapid advance. The Mendip lead deposits in Somerset were already being worked by the army in AD 49,[7] indicating a sweep through the territory of the Belgae and southern Dobunni in the preceding year or two. This could have been a significant result of the surrender of part of the Dobunni in AD 43 or of some unrecorded arrangement with native leaders in this area. In any event, the occupation of the Mendips carried Roman arms to the Bristol Channel, thus cutting off the south-western peninsula and providing a secure base for attack on South Wales. A port at Sea Mills near the mouth of the river Avon was operating by about AD 50.

The network of early garrisons in this region was evidently intended to be close-set and, for a time at least, legionaries were assigned to garrison duties in troublesome areas. Thus, a small legionary detachment occupied the fort at Hod Hill, according to the excavator alongside a cavalry formation, though a case can also be made for auxiliaries succeeding legionaries here. Such deployment of legionary detachments appears to contrast with later practice, but may have been commoner in the Claudian period than at present appears. Finds of appropriate equipment point to the presence of legionaries at Dorchester, though no structural evidence has yet been recovered. A site at Lake Farm near Corfe Mullen (Dorset) also dates from the late 40s, and here too a brief legionary occupation may have occurred. The problematic fort site of Waddon Hill near Beaminster should also rank among the early garrisons, though its bewildering internal planning gives no clue as to the character of its garrison. Again, the presence of legionaries is suggested by finds of equipment. The largely southern bias of the known forts is notable and may not be entirely fortuitous, for the larger strongholds of the Durotriges lay in the southern area of their territory.

In Eastern Britain, too, the advance was pushed forward with speed, here perhaps through less hostile peoples and certainly through a terrain which did not bristle with hill-forts. East Anglia as yet gave no hint of the troubles to come and *Legio IX* could strike north into the territory of the Coritani. The legionary forces were again deployed in substantial vexillations, perhaps varying from one or two cohorts to half the unit, or about 2500 men, with support, one might imagine, from auxiliary cavalry. A large fort for such a vexillation, of some 2000 men, was sited at Longthorpe, near Peterborough, on the River Nene.[8] A similar work, not yet excavated, lies at Newton-on-Trent, nine miles west of Lincoln, overlooking the Trent valley. Even before these bases were established Roman columns had probed northward to the Trent and along the limestone ridge of Lincolnshire. A small marching camp at Ancaster (Lincolnshire) shows the army following the ridgeway on the Lincoln Edge, later adopted by the builders of Ermine Street, while larger camps at Newton-on-Trent and Holme, near Newark, reveal forces operating in the valley amid concentrations of native homesteads.

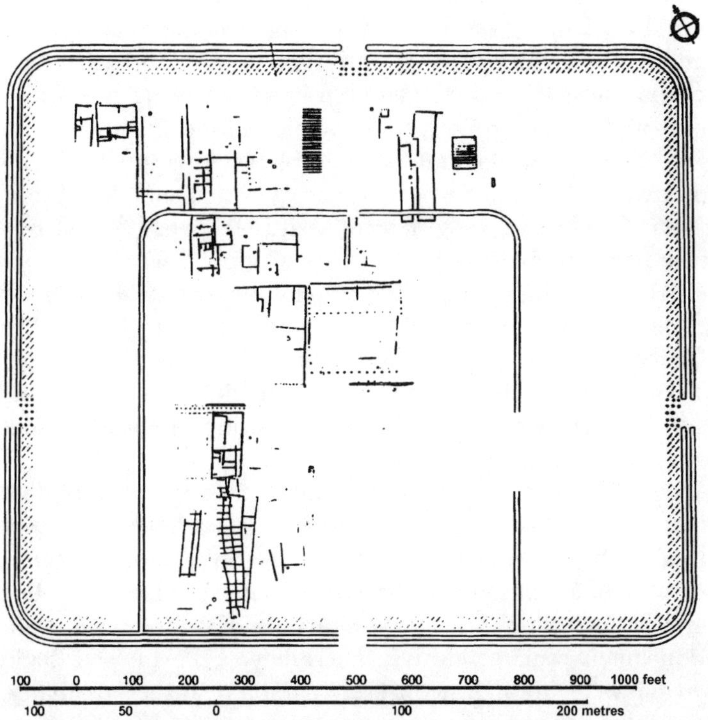

Figure 9 The military base at Longthorpe.

In due course, Coritanian territory was covered by a network of garrisons, in which the Fosse Way and Ermine Street figured prominently, but it would be gratuitous to assume that all the forts date from the governorships of Plautius and Ostorius, or even from the reign of Claudius.[9] Some can be shown to post-date the mid-50s. There is, however, no doubt that some of the Ermine Street garrisons were in position before 47. To this number belong the forts at Great Casterton, at Ancaster, covering the Ancaster Gap, and probably *Durobrivae* in the Nene valley. If the regular spacing of forts was maintained along the course of Ermine Street, a Claudian fort may be predicted at Lincoln. Although there is no trace of a fort here at this date, it seems incredible that so strategic a position was not seized. In support of an early base, possibly on low ground near the river Witham, there must be noted the presence of three tombstones of legionaries who had no cognomen.[10] The absence of cognomina is rare after the mid-first century and should be indicative of a Claudian date. The needs of coastal supply could be served by using the estuary of the Humber, where an early base may exist at or near Old Winteringham. Supplies could be moved far inland along the Trent, which is easily navigable as far upstream as Newark. Viewed overall, the pattern of garrisons established by the Claudian governors was designed to provide posts at intervals of no more than a day's march on the main routes, favoured positions being river-crossings. Away from the main routes, for example in Lincolnshire and around the Fenland margin, the interval was greater. An appreciable number of forts were placed at or near to native settlements, for instance at Leicester, Cambridge, Irchester and Ancaster, partly for purposes of control, partly to assist in the business of supply. We must beware of reconstructing a highly organized system of garrisons where probably none existed. These were early days, and it is unlikely that Plautius was already thinking of consolidation. For the time being, the northern front was reasonably secure. But in the west it will have already been clear that the task of conquering 'the rest' would be a fiercely contested affair.

If *Legio XX* and its auxilia were given the task of holding down the remains of the old realm of Cunobelin, operations in the centre of England and the western midlands devolved upon *Legio XIV Gemina*. A likely base for a thrust into the central plain of England is the Thames valley. An early military site has long been posited at London but it remains elusive. There have been finds of legionary equipment here (though not closely datable), so the possibility may be entertained that a legionary task-force was stationed at this most strategic of locations. The line of Watling Street, running north-west

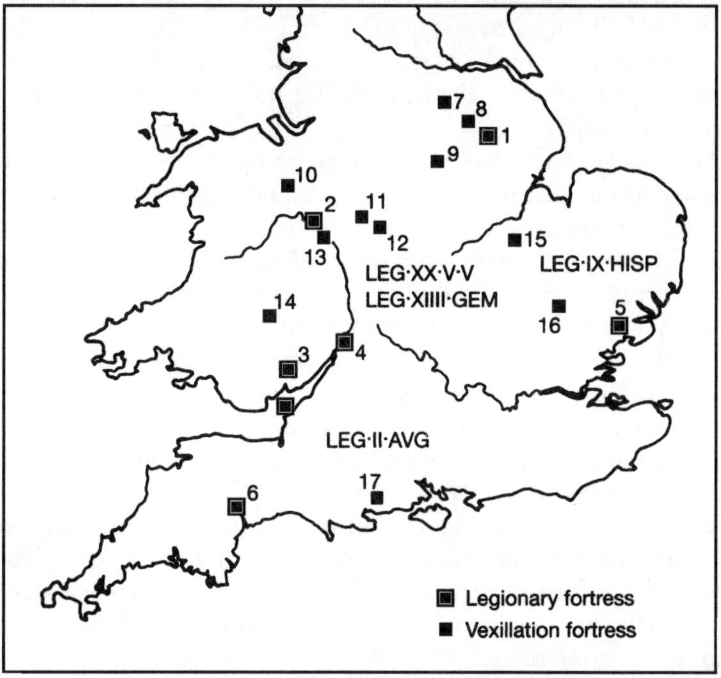

1. Lincoln. 2. Wroxeter. 3. Usk. 4. Gloucester. 5. Colchester. 6. Exeter. 7.Rossington Bridge. 8. Newton-on-Trent. 9. Edingley. 10. Rhyn Park. 11. Kinvaston. 12. Wall. 13. Leighton. 14. Clyro. 15. Longthorpe. 16. Great Chesterford. 17. Lake Farm.

Figure 10 Large forts of the period AD 43–65.

from London, has been seen as representing the general route of this legion, but this is pure supposition: none of the forts on that road necessarily dates from the legateship of Plautius. If, on the analogy of the operations of *Legio IX* in the east and of other units later, *Legio XIV* was deployed in a number of detachments, a legionary force is likely to have explored the Thames valley westward, not least because this route took them through the territory of the Atrebates and on towards the Dobunni, of whom some at least had already made their peace with Plautius. The route may be marked by a fort at *Calleva* (Silchester) and another at Dorchester-on-Thames. A major fort at Silchester would make good sense. The large timber structures found beneath the later forum may be the first indication of its presence. If the upper Thames were followed, occupation of the Cotswolds would have been the next objective, and beyond them the lower Severn valley. At Cirencester, a sequence of two or three forts has its origins in the governorship of either Plautius or his successor.[11] The territory of the Dobunni seems to have been rapidly enmeshed by garrisons and the routes connecting them, so that one might wonder whether all the tribe did not surrender in 43 or very shortly afterwards.

The strategic importance of the lower Severn valley will have been instantly recognized by the Roman commanders, and the temporary base of a legionary force may be reasonably sought in the region. A plausible site for *hiberna* would be Gloucester, at the lowest convenient crossing of the Severn. A succession of military sites at Kingsholm, half a mile north of the later city of *Glevum*, began in the years before 50, but it is not known precisely when and there is no proof that this was ever a legionary establishment. But that Kingsholm was of considerable importance in the early phase of occupation is demonstrated by the fact that the road from Cirencester is aligned upon it and not upon *Glevum* itself.[12]

The dispositions of Plautius' armies can only be dimly comprehended as yet, and the recovery of much more early Claudian material from forts is required to bring them into sharper focus. On one fundamental question, a note of caution must be sounded. Despite the modern tendency to view the Fosse Way as part of a temporary frontier-system, there is no evidence that the construction of any kind of frontier formed part of Plautian strategy. His brief, so far as we are informed of it, was conquest, and his four years were taken up with that above all else. What his commanders learned about the tribes of Western Britain must have convinced them, if they needed any persuasion, that much hard fighting lay ahead. The tribes of Wales could never be kept in check from the valley of the Severn. There were sound military reasons, then, for pressing on with the conquest of Wales (and that is precisely what the next governor proceeded to do) so that, as Tacitus was to remark in a later context, liberty might be banished from the map. There were economic reasons, too. Most of the desirable minerals lay north and west of the Trent-Severn line, and no procurator would be content to leave those resources in the hands of native chieftains, however well-disposed towards Rome. There are no discernible grounds for thinking that Claudian policy aimed at no more than the subjection of lowland England. When Plautius left for Rome and his *ovatio* in 47, the conquest of Britain was well begun, but there was to be no halting-place yet.

The province now passed to P. Ostorius Scapula. Nothing is known about his family save that his father or grandfather had been one of the first pair of praetorian prefects in the reign of Augustus. Britain was to be his last post, for he died in 52 while still holding the command. His governorship was to be one of constant warfare against the western tribes, bitter campaigns in which casualties were probably heavy and progress slow. In the autumn or early winter of 47, shortly after Ostorius arrived, hostile tribes fell on the territory of 'allies'. This could mean the lands of the Cornovii of the upper Severn or that part of the Dobunni which lay west of the lower Severn. The raiders were firmly driven out by the auxiliaries sent against them.

Since the governor intended to go forward into the Welsh mountains, he had need of a stable province behind him. It may be that the attack on the allies had revived something of the innate warlike spirit in those warriors who now found themselves cut off from their ancestral pursuits. At all events, Ostorius determined to disarm the peoples already overrun and to tighten the Roman hold on the territory up to the Trent and Severn. Precise interpretation of what Ostorius was aiming at depends on how the notoriously corrupt sentence of Tacitus is emended.[13] The text of the crucial manuscript reads *cunctaque castris Antonam et Sabrinam cohibere parat*. Heraeus and Bradley improved this to *cis Trisantonam*, but there is no need to drop *castris* altogether: indeed, the sense is improved by leaving it in. If included, it indicates that Ostorius was consolidating the rearward areas by building forts, the implication being that the territory south and east of the Trent and Severn had already been pacified by Plautius.

Ostorius' measures brought the Iceni out into open revolt, and later neighbouring peoples joined them. This should have been in 48, the governor having arrived in the autumn or late summer of 47. It is not surprising that the lead was given by the Iceni. They had not been reduced in battle and now felt the curtailment of their limited independence the more keenly. With the support of a hasty muster of dissidents from adjacent areas, the Icenian warriors briefly held a rural stronghold against Roman infantry. Again, a British force was entrapped within its own earthworks and soon overwhelmed, despite a fierce resistance. The decisive victory ended Icenian resistance and dissuaded others who were contemplating similar action. Garrisons were presumably left behind on their territory, and Roman attention again turned to the Welsh hills.

The first target was the Deceangli, whose lands lay between the Clwyd and the Dee. They were quickly overrun, the hill-men avoiding open battle. The geography of this campaign is unknown, there being no marching camps which can plausibly be linked with the operations of a force at this date. It is a reasonable guess that

Ostorius used the valley of the Dee as his line of march, which would indicate a logical strategy of sealing off the Welsh tribes from the north as well as from the east. In tackling the Deceangli early on, there was the added prospect of gains in minerals – silver, lead and copper.

The possibility, and the dangers, of collusion between the Welsh hillmen and the Brigantes were now made clear. Ostorius had almost reached the Irish Sea when trouble arose among the Brigantes, enforcing his return. For the time being, the forward movement was halted. Whether this turn of events had been influenced in any way by Caratacus, shortly to be revealed as the guiding spirit of British resistance in the west, cannot be known. It would not have been beyond his wits. The Brigantian rising, however, did not last long, pro-Roman members of the tribe apparently being able to bring the more warlike spirits to book without Roman assistance.

The war against the hillmen of Wales was resumed in 49, this time in the south, the enemy being the Silures. Caratacus again emerges on to the scene. His activities between 43 and 49 are unrecorded. He may have been behind the incursion of 47 into allied territory, as well as the events of the preceding year. His prestige among the Silures was high and he was keenly aware of the need to keep the spirit of independence alive in other tribes. When Ostorius moved against the Silures, he decided to move up a legionary force to this front. The regiment which could most readily be spared was that still in occupation at *Camulodunum*, probably *Legio XX*, as has already been suggested. The disturbances of two years before had shown that the total removal of troops could not be carried out with confidence. The solution arrived at, following long established practice, was the foundation of a veteran colony, the site chosen (as in the case of Cologne a year later) being that originally occupied by the legionary fortress at *Camulodunum*. The foundation of the *Colonia Victricensis*, as its title apparently ran, as a *specula ac propugnaculum imperii* in an area still requiring vigilance, was firmly in the tradition of the colonies at Aquileia, Placentia, Cremona and Narbo. Most probably veterans from all four of the legions in Britain were settled at *Camulodunum*, not merely men from *Legio XX* alone. There were provincial *incolae* as well, though in what proportion to ex-soldiers cannot be guessed at. The land assigned to the new colony must have been extensive. If the analogies of Cologne and Trier may be justly referred to, the entire tribal territory of the Trinovantes became the *territorium* of the new city, the pick of the *agri captivi* going to the colonists. It was this that brought retribution a decade later.

The obvious base for operations against the Silures was the lower Severn valley and the new fortress of *Legio XX* is to be sought there, perhaps at Kingsholm near Gloucester, though this has not yet been demonstrated. Tacitus says nothing about Roman successes in the campaign. The emphasis is all upon the prestige and cunning of Caratacus. In the following year, 51, the scene shifts to the Ordovices of central Wales, probably at the prompting of Caratacus. There, either in overconfidence or frustration, he risked a set battle. Like almost all the major battlefields of Roman Britain, the site cannot be fixed with certainty. The upper valley of the Severn is one possibility, but several small valleys which join it have an equal claim. The area of Montgomery, where three valleys meet, has had its supporters. More recently, a site on the river Tanat at Abertanat has produced evidence of military activity in the early 50s and the location suits well the scene-painting of Tacitus. The complex of works at Abertanat and nearby Llansanffraid must in any event be associated with early campaigns directed along the upper Severn. Whatever the site, British valour was again not enough and the Roman victory was total, but for the capture of Caratacus himself. Leaving his relatives behind in captivity, he escaped to the Brigantes, the only refuge now remaining. Whatever hopes he may have cherished came to nothing, for Cartimandua's precarious hold on her kingdom needed Roman support. Caratacus was handed over to Ostorius, and later he, his family and his followers adorned a spectacle set before the populace of Rome by Claudius, still basking in his British triumph. Spared by the emperor, his later years are unrecorded.

If Ostorius expected that the removal of Caratacus from the action would soon bring the war to an end, his hopes were vain. The will to resist was still strong among the Silures and the legate himself was in the last months of his life, already ill or exhausted. There was a serious reverse for Rome when a legionary detachment, under the command of a *praefectus castrorum*, was surrounded while engaged on fort-building. Before help arrived, it had lost nine of its officers, including the commander, and many men. Later successes for the Silures enabled them to spur other tribes into active rebellion. The fighting of 51–2 was bitter and exhausting. How difficult Ostorius found it can be measured by his despairing views of what should be the fate of the Silures: extermination or transportation to Gaul. When he died in 52, the tribe had still not been broken, and the western marches of the province were as insecure as ever.

There are possible traces of the passage of Ostorius' armies along the routes into the hills, though dating evidence is poor and little is known of the forts apart from their defences. The Silures could best be approached through the Wye valley, and to the campaigns of 51–2 may belong a large fort of twenty-five acres at Clyro, west of Hay-on-Wye, and another of sixteen acres at Clifford, two miles to the north-east. These are likely to represent successive campaigns along this route. A large base of thirty-six acres built at Cardiff in the mid-50s seems to indicate an intention to campaign westward along the Glamorgan plain, probably with support from the sea; but there is no doubt that the main route out of South Wales was along the Wye valley.

In the central and northern marches, a number of camps and forts have now been discovered, mainly from the air,[14] permitting us to form a general impression of the routes used in the operations, even though these numerous works cannot yet be placed in their proper sequence. A striking series of large camps, thirty-five to forty acres in area, can be traced from Wall (Staffordshire) along Watling Street to Burlington and Wroxeter and thence north-westwards to Whittington near Oswestry and on through the Dee valley to Penrhos near Corwen. If these belong to the same campaign, this looks like an encircling move around the northern flank of the Ordovices for which a date in 51–2 is likely enough. Close to the same route lies a large fort at Rhyn Park, near Chirk, which should represent the movement of a large force using either the Ceiriog valley or the gorge of the upper Dee. The storage-depot at Llanfor lies on the other side of the Berwyn mountains and marks a route west from Rhyn Park along the Dee valley. The Severn is another obvious route of penetration into the central hills. There is no evidence that Wroxeter was occupied in this governorship, but at Leighton, three miles to the south-east, there is a fort large enough to house a legionary vexillation and an earlier marching camp. Several of the smaller valleys may also have seen the passage of troops at this date. In the Teme valley at Brampton Bryan (Herefordshire), for example, a large camp of sixty-four acres should belong to this period and suggests the advance of an army towards the Ithan, in concert perhaps with a force using the Wye valley to the south.

Claudius acted quickly to replace Ostorius, appointing the experienced Aulus Didius Gallus. He may not have been intended for the British command, having held the consulship as long ago as AD 36 and being now in his mid 50s. However, he already had experience of Britain (*page 56*), and had held provincial commands in Moesia and elsewhere. His greatest claim to popular fame was his capture of Mithridates. There is no reason to think that he was a helpless old dodderer, as Tacitus hints, content only to act through his subordinates. The legate found on arrival that the Silures were as formidable as ever; they had successfully struck at a legion (perhaps *Legio XX*) and followed this up by widespread raids. Didius probably realized that there could be no quick success and decided upon a policy of containment and modest advance where this proved possible. Fort-building and the improvement of communications might now be overdue since the legionaries had had so much campaigning to do. Further, the weakness of Rome's ally Cartimandua became ever clearer after her surrender of Caratacus in 51, and for the time being the Brigantian problem defied solution. For the first time, a governor had to contend with two threatened fronts. After internecine fighting, Roman auxiliaries were sent in to assist Cartimandua. Later, probably in a subsequent governorship, legionaries were needed to preserve her position.

Didius' measures of consolidation in the west probably involved the foundation of a legionary depot at Usk.[15] Although this base covered fifty acres, it cannot have housed a full legion as so much of the interior was taken up with store-buildings. It is better interpreted as a stores-depot for units operating in the valleys of South Wales from about AD 55 to the mid-60s. This took the place of the base at Kingsholm, now too far to the rear to be of use. On the upper Severn, regrouping brought a new fortress for *Legio XIV* at Wroxeter. This lies deeply buried beneath the later city and little is known of its layout. Elsewhere in Eastern Wales, the work of Didius may one day be recognized in some of the numerous auxiliary forts which have recently been recorded from the air, but which remain undated. A relatively dense network of forts is now appearing in South-east Wales and Herefordshire, with control-points only twelve miles apart. Dates are not yet certain but most must belong to the 50s and early 60s. In the South-west, advance was certainly made in the early fifties for by AD 55 or probably a little earlier a legionary fortress was established at the head of the Exe estuary at Exeter, presumably by *Legio II Augusta*.[16] Campaigning in Devon north of Dartmoor is represented by a large fort at North Tawton, while later garrisons, but probably still earlier than AD 60, were based in forts at Okehampton, Bury Barton, Tiverton, Cullompton and Hembury, all of these commanding the main routes in the peninsula. West of Dartmoor, there are as yet no clear signs of military intrusion before AD 60, though a striking series of Roman bronzes and pottery found in a native enclosure at Carvossa, near Probus, Cornwall, is strongly suggestive of close contact in the mid-50s. About this time too, or earlier, a Roman force took over the hill-fort at Hembury, constructing its own buildings in the interior.

The death of Claudius in 54 and the accession of Nero brought no alteration to Roman policy towards the western tribes. Suggestions that early in his reign Nero contemplated withdrawing the Roman army from Britain, and then abandoned the idea for fear of damaging the *fama* of Claudius, do not carry conviction. It is unlikely that Seneca and Burrus would have given countenance to such a project if it had entered Nero's mind. The only circumstances in which the abandonment of an entire province would be considered were either a great military disaster, such as that of AD 9, or a provincial rebellion. Much had by now been invested in Britain, some of it in hard cash – including some of Seneca's own (*page 86*). There would be no withdrawal now without some overpowering military reason.

In 57 or 58, Didius made way for the well-connected Q. Veranius. His most significant earlier post was his five-year tenure of the command in Lycia and Pamphylia. This governorship had involved him in mountain warfare, although it is not clear how serious this was. It was also fought more than a decade before his tenure of Britain. Nevertheless, there are unlikely at the time to have been many commanders with much experience of campaigning in hill-terrain, and it is notable that two of them were sent successively to Britain, Veranius and Suetonius Paullinus. The movement forward was to be resumed.

Veranius did not get the two years which he believed were necessary to complete the conquest of Wales, dying within his first year as legate. Precisely what his campaign of 58 achieved will never be known, but its target must surely have been the Silures. His successor, Suetonius Paullinus, campaigned with success against more than one tribe in 58–9 and felt confident enough of his hold on the south to attack Anglesey in 60. The Silures were thus now firmly held in check and they do not figure as opponents of Rome. Their subjection had taken a dozen years and the cost to Rome in military commitment, and in casualties, was disproportionately high when set against the slight gains to the security of the province as a whole.

Suetonius Paullinus' attack on Anglesey represented the most ambitious advance for a decade. Probably striking through the territory of the Deceangli, the expedition reached the Menai Straits and found the enemy drawn up on the far side, their numbers swelled by warriors who had retired there in the face of the Roman advance. Not for nothing was Suetonius regarded as a serious rival to Corbulo – the military idol of the day. The preparations had been carefully made. Flat-bottomed boats had been built and these ferried across the infantry. The mounted troops used whatever fords existed, though some had to swim across beside their horses. Once across, after understandable hesitation in the face of the black-clad Celtic women and Druids calling down curses from heaven on the invaders,

Suetonius' men launched themselves into the fray. For all its fearsome aspect, the motley army assembled on Mona was not equipped to withstand the onslaught. The battle was soon over and the island garrisoned. The legate expected to be able to press on with the conquest of the rest of Wales. But far away to the east a maelstrom had burst forth, and Rome's hold on Britain was to be severely shaken.

5

Revolt and Conquest Renewed

The revolt which broke out in Eastern Britain in 60 was, next to the Batavian revolt a decade later, the most serious rebellion against Roman rule in any province during the early Principate.[1] Tacitus described the uprising in considerable detail and paid particular attention to what drove the two tribes to throw their remaining strength against Rome. Roman administration comes out of the affair very badly. Exactions had been harsh and abuses of several kinds abounded. The very men whose cooperation Rome had to gain, the tribal leaders, had been most heavily oppressed. The Trinovantian nobles had lost much of their land when the *colonia Victricensis* was founded in 49. Five or six years later the construction of the great temple of the deified Claudius cost them dear, and this came over and above the expenses of the Imperial cult centred on *Camulodunum*. The Iceni had hitherto been shielded from the worst effects of subjection to the Roman state. But the little kingdom over which Prasutagus ruled until about 60 was not to retain even its token independence after his death. Nero's attitude towards allied kings was not that of Claudius. Tragically, it was with brutality and greed that the territory of the Iceni was taken over by agents of the legate and the procurator. In the face of these outrages, the tribe united behind Boudicca, the widow of Prasutagus, and in her the revolt found its figurehead.

The Trinovantes and Iceni had their own peculiar reasons for turning on their masters. There were, however, other circumstances which affected a wider circle of provincials, including many who had readily accepted the rule of Rome. Sums of money had been lent to leading Britons by Roman financiers, prominent among whom was the philosopher Seneca, Nero's tutor, and much of this money was now being recalled. The story has been doubted or played down by some modern writers, but there is nothing inherently unlikely about it. Roman capital was frequently placed at the disposal of native landowners in the early days of Roman rule, often with good effects, sometimes with ill. Why the loans should be suddenly called in is obscure, unless it was because the magnitude of the military task which still faced Rome in Britain began to be more clearly appreciated among Roman capitalists, causing a loss of confidence in their British investments. As in the case of the revolt of Florus and Sacrovir in Gaul in AD 21, debt and consequent exaction to recover it probably played a significant part in the Boudiccan rebellion. The exactions were not confined to private speculators. The provincial procurator, Decianus Catus, was at this same time trying to call in money which Claudius had paid as subsidies to British leaders. To hard-pressed provincials, plunged into debts of this magnitude, there seemed to be no way out except by taking up arms.

The course of the rising is starkly clear in the pages of Tacitus and Dio and it needs no embellishment. The *colonia* at *Camulodunum* quickly fell to the rebels and was destroyed. Suetonius Paullinus rushed back to the south-east but immediately saw that London and *Verulamium* could not be saved. The legions and most of the auxiliaries were dispersed far to the north and west. Nearest to the threatened region was part of the Ninth legion but a thrust under its commander, Petillius Cerealis, was easily beaten off. London and *Verulamium* were overwhelmed and suffered the same fate as *Camulodunum*. But the rebels had yet to face a Roman army prepared for battle. Although Paullinus could only muster some ten thousand men, he decided to risk battle as soon as he could. On a battlefield which may not have been far to the north-west of *Verulamium*, his small army defeated and destroyed a huge force of Britons, with only slight losses of its own.[2] Eighty thousand Britons perished, ten thousand more than Roman and allied victims, in the three ravaged cities. The revolt was over. For a brief time the loss of Britain had seemed a possibility, and Rome owed much to the coolheaded leadership displayed by Paullinus. But what above all else saved the day for Rome was the reluctance of the other southern *civitates* to throw in their lot with the rebels. Despite the aggravations of provincial administration, loyalty to Rome held, however feebly that flame burned. Perhaps the most surprising facet of the Boudiccan rebellion is that the bitter passions unleashed in East Anglia found no answering response elsewhere.

The reprisals to which Paullinus now gave full rein were so harsh that the procurator who succeeded Decianus Catus, C. Iulius Alpinus Classicianus – fairly certainly a Treveran noble – was moved to protest to the emperor. One of Nero's freedmen, Polyclitus, was sent to Britain to examine the facts of the case. Shortly afterwards,

Paullinus was relieved of the British command and recalled, though without losing either prestige or Imperial favour.

The repercussions of the revolt were felt in many spheres, and ripples from the centre may have reached remoter shores. The immediate effect on the progress of the Roman advance was to bring it to a virtual halt for a decade, although there were still sound military reasons for pressing forward. Suetonius had softened up the Welsh tribes for the final blow. The Brigantian frontier was in turmoil, and it was by now obvious that the tribe would have to be brought into subjection in due course. But the next two governors of Britain made no decisive move in either direction, presumably because they did not feel confident enough to commit a major part of their forces to long campaigns on the fringes of the province. Roman losses in 60–1 had not been light. A draft of 2000 men from the Rhine provinces was brought in to bring *Legio IX* back to strength, and ten auxiliary units, eight cohorts and two *alae*, were also transferred to Britain to stiffen the garrison. Casualties among the civilian population were officially given as 70,000, not an impossibly high figure if it included *peregrini* who did not support the rebels, as well as veterans and other immigrants. Many must have fallen at *Camulodunum*. London and probably *Verulamium* had warning of what was coming and many will have made their escape. Whether other towns and cities in the south-east were destroyed or attacked we do not know. A destruction level of this date has been identified at Winchester. Obviously, it would be the East Anglian communities that were most at risk, but it would not be surprising if disaffected spirits in other tribes took the chance to express their feelings.[3] It was only seventeen years since the invasion, and many who had opposed Plautius would still be in vigorous middle age. But if there was widespread destruction elsewhere, it has not yet been revealed in the archaeological record. Apart from the destruction levels identified at Camulodunum, Verulamium and London, direct archaeological evidence for the revolt is sparse. Damage to other sites cannot be dated with precision to AD 60/1 so that no firm link can be established with the rebel assault or with Roman reprisal. Several hoards of coins and metalwork, however, found in Norfolk, north Suffolk and north Cambridgeshire do seem to be referable to these events. (Interestingly, the territory of the Trinovantes in Essex and south Suffolk has not produced similar hoards.) Some of these deposits are large. One at March (Cambs.) contained 872 silver coins of the Iceni; another at Lakenheath (Suffolk) consisted of 410 silver Icenian pieces, 3 Iron Age gold coins and 67 Roman denarii. Two smaller hoards end with denarii of AD 55/60 and 59/61 and must date from the revolt or its aftermath. At least six hoards of fine metalwork are also known from Norfolk and Suffolk, four of them found within 12 miles of the major Iron Age settlement at Thetford (above, p. 36). These are more difficult to date than the coin-deposits, but all could have been concealed about AD 60 or shortly thereafter.

More fundamental was the influence of the revolt on the tenor of Roman policy towards the Britons and the part it played in provincial affairs. It often took blatant cases of maladministration to reveal the limits of what a provincial population would bear. It would be naive to suppose that the replacement of Suetonius by a governor who was not bent on redress brought about any new relationship between the provincials and Rome, or any notable amelioration of their lot, but it does seem as though a somewhat more sensitive understanding of the governed did grow out of the hideous events of the rebellion. The more tangible signs of this new awareness of Roman responsibility are evident in the Flavian period, above all in the active encouragement given to urban communities to administer their own affairs within the framework of a Roman city, but also in the growth of *villae rusticae* of which Varro and Columella would have approved. The seed-bed for these important growths was prepared in the sixties by sensible, if unspectacular, administration.

The successor to Suetonius was P. Petronius Turpilianus, who came to the province direct from his consulship in 61. 'After he had quieted the earlier unrest, he was not emboldened to do anything further.' If Petronius did indeed restore order in the aftermath of 61, Tacitus is paying him a considerable and unconscious compliment. That he did nothing may not be the literal truth, for he was awarded the *ornamenta triumphalia* on his return in 63. The succeeding six-year governorship of M. Trebellius Maximus was, we are told, characterized by *comitas*, a quality much needed at the time and one appropriately shown to provincials rather than to enemies. Trebellius had no military commands behind him and thus, like Petronius, was an exceptional choice for Britain. But he had served as a *censitor* in the Three Gauls and this experience could have been turned to good effect in Britain. He may have been responsible for the first thorough census taken in the province. His tenure was unusually long, too long for him to have been the disastrous administrator Tacitus makes him out to be. He did, however, lack authority and was twice faced by rebellion among his own senior staff, the lead being taken by the ambitious Roscius Coelius, legate of *Legio XX*. On the first occasion, a compromise was reached. On the second, in 69, Roscius Coelius took advantage of the 'long year' of conflict and confusion to gather around him such forces as he could muster. Trebellius found himself isolated and was compelled to flee to Vitellius. He could not have expected to be restored to the command after a six-year tenure, and Vitellius found a new legate, M. Vettius Bolanus.

Trebellius had faced the inevitable problems of an unmilitary administrator put in charge of a powerful army which included experienced senior officers who did not easily brook inaction. Before this, provincial armies had found a lull between campaigns irksome: the building of roads and the digging of canals gave less heady excitement than fighting. The governor was doubly unfortunate. He lost his province and retired in disgrace. His apparent failure is there for all to read in the starkly illuminated pages of Tacitus. And yet Trebellius may have carried out his appointed task well and advanced the cause of Rome far more than many a diehard soldier.

Archaeology refutes the bare record of Tacitus, which asserts that the years 61–9 were devoid of military initiative. Apart from reorganization consequent upon the revolt, there were major changes in the disposition of the legions and some shuffling of the *auxilia*. There appear to have been no significant accessions to provincial territory, however, and it is this above all which soured Tacitus' view of these two governorships. The peoples of East Anglia still required watching, and forts which may have served this purpose existed at Ixworth, Coddenham (both in Suffolk) and Chelmsford (Essex). A large fort of more than twenty acres is known at Great Chesterford (Essex); this could have served as the headquarters for the operations which followed the rebellion. Its precise date, however, has not yet been determined.[4] Other posts are to be expected in Norfolk, perhaps at Caister-by-Norwich and on the coast, where many small estuaries offered harbours for supply ships. On the western edge of the Fenland, the large fort at Longthorpe was given up shortly after the revolt and replaced by a smaller post. *Legio IX* now based itself at Lincoln, the date of the fortress on the hill-top being about or shortly after 60. Little is known of this legionary base apart from its defences and the fact that its area (41 acres) was less than was normally found necessary for a complete unit. Either the legion was under strength when it built the Lincoln fortress or a detachment was doing duty elsewhere.

On the south-western frontier there were other changes. At least one fort was established in Cornwall by AD 65, at Nanstallon near Bodmin.[5] There must have been other garrisons in the far South-west, possibly at the estuary heads, but they have not been located. The native enclosure at Carvossa, near Probus, has produced an impressive range of Roman metalwork and pottery of the Neronian and early Flavian period, and may have housed Roman troops for a time. The absence of known forts in Cornwall is in sharp contrast to the situation in Devon, where several forts are recorded on the routes to north and south of Dartmoor and on those leading to Exeter from the north and east. Few of these have been examined on any scale but those near Tiverton and Bury Barton, near Lapford, appear to be Neronian, founded in the late fifties or early sixties. As yet, there are no certain signs of the exploitation of tin and other minerals in Cornwall at this date. Wales was still a problem, though not as formidable as a decade earlier. The base at Usk continued to be held and in the governorship of Trebellius, after 66, a new fortress was built at Gloucester.[6] In that year of 66, *Legio XIV Gemina* and some auxiliary regiments were withdrawn from Britain for Nero's projected eastern campaigns and, though it returned briefly three years later, it was already evident that Britain would have to be held by three legions instead of four. The fortress at Wroxeter was now held by *Legio XX* or by a detachment.

Behind the forward positions, many of the forts occupied earlier were still maintained. In the area between the upper Trent and the Welsh marches there are signs of reorganization, still dimly recognizable but suggestive of far-reaching plans. On the upper Trent itself, a potentially important site lies at Trent Vale (Staffordshire). This fort (a safe assumption) stood in a narrow corridor through which the Cheshire plain could be reached. The early date of the site (probably its occupation was confined to the reign of Nero) is underlined by its remoteness from the developed road-pattern. Much better known is the complex series of works at Baginton, near Coventry. This fort is on no obvious route, lying six miles north-west of the Fosse Way. The earliest fort may have included legionaries in its garrison. After a few years, the fort was reorganized as an exceptional addition was made to its plan, a circular space fenced off by stout timbers. This has been identified as a training area for cavalry, an attractive suggestion as the Baginton fort is far removed from the battle-fronts of the day and would thus suit such a purpose very well.[7]

Alterations on the front facing the Brigantes are only dimly perceived as yet. About 60, a fort was sited at Broxtowe in the broken terrain at the southern end of Sherwood Forest. As at Baginton, the first fort was a large work and the site was not connected to the developed road-network. Another large work of Nero's reign lay in the Derwent valley at Strutts Park, a mile and a half north of Derby, where several routes converged. Most important for Rome's immediate purposes were the through routes, the Derwent valley and the line of Ryknield Street, certainly in existence in the reign of Nero, most probably in the 60s but possibly earlier. A Neronian origin for the fort at Chesterfield is assured and is virtually certain for Templeborough, near Rotherham.[8] The occasion or occasions for these foundations cannot be accurately defined, but they are likely to be connected with the unhappy history of Cartimandua (*page 67*), shortly to be brought to a conclusion.

Vettius Bolanus came to Britain in 69 having served as a legionary legate under Corbulo. Any provincial commands held before Britain are unknown. Corbulo had given him increasing responsibility as his abilities became evident, recommendation enough for a provincial command. Tacitus thought little of his performance in Britain: neither in dealing with the enemy, nor in quelling his undisciplined troops was any initiative shown. Vettius may have felt himself inhibited throughout much of his governorship by the uncertainties issuing from the civil wars. Moreover, there had already been transfers of troops from Britain and Vitellius later requested more, although by then Vettius' allegiance was wavering. There are, even so, strong hints that he did more than hold the ring for three years. In a poem addressed to the governor's son, Statius lists among Vettius' exploits a progress through Caledonian fields, of forts established and of trophies dedicated in Britain, including a breastplate taken from a British king. The detail can scarcely be insisted upon, but a Roman audience would not have swallowed a mere invented tale of successful warfare in a notoriously difficult province. The adjective 'Caledonian' was chosen because when the poem was written (in the 90s), Caledonia was news. If 'Brigantian' is read instead, the scene of Vettius' operations is more credibly defined. At the very least, then, here is allusion to successful operations against an enemy in Northern Britain, and the fame of this success still attached to the governor when a later conquest of the north had been carried out.

It may one day be possible to define the theatre of Vettius' operations more closely. A large fort at Rossington Bridge, near Doncaster, may mark penetration of southern Brigantian territory about 70, but the site, which covers more than twenty-five acres, is still undated. A foothold north of the Humber would be the logical preliminary to advance through the Vale of York, and the earliest work at Brough-on-Humber may be one result of such a plan. But it is uncertain whether Vettius or his successor took that step.[9] A site which should come into the reckoning is York. The foundation of the legionary fortress for *Legio IX* at York is usually assumed to have been one of the first acts of Petillius Cerealis in 71. There is no evidence for so precise a date, for it would be virtually impossible to distinguish between a work of 71 and the mid-70s, or between 71 and the late 60s, on ceramic grounds alone. There is at least one firm indication that Roman troops were stationed at York before 70. Considerable numbers of Claudian bronze coins have been found here, so many that it becomes implausible to dismiss them all as old issues lost during the Flavian occupation of the site. Other sites which yield Claudian bronze in such quantity were certainly occupied in the reigns of Claudius or Nero. There is also a little pottery from the early levels at York which could well date from before 70, though much more material is required to clarify the matter. How early this putative pre-Flavian occupation of York began is a question which can receive no answer as yet. The period of Vettius Bolanus' command has the most convincing claim. Vettius was probably involved in the final rescue of Cartimandua, a fact which may point to him as the founder of *Eboracum*. Other possibilities must be entertained. The site may have been held much earlier, not necessarily by *Legio IX*, during operations in support of the Brigantian queen. The fortress may thus have taken over a position already long used, perhaps by auxiliaries. No firm evidence bearing on the date of the fortress is yet available. There is certainly no need to cling to 71. The later governorship of Petillius Cerealis or that of his successor Frontinus is just as reasonable.[10]

The dashing and somewhat careless Q. Petillius Cerealis Caesius Rufus now took over the province, having recently been in the public eye as the subjugator of the Batavian rising. A prominent Flavian supporter, and probably the son-in-law of Vespasian, his military service had been long and taxing: legate of *Legio IX* during the Boudiccan rising, the Flavian march on Rome, the Batavian revolt. In one place, Tacitus grudgingly admits that his career had been 'not inglorious', but elsewhere Petillius Cerealis appears as a general whose successes were due to luck or divine intervention and his failures to an elementary lack of caution. It is clear that Tacitus disliked him intensely, for reasons about which we can only speculate.[11] Aside, therefore, from the understandable tendency to play down Cerealis' achievements so that Agricola's might shine out the more brightly, Tacitus was seemingly moved by some strong feeling against this man, whether transmitted from Agricola or more personally inspired it is impossible to say. It has been suggested that Cerealis may have been consul in 83 (for the third time) and was thus in a position of influence at a crucial time in Agricola's governorship.

Archaeology throws remarkably little light on the operations of Cerealis, in which he overran a large part of Brigantian territory, fighting many battles and scoring some successes. For a task of this magnitude, three seasons of campaigning were not enough and it was left to the successors of Cerealis to complete the conquest. There is a curious scarcity of forts and other works, even in the southern Pennines and the Vale of York, which can reasonably be linked with the army of Cerealis. The problems surrounding the date of the fortress at York have already been remarked on. If York was chosen as a base for *Legio IX* in this governorship, it becomes difficult to account for the existence of a large fort at Malton, in the Vale of Pickering. Malton is better viewed as a campaign-base of Cerealis' army, with garrisons in south Yorkshire, at Doncaster, Brough-on-Humber, Hayton and Castleford, representing consolidation after rapid movement. These forts represent a definitive occupation of the southern Vale of York, a fertile territory and a useful springboard for northward assault. A subsidiary function may have been to protect the land of the Parisi from the Brigantes, but this consideration is unlikely to have ranked high in the list of Roman objectives. Routes across the Pennines were of crucial importance in this phase of conquest; some forts on these routes, such as Bowes and Wensley, may be foundations by Cerealis. But dates for these have not yet been obtained. Apart from Malton, another site in the Vale of Pickering which must come under consideration in the context of early Flavian, or even late Neronian, campaigns is that at Cawthorn.[12] Here a group of temporary camps has in the past been interpreted as practice-works. But they are much more convincing as campaign-bases, not least as they have produced evidence of occupation. One of the works, moreover, is a fort, analogous in plan to Great Casterton, not a temporary camp. It can only reasonably be linked with operations and subsequent occupation in eastern Brigantian territory.

The territory of the Parisi was probably already firmly held and may indeed have served as the base from which the rescue of Cartimandua had been organized. But in Brigantian territory, not a single fort has produced evidence of a foundation as early as Cerealis. Even the three marching camps in Stainmore commonly assigned to this governor *could* be later. If the hand of the impetuous legate cannot be discerned in Roman works, it has for some time been assumed that at least the scene of his decisive encounter with his opponents has been identified. At Stanwick, near Scotch Corner, Sir Mortimer Wheeler's examination of the large and impressive earthworks revealed three phases of construction.[13] The first comprised an enclosure of seventeen acres resembling a hill-fort in design, dating from the first half of the first century AD. Soon after the middle of the century, an extensive area was taken within new ramparts, increasing the area to 130 acres. Later still, a huge area of a further 600 acres was enclosed by a bank and a ditch, not completed before the site was entirely abandoned. Wheeler argued that the Stanwick earthworks in their later phases were the hosting-place of Venutius' army and that the final, unfinished *enceinte* represented a last-ditch stand against the northward advance of Cerealis from the Vale of York. In its essentials the story has appeared attractive to most later writers, but it is underpinned by assumptions not facts. Apart from our ignorance as to whether or not Venutius was still the leader of the Brigantes after 71, there is no proof that the Roman army ever attacked the works at Stanwick or were confronted by a British force there. More serious still, there must be doubt as to whether the earthworks were still occupied in strength at this date. Very little material which *must* be dated to the early Flavian period has been recovered from phases associated with the earthworks and there is a dubious air about Wheeler's suggested sequence of rampart-construction. Some of the Roman pottery of Neronian to early Flavian date found here could be explained as relics of a military unit placed at this strategic junction, though more tangible traces of a fort are yet to be sought. The least convincing aspect of Wheeler's interpretation of Stanwick requires us to believe that the Brigantian leader was so unwise as to intend to hold a huge stronghold of more than 700 acres against Roman troops. Even if his own tactical sense did not counsel otherwise, he would need to have been astonishingly stupid not to have learnt from the harsh experience of the southern Britons over the previous thirty years. Whatever role Stanwick played in the early Flavian assault on the Brigantes, archaeology has yet to define it clearly. It may prove to have had less significance in the 70s as a native centre than as a strategic point held by a Roman garrison.

The operations conducted by Cerealis were probably sweeping attacks, covering so wide an area that no time was left for consolidation and the building of forts. This kind of *Blitzkrieg* is precisely what the earlier exploits of this general would lead us to expect, and it would satisfactorily account for the scarcity of early Flavian military sites on the ground. Tacitus mentions only warfare against the Brigantes, but Cerealis will not have neglected the occupation of Wales, and some of the forts traditionally assigned to the governorship of Frontinus could well have been founded before 74. It may be that Cerealis had to devote so much attention to the western mountains that he could not spare sufficient forces for the occupation of the Brigantes. That is beyond demonstration at present, but it will serve as a reminder that the legates of Britain had still to contend with two troublesome fronts at once.

S. Iulius Frontinus arrived in Britain in 74 or possibly late in 73, probably directly after his consulship. Tacitus' one sentence on his tenure gives him the palm for the subjection of the Silures, but once again this should not be seen as the only theatre of operations. North Wales and the southern Pennines cannot have been disregarded. A detailed reconstruction of Frontinus' work cannot be attempted. It is clear, however, that new legionary fortresses were established by him at Chester, controlling routes into North Wales and along the western flank of the Pennines, and at Caerleon, thus securing the fertile Glamorgan plain, from which several valley routes lead into the hills. It has already been observed that the base at York may also owe its foundation to Frontinus. The significance of the fortress at Wroxeter was now greatly reduced, though it may still have been held while the fortress at Chester was being completed, if not for longer.

A substantial number of auxiliary forts in the network which covered Wales in the Flavian period were either begun or completed

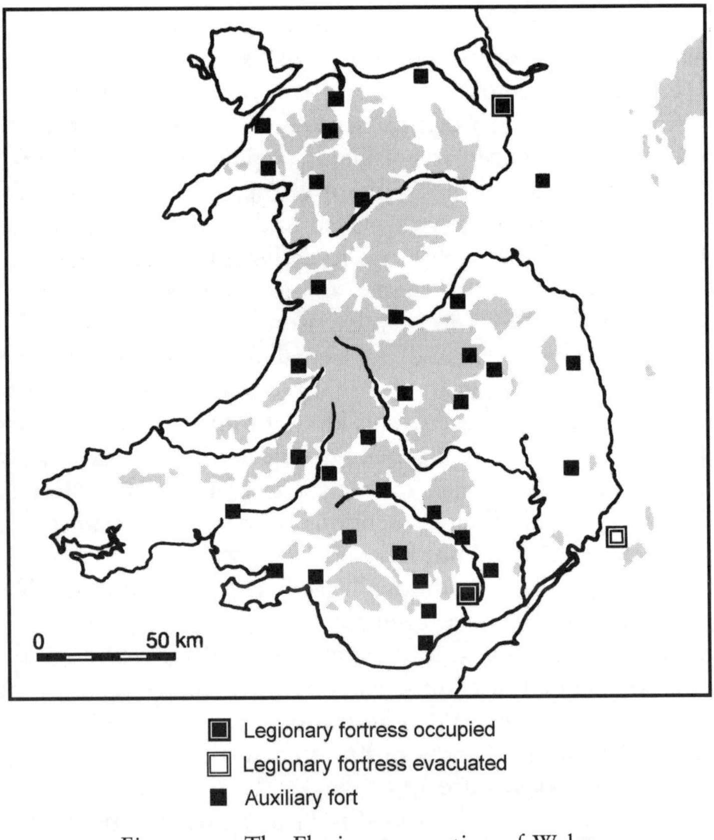

Figure 11 The Flavian occupation of Wales.

in this governorship, enabling the next legate to devote most of his time to the northern frontier. The map reveals how thoroughly Wales was garrisoned in the 70s. All the main valleys were controlled, in several cases by moving the sites of forts from positions initially chosen during the early campaigns. Few of the forts are extensively known, the only complete plan being that of Pen Llystyn (Caernarvonshire) commanding the base of the Lleyn peninsula.[14] It appears to have been planned for a cohors milliaria. Other forts of this period seem in the main to have been designed to house single units rather than detachments. A small number, including Caersws, Llanfor, Llwyn-y-Brain and perhaps Forden Gaer, are larger than seems necessary for an auxiliary unit, being seven acres or more, but little is known about their internal arrangement. In Central Wales, the longer intervals between forts were covered by small fortlets which might have housed patrols.

6

Britannia Perdomita

The conquest of the North

The new governor chosen to succeed Frontinus could scarcely have been better equipped by experience for command in Britain. Gnaeus Iulius Agricola had served under Suetonius Paullinus as *tribunus laticlavius* in 58–61 and under Cerealis as legate of *Legio XX*, both posts being held in times of energetic campaigning. He had passed on to the governorship of Aquitania in 74 and to a suffect consulship in 77, before returning to the province in which his range of administrative and military gifts would find full scope.[1] Agricola was now thirty-eight and seemingly destined for the highest commands. Aside from his military achievements and schooling, his straightforward nature, which owed much to his early education in Massilia, embodied the best characteristics of the new men who had emerged after the Civil Wars. He was immensely industrious, fair and honourable in his dealings, generous towards subordinates and understanding in his approach to the provincials. Such humane qualities are not always combined with military expertise, but Agricola was beyond question an astute and competent soldier. We know few provincial governors of the early Empire as well as we know Agricola and it is difficult to conceive of a better representative of the men who became *legati Augusti propraetore*.

Agricola's first objective was the completion of the conquest of North Wales and the occupation of Anglesey, terrain which the commander had seen nearly twenty years before. The long resistance of the Ordovices was punished by the severest treatment – annihilation according to Tacitus. That may be an exaggeration, but there is no doubt that Agricola intended this action to mark the end of the long struggle against the Welsh tribes. The decisive swiftness with which Agricola had struck in his first season was an earnest of things to come. The legionary fortress at Chester was being completed and would now keep watch on that long troubled region, aided by a garrison retained in the base at Wroxeter.

The Brigantes, overrun five years earlier but not yet pacified, were now the principal threat to the security of the province. The campaign of 78 quickly dealt with them, carrying Roman arms up to the Tyne–Solway isthmus and leaving behind a network of garrisons over most of the tribal territory. The Cumbrian mountains were not yet penetrated but simply sealed off along the Eden valley from the wild fells to the east. The logical approach to the occupation of the Pennines is to send two armies thrusting through the Vale of York and the Lancashire plain into the Eden valley, these two routes being connected by several east-west gaps through the hills, notably Stainmore and the valleys of the Aire and the Wharfe. These realities were fully appreciated by Agricola. The army assembled for the northern venture may have been the largest force any legate had had at his disposal since the early days. Campaign units could be drawn from four legions (II, IX, XX and II *Adiutrix*) and a large number of auxiliary units were freed for active service by withdrawing garrisons from the southern *civitates*, only to be countenanced if the tribal authorities could ensure internal security. The lessons of 60–1 had been well learnt and Agricola did not have to look back over his shoulder.

The Tyne–Solway line was reached by the end of 78. The army was now operating far in advance of its bases at York and Chester and thus the establishment of campaign-bases in the isthmus would have been a reasonable provision. A large work at Red House west of Corbridge and another at Carlisle may have fulfilled this function. The fort near Corbridge was probably large enough for at least a legionary vexillation, and the provision of a fine, stone bath-house suggests that the intention was to hold the site on a permanent basis. The Brigantes were now firmly held down, but there was to be no halt here. The death of Vespasian in the summer of 79 brought no change to military policy in Northern Britain. We are not told what Agricola's mandate was, but the continued advance is reasonably interpreted as the belated pursuit of the aims which Claudius had enjoined on Aulus Plautius in 43; to proceed to conquer 'the rest'.

Beyond the Brigantes lay the Votadini, Selgovae and Novantae, not named by Tacitus but certainly the *novae gentes* against whom the campaign of 79 was launched. Again, approaches along two major routes seem probable, one force passing through Northumberland to the Tweed and thence to the Forth, the other striking through Dumfries and Peebleshire to meet the other column in the narrows between Forth and Clyde. The territory overrun was not far short in size of that of the Brigantes; the weather had been bad, and it was not surprising that another season was needed to construct forts and consolidate what had been won. We hear nothing about the nature of the resistance. A small number of large hill-forts existed in the Scottish Lowlands, such as Traprain Law and North Eildon, but the large number of single homesteads surrounded by palisades or earthworks may have given the Roman forces a good deal of trouble, scattered as they were in a largely roadless terrain.

As in the Pennines, occupation was based upon a nexus of forts and roads, breaking up the terrain into easily penetrated blocs and making native concentration very difficult. The subsequent history of relations between Roman and native in the Lowlands indicates that if attempts were made to pacify the Selgovae and Novantae by diplomacy they met with no success. There was to be no alternative to the presence of Roman garrisons. Even the territory of the Votadini, often considered to have been more amenable than their western neighbours, was under watch from the garrisons on Dere Street, and there is no real reason for believing that their first contact with Rome was friendly, whatever their later relations were.

In a famous passage, Tacitus states unequivocally that the isthmus between Clyde and Forth was 'strengthened by forts' and that the line would have served as a frontier if Imperial aims had not demanded further conquests.[2] But archaeology has so far revealed very few sites in this narrow neck of land which were certainly founded by Agricola. Camelon and Mollins are the only certain examples known at present, though the Agricolan forts at Inveresk on the Forth and Barochan on the Clyde could also be regarded as covering the isthmus. Other Flavian forts may yet emerge along the line later taken by the Antonine Wall, in which connection it is worth note that Flavian pottery has been recorded from the sites at Mumrills, Cadder and Castlecary. Tacitus' words have sometimes been taken to mean that the emperor Titus had decided to confine Roman occupation to the land south of the narrows. If that thought crossed Agricola's mind and was conveyed in his dispatches to Rome, it was not acted upon, and there are no convincing grounds for believing that the original plan for total conquest had been modified. The signs are that Agricola was only now making contact with the most formidable of the northern peoples, the Caledonii, and only their conquest would allow the Romans to secure a hold on the Lowlands and the central plain.

Before the advance northward was resumed, Agricola mounted a seaborne attack on tribes which were hitherto unknown and unconquered. These operations in 81 have given rise to controversy, chiefly on their geographical setting. Most recent commentators on the

Figure 12 Agricola's campaigns (by year) in northern Britain.

relevant passage of the *Agricola* have placed the operation in Ayrshire and Galloway, seeing the tribes dwelling south-west of the Novantae as the peoples 'hitherto unknown'. This is just possible, but it imposes strain on the words Tacitus uses to describe the ground secured in the previous year: *omnis proprior sinus tenebatur.* If that is taken to mean precisely what it says, then all the Lowlands up to the Forth and Clyde had been occupied in 80, an interpretation which has the further backing of sound military strategy.[3] It follows that the naval expedition which Agricola led *prima nave* must have been directed across the Clyde, probably at Kintyre, Argyll and Arran, and it will have been from the Mull of Kintyre that Ireland was descried at the end of the campaign. The prospect of carrying Roman arms into Ireland was thus raised, and the flight of an Irish prince to Agricola might have seemed to offer a potentially useful pretext for intervention. It will never be known whether or not Agricola entertained the thought of sending an expedition to Ireland, but there is no reason for supposing that the idea was beyond consideration. There is, perhaps, an echo of Agricola's own view in Tacitus' remark that the occupation of Britain would be more secure if all the surrounding lands were in Roman control. Agricola may have proposed that Ireland should in due course be invaded. But if that proposal reached Rome after the death of Titus in September 81, it found a trenchant Domitian in charge, and he would have been less likely than his brother to have countenanced such a venture. The conquest of the larger island still called out for completion, and now at long last that objective seemed within reach.

Domitian's accession brought many changes in policy, both at Rome and in the provinces. Many leading figures who had enjoyed the trust of the earlier Flavians were summarily removed from office and many lost their lives. Agricola had already held his command for five years and need not have been surprised if he had been recalled. For in 82 Domitian was preparing for a campaign against the Chatti and Sugambri in pursuit of the military fame which had eluded him since his minor role in the Civil War. The army he was assembling for this war would inevitably include troops from Britain, thus reducing Agricola's strike-force. But the British war went forward and under the same legate, presumably because the end was clearly in sight.

The final campaign of Agricola reveals the careful preparation, based on thorough reconnaissance, and the skilful deployment of forces of an outstanding general. The fleet was used not only to supply the land troops but also to lay bare the heartlands of the enemy by sailing up the long estuaries, leaving only the mountains as a refuge. The Caledonians, however, began to mass together, perhaps for the first time. An army of more than 30,000 is said to have gathered, an impressive and not implausible figure. Their principal leader, or at least the only one mentioned by Tacitus, was Calgacus, probably given the command by the other chieftains. At first, the barbarians used their forces in several divisions, their intention being to harry the

Romans on a wide front. Agricola responded by splitting his forces into three army groups. One of these, headed by a weakened *Legio IX*, was attacked in its camp and the governor himself had to bring up a relieving force and drive off the Caledonians. The Roman advance continued for the rest of the season, taking the army well beyond the Tay and perhaps as far north as the Spey.

Several series of marching camps can with reason be associated with this drive into Northern Scotland.[4] The most distinctive type of camp, named after an example at Stracathro, had gates which were protected both by a curving external *clavicula* and a straight hornwork. These works usually cover between 25 and 40 acres and could have housed a legion and an accompanying force of auxiliaries. Another group, measuring about 30 acres, and with representatives at Finavon and Cardean, probably also marks the passage of Agricola's army. Yet another series, including Kintore, Glenmailen, Normandykes and Raedykes, stands out on account of their large size, between 100 and 120 acres. If these were indeed Flavian works, they could represent a regrouping of forces for Agricola's final campaign. There is, as yet, no evidence for camps of any date beyond the Moray Firth, which must condition any assessment of the setting of the final engagement.

It is well known that Agricola deployed a fleet in his northern operations, though very little is known about the manner of that deployment. The needs of military supply will have been huge, but the movement of troops could also have been effected by sea and estuary. The long, broad estuaries of the Forth, Clyde, Solway and Tay lend themselves to deep passage inland and easy control of the adjacent land masses by an arm in which the northern tribes were not proficient, or in which they fell far short of Roman expertise. In eastern Scotland there must have lain the site of *Horrea Classis* ('granary of the fleet'), noted by Ptolemy. This probably lay on the Tay estuary and underlines the vital importance of supply by sea of the land-based forces.

The necessary culmination of the campaigns in Scotland and, as everyone must have realized, the final act of Agricola's governorship, was to be decisive defeat of the Caledonian confederacy. The fleet was used to devastating effect in raiding the native lands and forcing the issue to a conclusion. Calgacus and his warriors followed British precedent in choosing a position for the battle well in advance and awaiting there the arrival of the invaders. Although the precise position of the battlefield of *Mons Graupius* cannot be deduced from the pages of Tacitus and no other source of information has yet revealed it, it is evident that Calgacus chose his site where his forces would best assemble, now that Rome held much of the coastal plain, and where a victory would enable him to hold on to some, at least, of the productive land of the region. A plausible case has been made out for the lower slopes of the hill of Bennachie as the battlefield, the Roman forces lying in camp at Durno, four miles away, and this is the best-candidate for the site so far proposed.[5] The battle was a relatively uncomplicated affray, in which neither Agricola's generalship nor the fighting qualities of his legions were tested. The legions, indeed, were held in reserve and took no part in the engagement. Caledonian losses were heavy: 10,000 killed, while Rome lost 360 auxiliaries. For the first time, so far as is recorded, auxiliaries had borne the brunt of a major battle while the legions looked on. It only remained for Agricola to take his army into the territory of the Boresti (perhaps in Moray), take hostages there, send the fleet around the northern end of the island, thereby establishing the fact of its being an island to Roman satisfaction, and visit the Orkneys and receive their surrender. Though no attempt was made to enter the Highland *massif*, there could be little doubt that *Britannia* was now *perdomita*.

Agricola made his way by slow stages to winter quarters away from the scene of his victory. After a six-year governorship, he can only have been expecting the recall which duly followed. Triumphal ornaments were awarded to him by Domitian, possibly in confirmation of an earlier grant by Titus, but his public career was over. His immediate predecessors in the British command passed on to higher things. Agricola received nothing further. Eight years later he died at the age of fifty-three, by then no doubt embittered by the abandonment of his northern conquests as much as by his own effacement from the ranks of office-holders. The achievement of Agricola in northern Britain was immense and stands firm against attempts by some recent writers to reduce it. A seven-year tenure of an armed province like Britain was exceptional at this time; had it been inadequate in any respect, Domitian would not have been slow to terminate it. On any standard, Agricola's final subjugation of the Brigantes and his invasion and occupation of southern and central Scotland must rank among the most successful feats of arms of any early Imperial governor. It is not possible to arrive at any independent assessment of Agricola's attainments as a provincial administrator on the basis of Tacitus' memoir. But it is difficult, if not perverse, to call his generalship into question.

Archaeology is our only guide to the military dispositions which Agricola left behind him in 84 or which were shortly thereafter brought into being. It is most unlikely that Agricola had much time

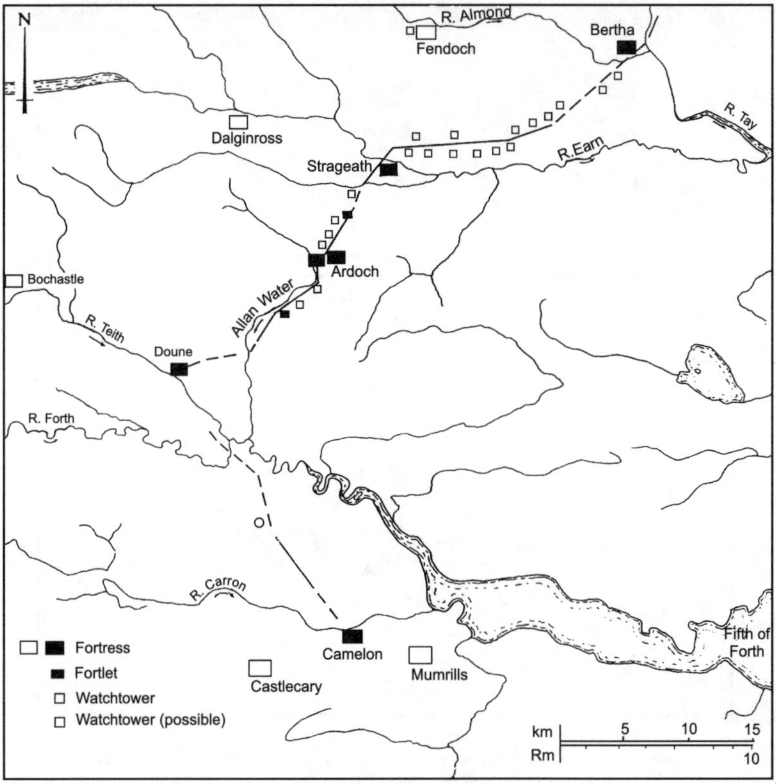

Figure 13 The Flavian Forth–Tay frontier.

to put into effect any coordinated plan for the occupation of the north, for *Mons Graupius* had been won late in the fighting season. No doubt the positions of some forts had already been chosen, but the main period of fort-building will have followed Agricola's departure, in the governorship of his unknown successor. The nodal point of the occupation was to be a new legionary fortress at Inchtuthil in Perthshire, the unit intended as its garrison being in all probability *Legio XX*.[6] Inevitably, the broad strategy was closely related to the main lines of communication, notably to the route which led north-eastwards from the Forth crossing at Stirling by way of Ardoch and Strageath to Bertha on the Tay, and thence along a course which stood clear of the mountains to as far north as Stracathro at least. Forts on this arterial road were not enough as they lay too far from the valleys leading down from the Highlands. These valleys were therefore blocked near their mouths by forts of which the base at Inchtuthil was one, effectively sealing off the Dunkeld gorge.

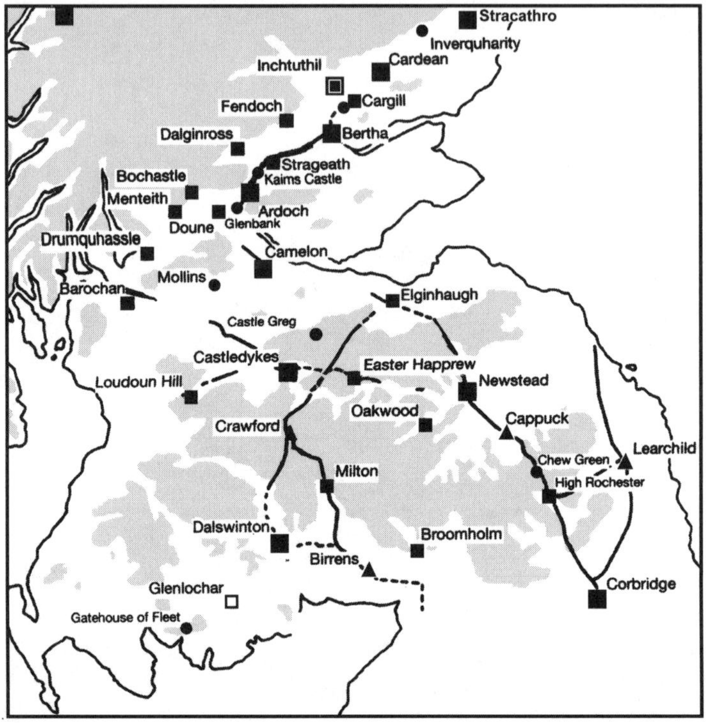

Figure 14 Northern Britain *c.*AD 85–90, after D. J. Breeze.

Auxiliary forts closed off the other principal means of egress from the mountains. Thus, Dalginross covered Strathearn, Fendoch the Sma' Glen, Bochastle the Pass of Leny, Menteith the upper Forth valley and Drumquhassle guarded the gap of Strathblane and the path followed by the Endrick Water towards Loch Lomond. The known pattern of occupation of one of the most fully excavated Flavian forts in Scotland indicates that garrisoning could be more complicated than is often assumed. Aerial survey of the fort at Strageath reveals complex defences and a series of annexes matched only by the fort at Ardoch. Within the fort, the garrison seems to have included more than one auxiliary regiment, some of the troops probably being outstationed in the towers on the Gask Ridge. The fort at Bertha, sited at the confluence of the Tay and the Almond, must have played a significant role in the Flavian occupation of the region, as is suggested by its large size (3.7 hectares: 9.1 acres). Bertha was seemingly the terminal fort of the Forth–Tay line and it is unfortunate that so little is known of its history. As with so many other aspects of Flavian Scotland,

Plate 1 Gold coin of the emperor Claudius commemorating the conquest of Britain. University of Durham.

Plate 2 Tombstone of Sextus Valerius Genialis, a Frisian, found at Cirencester, first century AD. Corinium Museum, Cirencester.

details of chronology are difficult to define within the narrow framework of AD 81–87.

The Inchtuthil fortress is the only timber legionary base in the entire Empire of which the plan is virtually completely known, the gaps being the result of historical circumstance, not incompleteness of record. Apart from the many-sided interest attaching to the fortress itself, the site is a complicated one. Close by lies the camp occupied by the construction parties, a stores compound and an administrative block for the supervising officers. Within the fortress, all the sixty-four barracks were present, together with four of the tribunes' houses, six granaries, hospital, *fabrica* and an unusually small *principia*. All the buildings for the use of the troops had been built and a stone wall added to the early turf rampart, when suddenly work ceased and demolition was ordered. The fortress had not formally been put into commission, for the commander's residence had not been erected and his bath-house in the command-post had not had its water-supply installed. Stocks of pottery and glass had been placed in the stores, so that some troops at least had moved in before the entire site was levelled and the legion withdrawn.

Building of the auxiliary forts had obviously proceeded much faster and those so far known appear to have been completed. All were large enough to house full-size auxiliary units, though little is known in detail of the character of their garrisons. In these works, too, occupation was brief, so brief that metalled roads had not been constructed to link the forts at Fendoch, Dalginross, Bochastle and Menteith with the main road. Fort-builders and early garrisons had made shift by using cleared tracks, as in Augustan Germany and Claudian Britain. The dispositions made by Agricola, or his immediate successor, may well have taken the form of successive linear systems of forts between the rivers Forth and Tay. The first of these could have lain along the line of the Forth–Clyde isthmus (Castlecary, Mollins and Cadder). This might then have been replaced by a forward line at the base of the southern Highlands (Drumquhassle, Malling, Bochastle and Doune) which extended northward to the Tay. Such a cordon makes good strategic sense and may have been further recommended by defence of the fertile territory occupied by the Dumnonii in Fife. While this outline of military occupation in the years 84–87 seems reasonably secure, it must be stressed that many of the component forts have been discovered only in the past fifteen years and most have not yet been examined. There is no doubt that others have still to come to light.

One final element in the Agricolan (and later) arrangements for the occupation of Scotland remains to be considered, one which

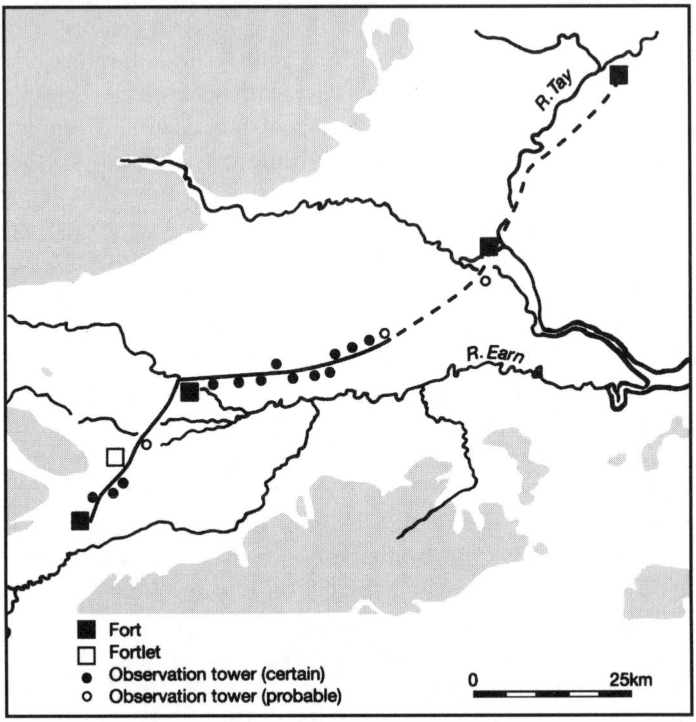

Figure 15 Roman posts on the Gask Ridge, Perthshire.

introduced to Britain a scheme of works which was just entering Roman practice in forward areas. The road leading from Strageath towards Bertha runs along the low Gask ridge, along the northern side of Strathearn. In the eight and a half miles from Strageath, no less than ten small observation posts are known, each consisting of a square timber tower surrounded by a square or circular earthwork.[7] The spacing between the towers is variable, from about a mile to half a mile, the sites being carefully chosen for their intervisibility. The evidence of date for the Gask Ridge towers is not impressive, but it points to the Flavian period and no later. No closely comparable series of towers is known in Britain at this date, although another group of three posts lies on the road between Ardoch and the fortlet at Kaims Castle. Why the Gask Ridge was singled out for this elaborate and exceptional provision is not clear, although the ridge does provide commanding views to north and south. The works which the towers most closely resemble are the signal-towers on the Taunus sector of the Upper German *limes*, which also date from the reign of Domitian. These stand at intervals ranging from 500 to 1000 yards according to the intervening terrain. The arrangement may well lie behind the report of Julius Frontinus that Domitian laid out *limites* (i.e. tracks) through enemy terrain, denying the barbarians their refuges and thereby reducing them to subjection. The same strategy underlies the Flavian dispositions in Scotland, as had already been enunciated by Agricola. It is striking to find such similar works appearing in two frontier regions at the same time. Frontinus gives the palm to Domitian in Upper Germany, but did he borrow the idea from Northern Britain, perhaps under suggestion from an officer who had served in Agricola's army? In the strict sense of the term which Frontinus used, the Gask Ridge road and its towers was indeed a *limes*, differing from the system on the Taunus in being sited behind the foremost positions. The idea of the closely held frontier still lay in the future. If Agricola's conquests had been held for a longer period, into the reigns of Trajan and Hadrian, the attempt might have been made to seal off the Highlands by a stronger cordon of forts, linked together by towers of the Gask Ridge type – thus producing a frontier system on the same model as that of Upper Germany and Raetia, modified to suit local topography. But the urgent needs of other Imperial frontiers supervened.

Retrenchment and reorganization

The archaeological evidence for an orderly withdrawal from the north, accompanied by a systematic dismantling of forts, is abundant and unequivocal. Most graphic, because of the larger scale, are the details of demolition observed at Inchtuthil: the removal of the main timbers of the buildings and gates, the nails bent with a claw-hammer, the remains of bonfires of useless timber, the smashed stocks of pottery and glass, the mass of surplus nails and iron tyres buried in the *fabrica* to deny use of the metal to the enemy. Similar evidence comes from the auxiliary forts which have so far been examined e.g. from Fendoch, Strageath and Cardean. The date can be fixed with fair precision. The latest coins from Inchtuthil were minted in 86 (one possibly in 87) and had not circulated for more than a year or so before they were lost. If they were associated with the demolition of the fortress and not with its construction, the final act of abandonment can hardly be placed later than 87–8. Coin evidence from the auxiliary forts is entirely in accord, *asses* minted in 86 and lost while still new being found at Stracathro and Dalginross north of the isthmus and at Crawford, Barochan and Newstead to the south.

The accumulation of evidence pointing to the same year from so wide a range of forts is unusually impressive. Only one coin, from Inchtuthil, may be as late as 87, and even this is doubtful. All the rest point to 86 as the crucial year.[8]

The precipitate withdrawal of the northern legion and its *auxilia* was in response to two disastrous reverses on the Danube frontier in 86–7. *Legio II Adiutrix* was the unit transferred from Britain, and the fact that one of its centurions was decorated in the Danubian war which ended in 89 provides a little further support for an abandonment of the northern conquests in 86–7. This transfer meant that the fortress at Chester was vacant; it was now filled by *Legio XX*, for as long as that unit retained its identity. Redeployment of auxiliary regiments in lowland Scotland must also have followed, for auxiliaries will also have left for the Danube at this date. The repercussions on the forts in Southern Scotland were profound, as can be inferred from our present knowledge of changes to their planning, though a

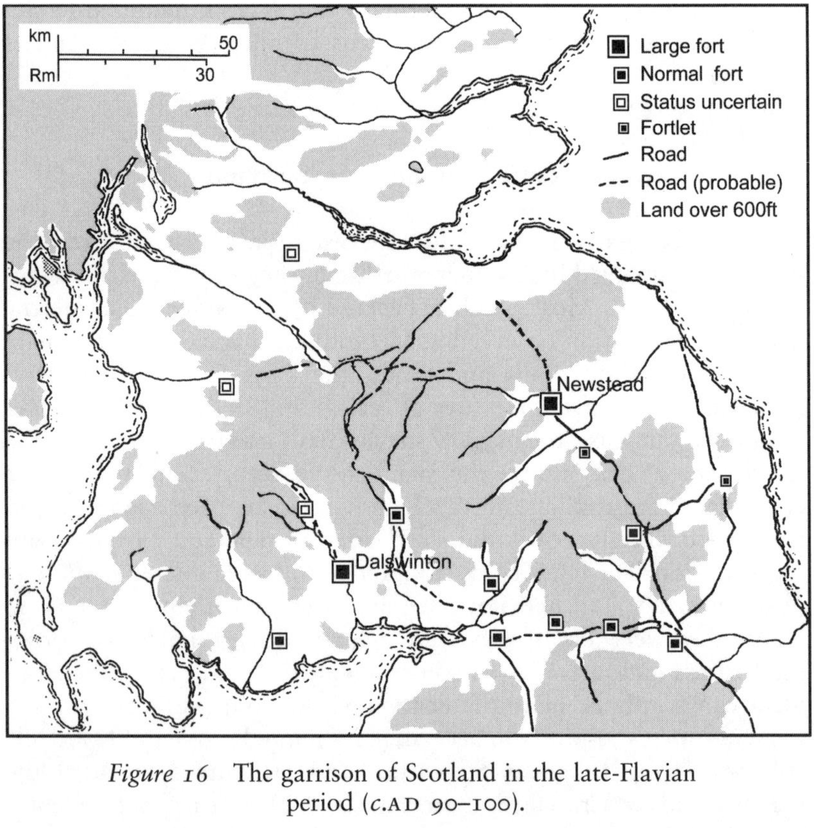

Figure 16 The garrison of Scotland in the late-Flavian period (*c.*AD 90–100).

detailed coherent account cannot yet be assembled. The four large forts of Newstead, Milton, Dalswinton and Glenlochar played an important part in the new dispositions, presumably housing garrisons with a cavalry complement, or even entire *alae* brigaded together with infantry, their function being to patrol the valley routes, perhaps as far north as the Forth–Clyde isthmus. Outposts further north may have existed, at Ardoch and Loudon Hill for example, but are not yet certainly attested. Some of the forts south of the isthmus were abandoned in these years, including Oakwood and Castledykes, but most seem to have been held until the beginning of the second century. Of the four large forts, the largest and best known is that at Newstead. This is of unusual size (over fourteen acres) and had exceptionally powerful defences, including a massive rampart forty-five feet thick. This is so abnormal as to suggest a serious threat of unrest among the inhabitants of the Lowlands. The size of the fort and the presence of legionary equipment there in some quantity point to a legionary vexillation as the garrison, perhaps in combination with an auxiliary *ala*.[9] At Dalswinton, too, the fort was large enough (over ten acres) to house a detachment of legionaries with auxiliaries in support, or possibly two *alae*. The presence of legionaries in these positions was probably deemed essential, as the Selgovae and Novantae had not been entirely beaten down and the nearest legionary base lay far to the south at York. So remote from the front was the base of *Legio IX* that it may reasonably be wondered whether there was not a legionary force established further north. The supremacy of Dere Street as the main route into the Lowlands was underlined by the building of a new fort at Corbridge and by reorganization at High Rochester and Cappuck. Attention was also paid to the Tyne–Solway line, a new fort being built in about 90 at Chesterholm and perhaps another at Carvoran. The road known as the Stanegate, running from Carlisle to Corbridge is usually attributed to Agricola's governorship, but it could belong to this succeeding period of reorganization. East of Corbridge, the Stanegate may have extended at least as far as a fort at Whickham, near Gateshead, if not further down the Tyne valley. There is increasing evidence for an early Flavian fort of some size at Carlisle and by AD 83, if not earlier, there was a legionary force here.[10] It was later to be given a more prominent role in the defence of the north. The Roman grip on the Cumbrian mountains was made firmer about 90, with new forts established at Ambleside, Watercrook and elsewhere, thus completing a task left unfinished by Agricola.

The final decade of the century and the remaining years of Trajan's rule are illuminated by only the briefest reports in our sources.

Domitian's governor Sallustius Lucullus fell foul of the emperor, allegedly by naming a new lance after himself. The period of his governorship is not fixed for certain, but it is likely to have fallen between 90 and 96. He may, then, have fallen victim to Domitian's terrible purge of 93–6 or, just possibly, he might have been implicated in the plot hatched by Saturninus, the governor of Upper Germany, in 89, since that conspirator will naturally have looked for support from neighbouring legates. It is tempting to see in the exceptional military honours won in a *bellum Britannicum* by C. Iulius Karus, while serving as prefect of *Cohors II Asturum*, a connection with these events in Britain. Perhaps Iulius Karus played a vital part in the downfall of Lucullus, thus earning outstanding honours which are otherwise difficult to explain. At all events, Karus' feats in the *bellum Britannicum* are to be dated to the reign of Domitian, between 90 and 96, and not to a later occasion.[11]

The absence of Britain from recorded history in the later reign of Domitian and in the reigns of Nerva and Trajan is not a matter of chance. The Danube frontier was the military *Schwerpunkt* of the period, occupying Domitian early in the 90s and Trajan in the years 101–6. On no western frontier can Trajan be discerned in the role of *propagator Imperii*. In Germany and in North Africa, his armies were engaged in reinforcement of the positions inherited from the Flavians. In Britain, the disengagement which had closely followed the recall of Agricola was continued and shortly confirmed by further retrenchment.

The men who held the British command in the 90s and later were thus not chosen for their generalship. Domitian could not safely send to Britain, Syria or Germany commanders whose fame was already established. The legates appointed by Nerva and Trajan likewise have no known claim to military glory. T. Avidius Quietus (*c.* 98–?) was well known for his refinement and his learned interests, but no experience of active campaigning is recorded for him and by now he must have been fifty or even older. What was expected of Trajan's first legate of Syria can be gauged from the fact that he was the eminent and now elderly jurist Javolenus Priscus who had earlier played a part in the Flavian organization of Britain.

Since vigorous campaigning was not envisaged in Northern Britain, the work of consolidation could go forward. Shortly after 100, however, there was a major change of plan, probably caused by a military reverse. At several forts excavation has revealed a layer of destruction caused by fire. The large forward positions at Newstead, Dalswinton and Glenlochar were involved, as were Cappuck, High Rochester and Corbridge on Dere Street. Doubts have recently been expressed as to whether these forts fell as a result of hostile action rather than of a deliberate decision to abandon the Lowlands and to retire to positions on the Tyne–Solway line. Once again, purely archaeological evidence cannot provide a clear answer. But the exceptionally rich and varied finds of equipment consigned to the ground at Newstead are more easily comprehended as the debris of an engagement than anything else, while the destruction level at Corbridge seems to have been too widespread to be accounted for merely by deliberate demolition. Beneath the burnt levels at Corbridge lay a hoard of gold coins, the latest of which dated from 98. The succeeding fort was being constructed in or after 103.

The date of the withdrawal, whether enforced or not, should thus fall between 100 and 103, or very shortly afterwards. In the reorganization which followed, the Stanegate was evidently invested with a role which roads were increasingly being called upon to play in policing of frontier districts. The details of the Trajanic frontier arrangements are still a matter of debate as few of the sites along the line of the Stanegate have been examined by modern excavation. There is general agreement that the road and its associated posts did form part of an inchoate frontier scheme, though the scarcity of dating evidence for most of the crucial sites baffles any satisfactory examination of its history and mode of operation. It is certain that there are no clear signs of occupation immediately following on the events of 100–3 in the forts immediately north of the Stanegate. None of the forts on Dere Street nor on the road leading north from Carlisle were held in this period and none of the fort-sites which were later chosen by the builders of Hadrian's Wall has produced any evidence for a Trajanic phase, however transient. The Stanegate forts

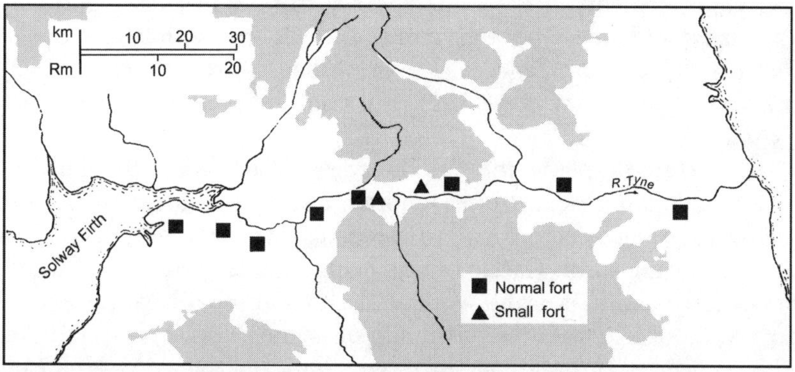

Figure 17 The Tyne–Solway frontier in the Trajanic period (*c*.AD 100–118).

and fortlets are thus revealed as the northernmost permanent garrisons held between about 103 and the building of the Hadrianic frontier from 122. Tenuous as this evidence is, nothing else is available at present.

Forts for full-size auxiliary units existed at Corbridge, Chesterholm, Nether Denton and probably Carlisle. Others have been inferred at Newbrough, Carvoran and Old Church, Brampton. Fortlets of less than an acre in area lay at Throp and Haltwhistle Burn, and the sites of a further four have been proposed but not yet proven. The plan of the Haltwhistle Burn fortlet includes only one barrack (for a century), an administrative block and a store-building. This type of fortlet is reminiscent of a number of sites of similar size on the Upper German *limes*, dating from the same time and later superseded by auxiliary forts. A small number of watch-towers on the higher ground to the north may also have formed part of the Stanegate system, a necessary provision for a road which did not seize the most commanding ground.

Other elements in the Trajanic scheme may be expected to emerge. To the west of Carlisle at least one fort is likely to have given protection to the southern shore of Solway. The fort at Kirkbride, probably a Flavian foundation, may have fulfilled the role. East of Corbridge, too, the map is blank, though a fort at Whickham near the south bank of the Tyne occupies a suggestive position. Even the course of the Stanegate itself, if indeed it extended east of Corbridge, is unknown. How systematic the Trajanic arrangement was will only be revealed by much more excavation of the posts on the Stanegate. If this road was intended to act as a control on native movement across the Tyne–Solway line, there should be more watch-towers to be located. If these did indeed exist, the Stanegate would include all the major elements of the contemporary frontier in Upper Germany and it would then be the more difficult to withhold from it the designation of *limes*. The prevailing picture presented by the Vindolanda texts (*page 100*) is of consolidation in the years AD 95–115.

That Trajan's plans for Britain were based upon the military arrangements inherited from Domitian and Nerva is apparent from the decision taken before 100 to reconstruct the legionary bases in a more enduring form. Caerleon was being rebuilt in 99–100, Chester in about 102 and after, and work at York was probably completed by 107–8, though there is the possibility of further work under Hadrian. This concerted programme can only indicate that no significant change in the position of the *castra legionum* was envisaged. Similar rebuilding was carried out at the same time on the auxiliary fort at

Gelligaer and elsewhere in Wales, at Castell Collen and possibly Forden Gaer. In Western England, the fort at Lancaster has produced a building record of Trajan's reign and the occupation of the Cumbrian mountains was further intensified by the construction of a fort overlooking Hardknott Pass.

There are hints of warfare in Britain during Trajan's reign, though it cannot be determined precisely when the outbreaks occurred. The transfer to Britain of *Cohors II Asturum* before 105 may be connected with the northern disturbances of those years, though earlier operations are not out of the question. Fighting later in the reign may have won the titles *Ulpia Traiana* for *Cohors I Cugernorum* and it is well known that the reign ended with heavy Roman casualties in an otherwise unrecorded war. The events of the first few years of the reign, however, did not prevent the removal of troops from Britain. A *vexillatio Britannica* occupied the fortress at Nijmegen on the lower Rhine after withdrawal of *Legio X Gemina* in 104. Its composition is not known, but the fact that it was responsible for a considerable amount of building at Nijmegen must indicate that legionaries were involved. Nijmegen has also yielded two tile-stamps of *Legio IX Hispana* and a mortarium-stamp of the same unit comes from nearby Holdeurn, clear evidence that at least a substantial part of this legion had occupied the Nijmegen fortress at some date after 107–8, the year of its last dated record at York.[12] The problem of when this legion left Britain and what its eventual fate was still baffles conjecture. It may have been withdrawn before the end of Trajan's reign, but, if that were so, another legion must have immediately taken its place at York. The warfare at the very end of Trajan's reign, only concluded by a Roman victory in 119, provides a likely occasion, but there could have been others. Losses in that shadowy war could have enforced removal of the legion to a quieter posting on the lower Rhine, to receive there fresh drafts of troops before it moved on. Its subsequent stations are quite unknown. It has been surmised that it was transferred to an eastern province and there suffered so severe a reverse that it was blotted out of the register of legions. This is a possibility, but one still entirely without support. The continued survival of the unit at least down to the beginning of the reign of Antoninus Pius, however, seems probable; it may not have met its end until the early years of Marcus Aurelius.

There is a strong possibility that other troops were moved from Britain in the years about 100, not by transferring existing units but by raising new units from the areas recently conquered and despatching them to Upper Germany. It has been persuasively argued by Prof. D. Baatz[13] that the *numeri Brittonum* who advertise their presence on the Odenwald-Neckar frontier in the Antonine period had arrived there about 100, the date at which the forts on this frontier are now known to have been erected. Apart from the striking similarity in plan between the Trajanic forts in the Odenwald and those of forty years later, certain forts in Upper Germany, including the Saalburg, Zugmantel, Hesselbach and Hüfingen, have produced distinctively British brooches dating from the end of the first century and the beginning of the second. The fact that these do not occur on civilian sites in Germany suggests that they should not be interpreted as objects of trade. Rather, they were carried to the German frontier by British recruits sent there to strengthen the garrison. The case is not yet decisively proved, but it is probable that the original *numeri Brittonum* were raised not long after the Flavian conquests in Britain and shortly thereafter drafted to Germany. There, the units were given distinguishing names derived from rivers and other natural features (*Elantienses, Triputienses, Curvedenses*), presumably because they comprised men drawn from many different tribes and septs and could not thus be accorded simple ethnic titles. There is no reason to assume that the Odenwald Brittones came exclusively from Northern Britain. The tribes of Wales and of Southern Britain would also be required to supply men for the *dilectus* under the normal arrangements.

Life on the northern frontier has been illumined with startling clarity by the discovery of a series of documents, written in ink on wooden tablets, in waterlogged deposits at the fort of Vindolanda on the Stanegate.[14] This cache of documents, letters and memoranda offers information of a quality unrivalled not only in Britain but in the Empire as a whole. It includes official and semi-official records and reports, accounts, letters to officers, including the unit commander, copies of letters from the commander, even a birthday party invitation. The wealth of data on military matters, valuable though this is, does not obscure more general issues, not least the degree of Romanization already evident on the northern frontier about AD 100. Among individual documents, pride of place is taken by a strength-report of the first cohort of Tungrians, in garrison at Vindolanda. Out of a total of 752 soldiers on the strength, 337 were at *Coria*, probably Corbridge, 12 miles to the east, 6 were at London, 46 in the governor's guard, perhaps at York, and 31 were sick or wounded. That more than half of the unit was deployed elsewhere is a salutary reminder of the fluid military situation, even in a relatively quiet phase, and enjoins caution on deductions of unit-strength from fort-size.

The activities of soldiers at Vindolanda, and thus more generally along the frontier, are revealed in far greater detail than ever before. We read of troops in workshops, builders despatched to the bath-house, others sent to the kilns, to clay pits, to tents, a soldier seeking leave at *Coria*. The commanding officer, Flavius Cerealis, writes a letter of thanks to an influential colleague, receives a letter of commendation on behalf of an officer based at Carlisle and writes to a friend for nets to use in hunting. His wife Sulpicia Lepidina receives an invitation to a birthday party from the wife of another officer, a rare glimpse of the life of women on this remote frontier. There are many references to food, especially supplies to the garrison: eggs, beans, radishes, apples, olives, chickens, fish-sauce, honey, spices, pepper, corn, ham, venison, beer and wine. Clothing well suited to the northern climate is often mentioned: socks, underpants, drawers, tunics, cloaks, overcoats. Bulk supplies came in from some distance: leather from Catterick, goatskins, stone, wheel-hubs, axles, spokes, planks.

There are no surprises in the degree of military organization evinced in the Vindolanda texts. What is surprising is the extent and standard of literacy on the frontier at this date. The elegance of the Latin of some of the officers' letters is to be expected; less predictable is the good Latin of the soldiery, most of them Gauls and Batavians, and of those who served the frontier army. Here are the beginnings of the Romanization of northern Britain and the speed of its onset is impressive. It can scarcely be doubted that it soon had an impact on native British society.

The Britons of the frontier region figure only once in the texts. A fragment of a memorandum remarks that the natives possess many cavalry and the horsemen do not use swords or throw javelins. The reference is couched in unflattering terms, the Britons being called *Brittunculi*, wretched little Britons. This is usually taken to be a comment on the opponents of Rome, but might just be a scathing assessment of the potential of the local inhabitants as recruits to the Roman army.

In all probability, related to a *dilectus* and a preceding census were the activities of a *censitor Brittonum Anavionensium* in the middle years of Trajan's reign. The *Anavionenses* presumably took their name from a river *Anava* for which the best candidate is the River Annan in Dumfriesshire. Although this lay beyond the line of Trajan's frontier, it is more than likely that the Roman command still aimed at controlling wide areas of Southern Scotland, even to the extent of raising tribute and troops there. If we could be certain that the *Anava* in question was the Annan, a useful insight into Trajanic policy in Northern Britain would thus be gained. It is just possible that the Trajanic *censitor* played a part in the later phases of the operation which resulted in the despatch of Brittones to the Odenwald, though this cannot be proved.

The urban communities

The final quarter of the first century saw great progress in the urbanization of the province.[15] The growth of cities had, by and large, been slow thus far. There had been only one colonial foundation, and its recovery after the Boudiccan destruction had been slow. The development of London as a commercial centre, it is true, had been rapid: certainly by the Flavian period, if not before, the place was probably the largest urban community and already designated as the provincial capital. In the 70s or the 80s the *praetorium* of the governor was built there, and at the same time a magnificent forum was laid out over the site of an earlier public building and its piazza. The office of the procurator had probably been established in the city about or shortly after AD 60. The most remarkable development, however, was on the river-front, where a major port took shape, its timber quays and warehouses eventually extending for 500 yards along the Thames foreshore. About AD 100, a fort was constructed in the north-west sector of the city, the modern Cripplegate, housing a garrison of the governor's guards and military staff. Close to it, about 120, an amphitheatre was erected. It is now clear that the area of Southwark on the south bank of the Thames was developed at an early date, between AD 43 and 55, and not merely as a 'suburb' of London. Substantial masonry buildings were erected in the 70s and a still more ambitious structure went up in the second century on the site of the later palace of the Bishops of Winchester. This building was probably an official complex, including residential quarters, possibly forming part of the governor's or procurator's establishment. A fine inscription on marble found in its ruins attests the presence here of a vexillation of legionaries in the third century, either on garrison duty or a building detail, or more probably charged with general service on the governor's staff. The overall scale and character of the occupation of Southwark clearly demonstrates that the area formed an integrated part of Londinium and was no mere peripheral appendage. As in other large Roman ports, production centres sprang up, yielding goods in glass, leather and other media. There are other abundant signs of a burgeoning of urban life in London at this date, and the rise of the city was surely reflected in its legal status.[16] Precisely what that status was is not known for certain. It was not the *chef-lieu* of a *civitas*, nor can it have ranked as a mere village. Its likely rank was that of a *municipium*, though this hypothesis is not supported by any literary or epigraphic testimony. *Verulamium*, too, probably achieved this status in the Flavian period, rather than under Claudius.[17]

This was a age of public building. Most of the *civitates* of Southern Britain were provided with public buildings under the Flavians, especially those serving official functions, such as the forum and basilica. This is known to be true of *Verulamium*, Silchester, Cirencester, Winchester, Canterbury, Chichester and Exeter. Commercial and market buildings also went up, for instance at *Verulamium* and Silchester, and at some cities places of public entertainment were provided, as in the case of the theatre at Canterbury. Religious buildings also appeared, though the number of classical temples so far recorded is very small. The most important of urban social amenities, public bath buildings, were being built at an early stage in the planning of Silchester and no doubt elsewhere. In some growing communities, for instance at Wroxeter and Exeter, military baths may have been made available to the civilian inhabitants when military use was ended. The spa at Bath also received its first substantial buildings in these years, though the major series of baths here was to come in the 70s.

The final decade of the century witnessed the foundation of two further military colonies, at Lincoln (about 90) and at Gloucester (96–8), the sites of the earlier legionary fortresses being chosen for the new cities. It was almost half a century since the *colonia Victricensis* had been founded, and it is tempting to link the foundation of *Lindum* and *Glevum* with the general consolidation after the withdrawal from the north. There may also have been unusually large numbers of legionaries ready for discharge in the 90s, following the northern wars. The early buildings of *Lindum* are little known as yet, though the forum was identified in the excavations of 1978–9. More is known of early colonial *Glevum*. Here, some at least of the first settlers were housed in the barracks vacated by the withdrawing legion, a clear indication that official funds were not to be lavished on the comfort of the veteran colonists. In the other Flavian cities our knowledge of private housing is not extensive, but standards do not appear to have been high. Large masonry houses were uncommon, and in general the internal appointments of dwellings were simple.

Most of the early cities had no defences, so far as is known. Earthwork defences at *Verulamium* and perhaps Silchester appear to be exceptions, though both are pre-Flavian in date. The colonies of Lincoln and Gloucester were surrounded by the earlier legionary ramparts and at Lincoln at least those defences were given a stone facing, possibly when the colony was founded. But the majority of the peregrine communities were open settlements until a much later date. Uncertainty still surrounds the building of the city defences at Camulodunum, but a strong case has been made for construction in the twenty years following the revolt of Boudicca. Quite aside from the archaeological evidence for a free-standing masonry wall built in the later first century, the destruction of a colonia was not an event which Rome would have treated lightly. It would have been astonishing if *no* defensive provision had been made for Camulodunum in the years immediately after AD 61.

Although the archaeological evidence is beginning to tell us much about the physical form and progress of the early cities, it can say nothing about the legal and institutional organization of the tribal communities. The identification of a forum and basilica reveals only that a place had been advanced to a certain status. It does not tell us what that status was (and there are several possibilities), nor does it define when the promotion was made. An *ordo decurionum* could exist (and probably generally *did* exist) for some time before the familiar buildings housing that body were completed. Those public buildings would, indeed, normally be provided by the *decuriones* themselves. If they were few in number[18] or had limited funds at their disposal, the time-lag between the legal settlement and the building of administrative headquarters might be considerable. Real evidence bearing on the constitutions of the cities of Roman Britain, which inevitably means literary and epigraphic evidence, is so slight that it must be admitted at the outset that the questions we most wish to pose remain unanswered, despite the judicious use of evidence by analogy. At best, we can review the few facts and present the range of possible forms of constitution on the basis of contemporary practice elsewhere. The discussion remains within the realm of hypothesis, while we await the fortunate discovery of inscriptions which might illuminate individual cases.

We may be sure that the constitutions of the *civitates* owed their form largely to the treaties struck between the Emperor and the tribes at the time of their incorporation into the province. Nothing is known of the terms of those treaties, but there is no doubt that there would have been considerable variation, as for example between the Durotriges and the Dobunni. Some will have been modified in the light of subsequent events, as perhaps in the case of the Iceni. The variety of native response to the coming of Rome thus resulted in a varied pattern of tribal constitutions. Even in the *civitates* which offered resistance, however, after the dust of battle had settled, it is likely that much of the administration was left in the

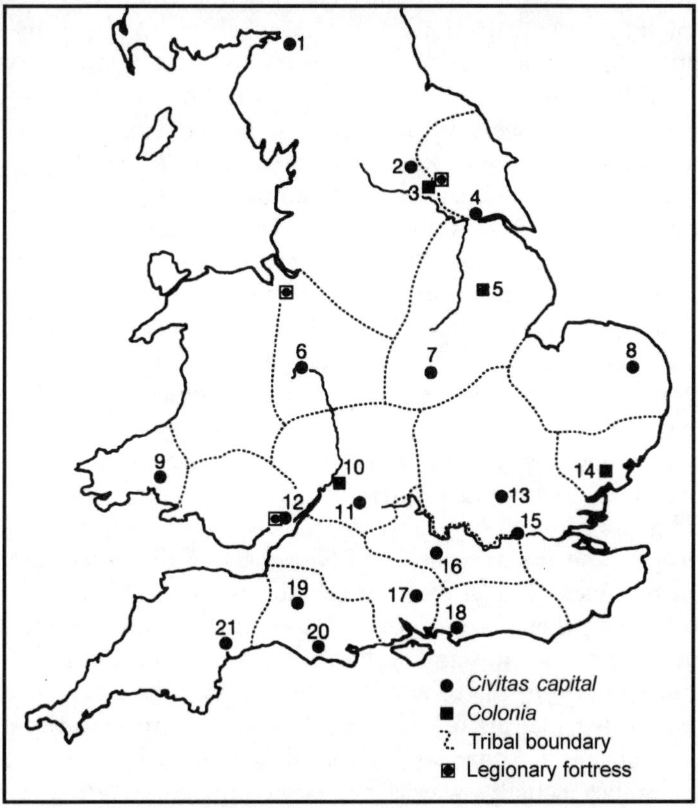

1. Carlisle. 2. Aldborough. 3. York. 4. Brough-on-Humber. 5. Lincoln. 6. Wroxeter. 7. Leicester. 8. Caister-by-Norwich. 9. Carmarthen. 10. Gloucester. 11. Cirencester. 12. Caerwent. 13. Verulamium. 14. Camulodunum. 15. London. 16. Silchester. 17. Winchester. 18. Chichester. 19. Ilchester. 20. Dorchester. 21. Exeter.

Figure 18 The *civitates* of Roman Britain.

hands of the tribal leaders and their followers. This was the practice followed elsewhere, and it is difficult to visualize what else could have been done. From an early date, then, the status of the men who were to administer the tribe was clearly defined and there was no sharp break with the past. There was a further reason why the running of the vital affairs of the *civitates* should have been left in native hands, namely the continuing strength of kingship among the British tribes. The prevalence of kingship meant that rulers and their retinues were the ideal (if not the only) instruments for carrying out such vital tasks as the raising of tribute and supplying recruits for the Roman army. To deprive such men of their power would not only set up unnecessary strains within the tribal order: it would also make the task of local administration all the more difficult. The apparently exceptional positions occupied by Prasutagus and Cogidubnus surely owed much to the central role played by kingship in British society. Their powers thus seem all the more understandable, and it is quite possible that there were others like them among the eleven kings mentioned on the Roman arch of Claudius.

Modern commentators sometimes give the impression that self-government was granted by Rome as a kind of prize for praiseworthy effort towards the establishment of communities that were Roman in essential structure as well as in outward form. This is simplistic and based on misconception. Roman encouragement for urban development was more hard-headed than that, springing mainly from the desire to create a practical basis for provincial administration in the most economical way. If the provincials were prepared, or could be persuaded, to assume the burden, well and good. This was what lay behind the promotion of Vienna to primacy among the villages of the Allobroges, and the attribution to Nemausus of the other communities of the Arecomici. It also lay behind the *saluberrima consilia* of Agricola and other Flavian governors in Britain. The need to leave Southern Britain secure and well-ordered while the north and west was brought within the province coincided with the emergence of a generation of tribal aristocrats which had grown to maturity under Roman rule and, in some cases, under Roman tutelage. How successful this policy actually was is not clear, but it is worth note that *curiales* and magistrates are not prominent in the epigraphic record in Britain. More significantly perhaps, individual local leaders do not figure on the monumental forum inscriptions from Verulamium (of AD 79 or 81) and Wroxeter (of AD 129).

What, then, were the possible constitutions for the British tribes? The more highly favoured provincial peoples could be classed as *civitates foederatae*, in which case they kept their own laws and were not subject to the rule of the Roman governor or to Roman taxation. Such communities still existed in the early Empire, though it is not clear whether they still retained their privileged independence. More numerous were the 'free and immune' states, *civitates liberae et immunes*, though by the mid-first century AD it is doubtful how real their immunity from the customary burdens actually was. Little is known about these communities in the western provinces. Below them in rank came the *civitates stipendiariae*, liable to taxation but still enjoying a measure of autonomy under their own magistrates. The form of their constitutions is not known in detail but they were probably modelled on those of Roman cities. Finally, occupying a position between the peregrine communities and Roman cities, there were the states endowed with Latin rights of citizenship, *Latium maius*. These were well represented in the west. Nero had made such a grant to the Maritime Alps and Vespasian to the communities of Spain. The citizens of these *civitates* remained peregrine, but those who held magistracies (and their families) became full Roman citizens, thus creating a social band to which the unprivileged could aspire. In the second century, full citizenship was accorded to the entire *ordo decurionum*.

It is likely that most of the Romano-British cities which developed in the later first century were either *civitates stipendiariae* or *civitates iuris Latini*. The former category, to quote the nearest analogy in time and space, included the majority of the Spanish communities in the early Flavian period and the same was presumably true in an emergent province like Britain. There may have been exceptions. The status of the Regini under Cogidubnus may have called for special attention, and the Iceni before 47 are another case where the original treaty arrangement may have allowed a measure of privilege, perhaps as a *civitas libera*.

The earliest recorded *legati iuridici* were appointed in the mid-Flavian period, the earliest known, C. Salvius Liberalis Nonius Bassus, being perhaps the first to hold the post, from the end of Vespasian's reign. The legal aspects of administration were by now proving burdensome and *legati pro praetore* may not have been equipped, by training or temperament, to deal with the complex and sensitive issues that might arise in a province like Britain, where tribal custom might be far from uniform, thus making assimilation to Roman law far from straightforward. It is notable that the two Flavian *iuridici* in Britain were both outstanding authorities in the law. L. Iavolenus Priscus succeeded Salvius Liberalis in the middle of Agricola's governorship; his subsequent, and rather unexpected, appointment in AD 90 to the Upper German command suggests that he had earned a reputation as a specialist in the problems attending transfer of authority to civilian communities, for only a decade later self-governing *civitates* were emerging immediately behind the German frontier. The presence of these two eminent jurists in Britain may have had much to do with the development of tribal organization in the service of Rome, which is rightly regarded as the major hallmark of Flavian administration in this province. It is hard to see how Frontinus and Agricola could have spared time for the *minutiae* of such a task. More probably, these fell to the lot of Salvius Liberalis and Iavolenus Priscus, Agricola in particular gaining his fame by being wise enough to listen to their advice. Some of the most awkward problems may have arisen over such matters as the ownership of land, the obligations of tenants to landlords and, in the newly acquired north and west, the legal status of the many peoples brought within the Empire in the previous decade.

Rural society in the first century

The spread of Roman culture in the countryside of Southern Britain was slow, as slow, probably, as it was in North Africa and slower than in the Rhine provinces. The growth of Roman-style farmsteads has not yet been detected in any area before the reign of Nero and only in certain regions did it begin so early. The initial response of a tribe to the Roman arrival must have been of great consequence in determining how the tribal *equites* fared immediately after AD 43, and these were the men in whose hands the development of estates largely rested.

Among the earliest discernible villas is a number in Kent and Sussex, all lying close to the sea and most of them situated on or near to navigable estuaries.[19] They include Eccles and Wingham in Kent, and Southwick and Angmering in Sussex, all originating in the period 55–80. Others, such as Folkestone, Eastbourne and Fingringhoe, Mersea and Rivenhall in Essex, were in existence well before 100. The coastal distribution of these villas may mean only that their owners were exploiting the alluvium of the coastal plains, but it might also be satisfactorily explained if some of their proprietors had commercial as well as agricultural interests. That *negotiatores* did come to Britain can be safely assumed, and some may have constructed comfortable houses near to the ports of entry. Furthermore, there are clear architectural links with contemporary villas in Gallia Belgica and one villa, Wingham, possesses at least one first century mosaic which is closely analogous to a floor at Haccourt in Belgium.

The *deductio* of veterans at *Camulodunum* in AD 49 transferred land from native hands to those of citizen-colonists, and some reflection of this might be expected in the archaeological record. First century villas have been identified in Trinovantian territory, though none is contemporary with the early years of the *Colonia Victricensis*. The Rivenhall villa existed by the Flavian period, developing out of an earlier settlement, and the less well known sites at Mersea and Fingringhoe were probably contemporary. Of their owners nothing is known for certain though a classical-style mausoleum at Mersea is suggestive of an immigrant. The evidence from Rivenhall points in the other direction, towards a native owner. Where, then, were the holdings of the veterans? A group of villas in the valley of the Colne below *Camulodunum* catches the attention and may one day supply part of the answer: for the present they remain unexamined.

The country residences of the Catuvellaunian nobles are more readily identified. Within a few miles of *Verulamium* several villas were founded in the years 60–80 and one, at Gorhambury, may go back to about 50. From about 75, the date at which *Verulamium* itself was beginning to grow again, there are clear signs of a more general conversion to Roman standards of building. The villas at Boxmoor, Gadebridge Park and Northchurch were all founded at this time. The plans of these villas were simple, but they represented a considerable advance in standards of comfort and convenience on what had gone before. The earliest rectangular building at Gorhambury was built in the same construction technique as the contemporary structures at *Verulamium*: wattle and daub walls over sill beams and with floors of clay and chalk. Though the plan is imperfectly known, it might have owed as much to pre-Roman as to Roman tradition. The most interesting of the early houses is at Boxmoor near Hemel Hempstead. This was a timber-framed building with four rooms in the main range, a projecting wing at each end and, running round the whole, a verandah. The building type is clearly not native and the likeliest architectural inspiration is to be sought in Gallia Belgica. Already in this early phase at least one room possessed painted plaster on its walls and a detached bath-house may have lain nearby. The first masonry villas appeared in the Flavian period at Lockleys, Park Street and perhaps Gadebridge Park. These were simple rectangular blocks without architectural embellishment. The temptation to call them 'cottage' villas, however, must be resisted for they were the foci for early estates, not dependent dwellings.

It is striking that the new canons of taste in housing, by whatever agency they were formed, are evident in the countryside and not in *Verulamium* itself. There were seemingly no allurements towards residence in the new city strong enough to attract the Catuvellaunian nobles from their rural seats. Given the extremely durable fabric of Celtic society – 'hierarchic, aristocratic, familiar' – that is perhaps not surprising. The city offered many more opportunities of advancement to their clients, the craftsmen, traders, the equivalents of Roman freedmen. Almost another century was to elapse before the homes of the wealthy began to figure prominently at *Verulamium* and at other cities and by then the ranks of the wealthy had been considerably enlarged.

The other region in which early villas have been observed is the coastal plain of Sussex, the territory of the Regini.[20] The great palace of Fishbourne dominates this landscape but there is good evidence for early houses of some pretension at Angmering, Southwick and perhaps Pulborough. The attitudes of prominent Regini no doubt owed much to those of Cogidubnus and his predecessors, but the extent of Roman influence on their villas in the first century is still astonishing. Most splendid of all is the Flavian palace of Fishbourne, built over the site of a large house begun in the sixties but never completed. The magnificence displayed at Fishbourne may plausibly be connected with the ruling house of the tribe, though that is not the only possibility. Roman *negotiatores* could also be very wealthy men, and the adjacent harbour could have been a great attraction for an Italian or a Gaulish immigrant. But that does not diminish the impression that the native leaders enthusiastically adopted many of the outward appurtenances of provincial culture at an early date. Even a rural religious centre might be refurbished in Roman form before 70, as a Roman temple on Hayling Island attests.

That the earliest villas occur in the south-eastern *civitates* is to be related to the longer contact with Rome experienced by the leading members of those tribes. It was to these regions that Roman traders had brought wine, pottery, bronzeware and glass in the first decades of the first century AD. After the conquest, Roman capital with all its allurements in prestige and social status would have been made readily available to any British noble who showed an interest in grasping it: the origins of many villas surely lay here. There are other considerations to take into account. We know remarkably little about the ownership of land in British society at this date (or indeed later), but it is possible that ownership was normally invested in the tribe, not in individuals, and that the tribal *equites* who controlled the use of land were unable to dispose of it. But South-eastern Britain had been in contact with Gaul for a century before AD 43, where even before Caesar's day there had been a perceptible shift towards private ownership of land. Since in the Roman provinces of Gaul this would have continued space, repercussive effects on Britain are reasonably certain. Pre-eminently in the south-east, then, the necessary economic conditions, and the social stimuli, for the foundation of villas existed by the time of the Roman conquest. Elsewhere, the process was to take longer, but the enormous potential of the new markets, first military and then urban, allied with the burgeoning of British agriculture under the encouragement of Roman capital, meant eventual prosperity for those *equites* who looked to the care and profitability of their estates.

No other *civitates* in Southern Britain have, so far, produced evidence for the development of villas in the first century. The midland peoples, Coritani, Cornovii and Dobunni, reveal no villas until well after 100. Further to the south-west, as might be predicted, Durotrigan landowners were not yet beginning to acquiesce in the Roman peace to the extent of constructing Roman dwellings. The same is true of the Iceni. In several regions outside the south-east, villas made no appearance for another century, a striking indicator of the regionalism of lowland Britain and the heterogeneous outlook of its tribes.

The exploitation of natural resources

The mineral wealth of Britain was rightly reckoned by Tacitus to be the *pretia victoriae* – even though Rome had earlier overestimated the riches of the island – and it is therefore not surprising that the major deposits of gold, silver, lead, iron and copper were exploited as soon as the territories in which they lay had fallen to the army. To some extent, as has been earlier indicated, they may have influenced the direction in which the Roman advance was turned. But there is growing evidence, too, for the rise of lesser industries and industrialized crafts in the first half century of the Roman occupation. This rise was not rapid in the first two decades of the province, but, from modest origins in those years, a number of concerns were able to thrive from about AD 70 onward. None grew into huge industrial organisms: that process was to take another century. The first century trades and workshops did, however, make a vital contribution to the rising prosperity of the new province as well as to the making of its Roman fabric.

We must begin with the metals for which Britain had long been famous. The lead and silver deposits in the Mendips of Somerset were being worked under military supervision within a few years of the conquest, for two ingots from the area are dated to AD 49. One outlet, at least, was to Gaul *via* the Channel coast ports. Civilian *negotiatores* and their agents were quickly on the scene. By AD 60, C. Nipius Ascanius had obtained a concession in the Mendip field and before long in Flintshire too, probably as soon as Suetonius Paullinus opened up that area. In the following decade, other private agents, including Ti. Claudius Trifer(na), worked the Mendip lead and later the ores of Derbyshire and Yorkshire. Shortly thereafter, an association of contractors, the *socii Lutudarenses*, seems to have taken over sole responsibility for the rich and accessible Derbyshire veins. The Elder Pliny, however, tells us that British lead was so abundant that its extraction was limited by law, implying that not all official control had been abandoned. The extent and importance of the yield of silver from the galena deposits is uncertain, but cannot have been great (0.01 per cent in Derbyshire). Lead was the principal attraction, for multifarious uses in building and plumbing and in the production of alloys.

Considerable, though scarcely massive, supplies of gold fell into Roman hands after AD 43, in the form of coined money and ornaments. Prospecting for the metal cannot have been successful until the conquest of Wales by the Flavian legates finally opened up the western estuaries (where gold might be obtained by panning) and, more significantly, the Cothi valley in Carmarthenshire. A large series of gold workings was developed at Dolau Cothi from the Flavian period, originally no doubt by the army, later apparently by civilian lessees. Determined efforts were made here to reach deeply buried veins, to drain the galleries by mechanical means and to treat the ore at the mine-head, thus revealing the importance of this site and perhaps, incidentally, the poor yields won elsewhere in Britain.

There is as yet no evidence for any highly organized and centralized working of metals into marketable goods in the first century. Rather, craftsmen working individually or in small groups catered for a fairly localized clientele. Among the more impressive instances of collaborative enterprise are the *fabri* at Chichester who had organized themselves as a *collegium*, perhaps by the early 50s, and who were presumably exploiting the iron of the nearby Weald, and the bronze-workers of *Verulamium* who before AD 60 had established themselves in recognizably Roman-style shops near the centre of the town. Less clear evidence comes from *Camulodunum*, though a brass founder was certainly working there, from London, where a goldsmith is attested in the 70s, and from Wroxeter, where there is more evidence for bronze-working in the Flavian period. This growth of metal craftsmanship is not confined to the cities. At Lullingstone in Kent, for example, a rural craftsman had assembled a group of copper/lead ingots. Far more compelling, however, is the widespread evidence for a continuance of Iron Age traditions in decorative metalworking (especially in bronze) conspicuously in Northern England but attested all over the province. The well known expertise of Iron Age smiths was so advanced that it would have been remarkable if the craft had withered after the conquest. In fact, thanks to the enlargement of the sphere of patronage after AD 43, the later first century saw a flowering in the minor art of bronze-work for the adornment of the person. Within the province, the products of the craft included brooches, some of them enamelled, dress-fasteners and other ornaments, horse-trappings and war-gear, some of which at least were used by Roman auxiliaries. Beyond the province to the north, the vogue was for flamboyant personal ornaments; massive armlets, neck-torcs and spiral bracelets. Later, when the northern regions were incorporated in the province, the skills of northern smiths were much in evidence in the metalwork used by the army and the wealthier natives.

Few industries reveal the history of their development in such detail as that of pottery-making. The impact of the army on this concern was immense, but it must not be allowed to conceal the continued importance of native traditions of manufacture or the significant rise of private workshops, in some cases at the instigation of immigrant craftsmen and capitalists. It is now clear that after the early years of occupation the legions supplied some of their vast need for pottery by organizing production close to certain of their fortresses. At Longthorpe before 60, a large number of pottery kilns sited outside the fortress supplied much of the better quality wares used by the troops there. At several of the later fortresses, including Caerleon, Gloucester, York and Wroxeter, distinctive wares have been identified and reasonably associated with workshops working under military supervision. By the end of the century, the legion at Chester had established its own works-depot at Holt, ten miles away on the River Dee, and here pottery, bricks and tiles were made, primarily for the Chester garrison. Arrangements for the supply of auxiliary posts have not yet been adequately studied but are likely to yield interesting results.

The importance of these military centres of production is obvious. Not only were they centres of Roman technical standards from which new types and production methods were disseminated, they also stimulated other groups of potters to enter the military market. Workshops in the Savernake area of Wiltshire, for instance, developed in the 50s, primarily to serve the military market in the west, and the same may be true of the contemporary kiln-sites in the Nene valley. In Dorset a local industry rooted firmly in the Iron Age also supplied Roman forts in the early years and later formed the basis of one of the largest of Romano-British pottery industries, that which produced black-burnished ware. The army must also have played a large part in opening up long-distance lines of communication by sea and river as well as on land, an obvious precondition for workshops seeking wider markets, both military and civilian.

The survival of the vigorous native tradition, especially in the south and east, was predictable, and there is no doubt that the bulk of production lay in the hands of British potters for whom AD 43 marked no immediate turning-point. But from the reign of Nero onward there is clear evidence for the activity in Britain of workshops established there by external agencies, and some of these were working on a large scale. The links, inevitably, had been created from Northern Gaul and the Rhineland. Interestingly, citizen potters (or owners) making mortaria were involved, such as the Valerii, who established workshops in South-eastern England, probably in Kent, from their base in the Bavai region. *Camulodunum* attracted the attention of other *entrepreneurs*, including G. Attius Marinus (who later moved on to another site at Radlett (Hertfordshire) and several men called Sex. Valerius, probably freedmen. The area south-west of *Verulamium*, especially the sites at Radlett and Brockley Hill, was chosen for the establishment of important potteries in the 60s and 70s and a wide range of wares was produced here, notably mortaria and amphorae.

The speed with which the best building stone was identified also argues for the intervention of external agents as well as military specialists, for there was no tradition in stone-building in the south of the island before the conquest. By Nero's reign, oolitic limestone from Northamptonshire and possibly Lincolnshire was in use for sculpture and tomb monuments at London and *Camulodunum*, and by the same date the virtues of Purbeck marble for inscriptions and ornamental uses had already been discovered. The first century legionary bases at Exeter and Caerleon show its use for sculpture and architectural details, while more conspicuous examples of its use are the *Verulamium* forum inscription and the Cogidubnus stone at Chichester. The qualities of Bath limestone for architectural details as well as monumental structures were also appreciated early on and it was employed in several cities by the Flavian period. These were the finest stones which Britain offered and all were in use before the end of the century. Less favoured materials with a more local distribution included the greensand of Kent and Sussex, chalk from the downland, Barnack rag from South Lincolnshire, and possibly Ketton limestone from Northamptonshire, all in use by 100 and all testifying to the rapid growth of one of the major new industries of the province.

There is a clear implication that craftsmen were imported for most of the skilled workmanship involved in the carving of masonry and for work in such media as mosaic, painting and gem-engraving. Legionary sculptors, well versed in the traditions of classical art, were responsible for military tombstones and other funerary monuments which set the first standards for stone sculpture in the island.

In the absence of any native tradition in this medium, the influence of these men on the early development of sculpture in the province was immense, though not absolute. A large body of immigrant craftsmen was employed on the palace at Fishbourne: mosaicists, painters, masons, sculptors and workers in stucco. Some must have come from Italy, or at least had acquaintance with what had been *à la mode* there shortly before, others from Gaul. The hand of an artist familiar with the Rhineland tradition can be traced in some of the architectural detail. The materials used also reflect the wide acquaintance of the craftsmen: marble from Greece, Italy and Aquitaine, fine stone from Normandy. Craftsmen work where they find patrons, and it is possible that Britain offered more lucrative outlets for skill than Gaul at this time, particularly in the growing towns.

7

The Frontier-builders

Hadrian's solution: *Romanos Barbarosque Dividere*

The sudden death of Trajan while campaigning against the Parthians brought to power P. Aelius Hadrianus, after a flurry of allegations that Trajan had died before nominating any successor by adoption. But Hadrian, then governor of Syria, was Trajan's next of kin and was in any case proclaimed by the army. The reign thus opened in an atmosphere of doubt and perplexity, and some of Hadrian's first acts cannot have improved his stock with the partisans of Trajan. The recent conquests of Armenia and Mesopotamia were abandoned. The leading military counsellors of the previous decade received no preferment or were removed. An equestrian friend of Hadrian was appointed to an exceptional command on the Danube and other adherents of the new emperor were shortly sent out to the other major commands. Even without the discontent and distrust stirred up by the execution of the four consulars in 118 – all of them generals of Trajan – the Senate found reason enough to hate the new regime. Even those who in the early days were allies of the *princeps* found it difficult to keep his trust or friendship. After three uncomfortable years in Rome, Hadrian set out on his great tour of the western provinces, his purpose being to review the resources of his Empire and to devise the most efficient means of maintaining provincial security. On all the frontiers, his aims and policies were determined early in the reign and there was no notable deviation from them in his lifetime.

There was fighting in Britain, in the north we presume, when Hadrian acceded and this was not over until 119, as an issue of commemorative coins shows.[1] Nothing is known of this war, but it was evidently a serious business for Roman casualties were heavy. It was shortly followed by the building of Hadrian's great Wall, the most ambitious Imperial frontier conceived by the mind of a single emperor. The first of Hadrian's governors of Britain was Q. Pompeius Falco, transferred from Lower Moesia in 118, probably with the specific task of bringing the province back under control.

In 121 Hadrian visited Gaul and the German provinces and in the following year passed to Britain, the first emperor to do so since Claudius in 43. He brought with him a new legate, his friend A. Platorius Nepos, fresh from the governorship of Lower Germany, whence also came *Legio VI Victrix* (from *Castra Vetera*), probably at the same time. The duration of Hadrian's stay in Britain is unknown but it is unlikely to have outlasted the summer months. He nevertheless found time to institute 'many reforms'. In Germany, there had been much to put right in the army, for there had been no serious warfare on that frontier for more than twenty years. This was not true of Britain, and Hadrian may thus have thought it more urgent to regulate, and perhaps stimulate, the progress of native communities towards self-government. For a variety of reasons, it was no longer the practice to found colonies, so that the development of urban centres and the administrative organs which resided there was now the peculiar responsibility of the tribal oligarchs. The emperor had a keen eye for improvement and economy in the bureaucracy, and here too there may have been much in need of review. Provincial administration easily became ramshackle under a system in which legates and procurators had barely enough time to discover what faults and abuses existed (if they were so inclined) before they moved on. Hadrian, already training himself to look for defects, was in a better position than any mandatory to apply a remedy.

Here and there may be discerned, or surmised, repercussions of the Imperial visitation. The forum and basilica at Wroxeter,[2] dedicated in 129–30, may have owed its inception to Hadrian's visit and can represent the emperor's interest in the provision of civic amenities for native cities. The large-scale drainage of the Fenland,[3] which was pursued with increased vigour from the 120s onward, is precisely the kind of scheme which would commend itself to an emperor who was himself '*immensi laboris*' as well as ever conscious of the desirability of creating wealth. The centre of the imperial estate thus created in the Fens may have lain at Stonea Camp in Norfolk. But above all else the northern frontier attracted attention as a major task requiring completion. Recent warfare had shown how inadequate was the Trajanic arrangement of frontier forces. Whether Hadrian came to Britain with a plan for a new frontier already formed in his mind or whether the idea was implanted during his visit cannot be known, just as there must remain uncertainty as to whether the Upper German palisade was constructed directly after his visit in 121 or rather later in the reign. But it is a reasonable presumption that Hadrian's Wall was a conception of the emperor himself and that the implementation of the grand design began in 122, though the possibility that work had already begun about 120 cannot be summarily dismissed.

More important for Hadrian himself in 122 than the building of a new frontier was the need to show himself to the army in Britain. Although he had some experience in warfare, he had, unlike Trajan, led no army in a war of conquest, and his policy towards the external peoples barred such enterprises for the future. Therein lay a danger to his Principate. Not since Nero had an emperor neglected to cultivate the regard of his troops. But, unlike his predecessors, Hadrian was envisaging a new role for the army, as guardians of firmly drawn frontier-lines, and he made this plain from the first years of his rule. Consequently, there was all the more reason for the emperor to reveal himself to the troops as a soldier like them, to share their diet and conditions, and to remind them that discipline and order were as vital in peace as in war. That is why 'he desired peace rather than war, yet he trained his soldiers as though war was imminent'. The policy was successfully carried through, and we hear of no reaction against it during the long reign. There may, however, have been repercussions for his successor (*page 127*).

The most imposing and, ultimately, the most complex of Roman frontiers was originally intended to run for 76 Roman miles from Hadrian's new bridge over the Tyne at Newcastle to Bowness-on-Solway.[4] A wall which ran almost from sea to sea across this isthmus was bound to cross very varied terrain, and although the common image of Hadrian's Wall is of the great barrier marching over the volcanic crags of the Whin Sill, that spectacular remnant of the frontier is only some twelve miles long. From *Pons Aelius* to the North Tyne at Chollerford, the Wall negotiated fairly undulating country, quite possibly carrying a considerable cover of trees at that time. In the central sector the Wall could generally command superb views to north and south, but west of the Irthing valley and on to the Eden a gentler landscape offered no obvious tactical line to the Wall builders. From Burgh-by-Sands to Bowness, the Wall confronted the flats of Solway, running above the high-water line for six miles.

In its original design the Hadrianic frontier was to be an intensively patrolled line, with fortlets ('milecastles' on the linear barrier, 'mile-fortlets' on the sea-coast) sited at mile intervals and, between each pair of fortlets, a pair of regularly spaced towers ('turrets' on the Wall, 'towers' on the coast). No such regular lay-out of frontier-works has

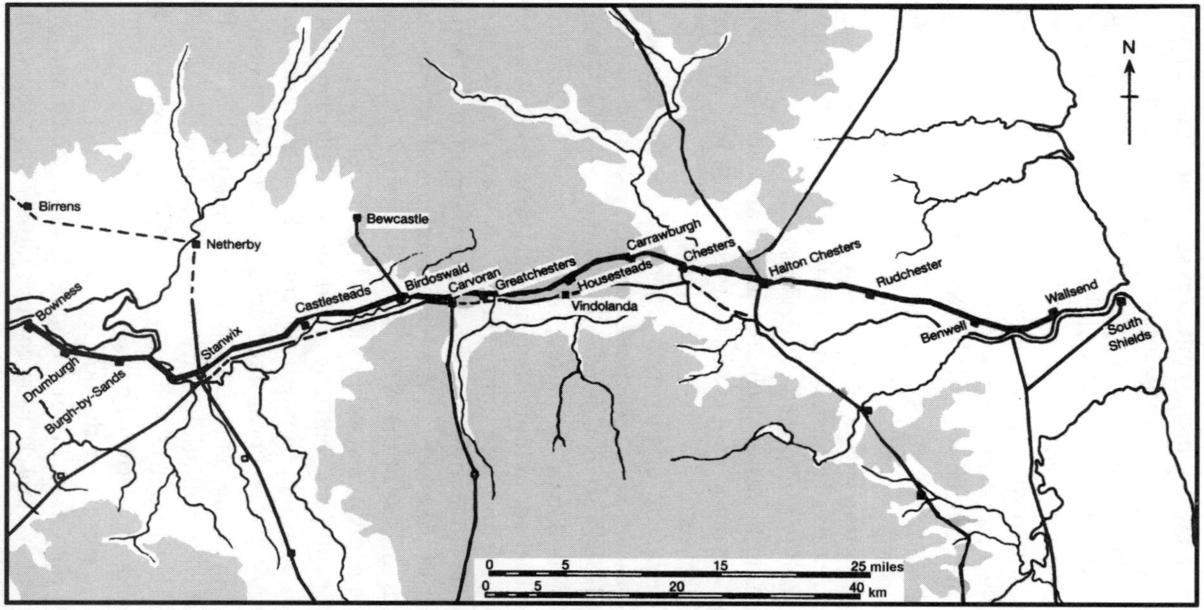

Figure 19 The Hadrianic frontier.

yet been observed on any other Imperial frontier. The connecting barrier was to be a wall of stone ten Roman feet (Roman foot = eleven inches) wide at the base from *Pons Aelius* to the River Irthing, and a turf rampart twenty feet wide from the Irthing to the Solway. Accompanying it was a ditch, omitted as superfluous on the Whin Sill and not completed in certain places where very hard rock was encountered, measuring between twenty-six and forty feet wide and up to ten feet deep. The stone Wall was probably at least fifteen feet high, perhaps somewhat higher, and the turf Wall need not have been much lower. The use of turfwork west of the Irthing valley still provokes discussion, but the most plausible explanation remains that limestone for mortar was not to hand west of the Red Rock Fault. Forts holding the main auxiliary garrisons lay to the rear in the central sector at first, but several were added to the frontier work a few years after work started, *c.* AD 125/6. This need not be seen as a radical change of plan rather than a series of adjustments as work proceeded. The first group of forts included twelve placed at intervals of about seven Roman miles, with variation at major river-crossings. Later additions, at Carrawburgh and Carvoran, were either inserted into longer gaps or sited to cover problem sectors.

The system of garrisoning adopted for the milecastles and turrets has not yet been recovered, for relatively few sites have been thoroughly excavated. Considerable variation has been noted in the troop accommodation of the few milecastles so far examined. Some may have housed no more than an eight-man *contubernium*, others have space for four such units. The turrets were plainly observation points like the stone towers on the Upper German and Raetian *limes*. How effective they were in the more broken and possibly wooded terrain east and west of the Whin Sill is debatable. Their often assumed use as elements in a system of lateral signalling along the line of the Wall is difficult to accept. For one thing, the milecastle garrisons were so small that only limited aid could be summoned in this way. For another, the practical difficulties of signalling in mist and low cloud are not to be underestimated. More probably, the turrets were to serve as observation platforms high above the Wall. When serious trouble threatened, the patrols would seek assistance from the garrisons in the rearward forts.

It is plain that the builders of the frontier were much concerned with the security of the Cumberland sea-coast and that a system of fortlets and observation towers, closely analogous with the milecastles and turrets, extended down the coastline at least as far as Ravenglass and Eskmeals at the mouth of the Esk. It seems likely that this chain of posts continued still further south, probably to the Furness peninsula and Morecambe Bay. As along the isthmus, the main garrisons were housed in forts, including Beckfoot and Maryport, with others added later, as at Moresby and Ravenglass. Further south, Lancaster may have lain at the southern end of the system, there being other forts yet to be located on the estuaries around the northern flank of Morecambe Bay. At the northern end of this coastal sector, a pair of narrow parallel ditches, set thirty to forty-five yards apart and enclosing the sites of the fortlets and towers, ran along the shore, from Bowness at least as far as Cardurnock. Although their purpose is not entirely clear, they may have held palisades, thus forming a definitive barrier against intruders coming from the sea. How long these defences were maintained is not yet known, but the ditches were more than once refurbished.[5] Some of the fortlets, at least, were abandoned within Hadrian's reign.

The final element of note in the original design of the frontier is a group of three garrisons outposted north of the western sector of the Wall, at Birrens, Bewcastle and Netherby. Since there is no trace of any Hadrianic outpost beyond the central and western sectors, it is a reasonable deduction that trouble was expected in the west, from the Novantae and Selgovae in particular. There is certainly no need to see these outposts as protecting part of the territory of the Brigantes:[6] they were sited here for purely military reasons.

The building of the Wall and its associated works had proceeded for some distance when there came a radical change of plan. The stone Wall had been substantially completed between Newcastle and the Dere Street crossing; its foundation, together with some of the superstructure, had been carried westwards to Housesteads on the Whin Sill, when a decision was taken which fundamentally altered the form of the frontier. Forts for complete auxiliary units were now added to the linear barrier, thus rendering obsolete most of the forts on the Stanegate. The forts on the Wall were not all constructed at the same time. It has been plausibly argued that the intention was to space twelve forts fairly evenly roughly seven miles apart along the Wall, some adjustment being made to the spacing where rivers intervened. Six of these primary forts were placed astride the Wall, with three of their principal gates north of the barrier. The others abutted on the rear of the Wall, in most cases facing north. The intention may have been to have *all* the forts projecting north of the barrier except where local topography forbade it, but this is not a necessary conclusion. The advance of forts to the line of the Wall was not done without modification to the scheme of milecastles and turrets. Turrets were dismantled to make way for the forts at Chesters, Birdoswald and Housesteads, while at Great Chesters a milecastle was

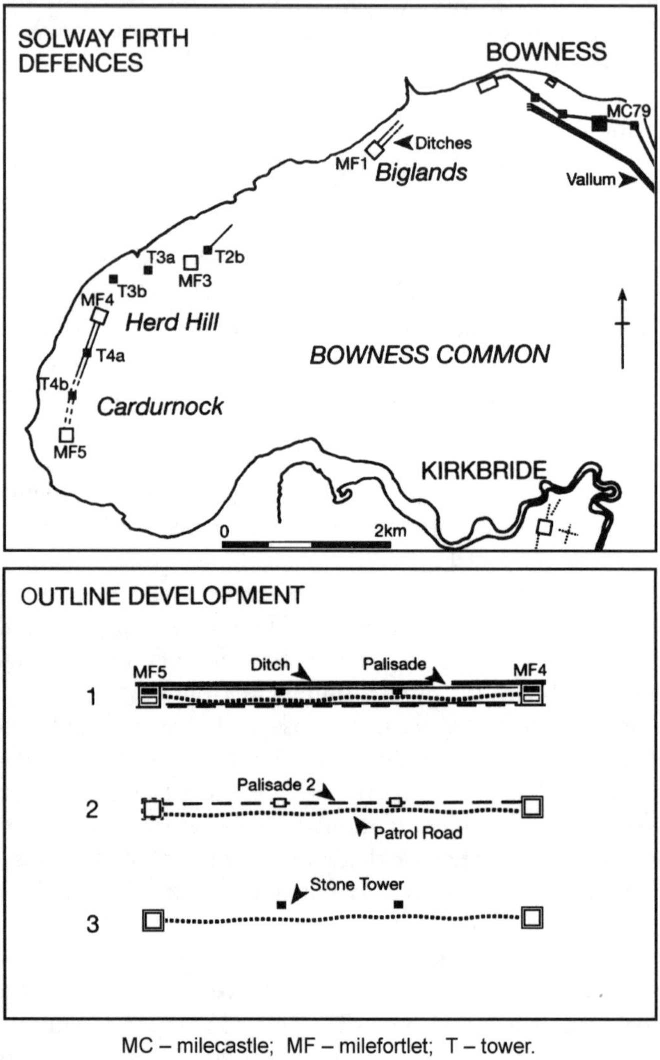

Figure 20 The Hadrianic defences on the Solway Firth, after G. D. B. Jones.

obliterated. At Halton Chesters, the Wall itself and its ditch had to be levelled to create a platform for the fort. The lapse of time between the inception of the frontier and the start of fort-building was brief. Two of the forts (Benwell and Halton Chesters) have produced building records of the governorship of Platorius Nepos, which ended in 125. Within the first season or two of work on the original frontier scheme, it would appear, the design was found to be inadequate and decisive steps were taken to put matters to rights.

It is not difficult to see why the first form of Hadrian's frontier was found wanting. A patrol garrison could not by itself deal with any serious inroad: they would need to call on the troops to the rear. But it was an absurdity that those troops were so close to the linear barrier and yet were still out of effective contact with what was happening on the frontier itself. The movement forward of the forts thus simplified the process of policing the Wall and the region beyond, though it did so by increasing the number of troops on the isthmus. It is as though a frontier rigidly planned on the drawing-board had been reshaped by men with more practical experience of the ground.

Another innovation immediately followed the building of the forts or the determination of their sites, one that is not closely paralleled on any other frontier and still gives rise to perplexity over its purpose and its history. The earthwork known to scholarship since Bede as the Vallum – and probably to the Romans as the Fossatum[7] – closely followed the building of the primary series of forts. The form of the earthwork is established in its main essentials, but there is still room for discussion on many points of detail, some of which might help to clarify what the Vallum was intended to do. A steep-sided, flat-bottomed ditch, twenty feet or more wide and up to ten feet deep, ran between two accompanying mounds, each about twenty feet wide and standing thirty feet from the ditch. The whole ensemble thus comprised a cleared belt about 120 feet across. Where the Vallum passed behind forts, substantial causeways were left in the ditch. These were guarded by large stone gateways forming control-points on the roads leading to the forts from the south. The arrangements at milecastles have been less satisfactorily demonstrated. Only at two (milecastles 50 and 51) have original causeways been identified, and one of these (51) is a dubious case. At several milecastles it is certain that such causeways did not exist, unless their place was taken by plank bridges or some such structure. On the whole, it is preferable to see the arrangement at milecastle 50 as special and determined by purely local factors.

Another of the much discussed features of the Vallum is whether or not there were patrol-tracks on the berms between the ditch and the mounds. The small number of excavated sections across the entire profile of the Vallum makes certainty impossible on this point, but the arguments often advanced for a track on the south berm do not seem convincing. Likewise, a track on the northern side of the ditch, though it could have offered the advantage of a link between the milecastles, is not established beyond all doubt by the evidence at present available. The absence of metalled tracks, of course, does not prove that the Vallum was not patrolled, though close surveillance would hardly be necessary in the many sectors where the Vallum ran close to the Wall. Equally, there is nothing to demonstrate that patrolling was envisaged from the beginning as an essential feature of the Vallum. It is not even certain that the areas of metalling found on the berms in various places were laid down as part of the original work. It follows from these observations that there is no warrant for the view that the Vallum acted as a service-track for the milecastles. The marked similarity between the layout of the earthwork and the engineering of a Roman road should not mislead us into believing that there was any similarity in function. If that had been the case, we might have expected the Military Way, later constructed between the forts, to have followed certain sectors of the north berm, for example. That did not occur.

The form of the Vallum, as it is at present comprehended, indicates its general purpose fairly adequately, though it would be a rash student of the northern frontier who claimed that he could see into the mind of the man who devised the Vallum. The great ditch and the widely spaced mounds were a formidable, though not insuperable, obstacle against approach from the south. Anyone found crossing it without authorization, whether soldier or civilian, would know he was in the wrong. Wheeled traffic and animals were directed to the forts where they could be controlled and supervised by sentries at the major crossings. Only in the sector between milecastles 34 and 48, where the Vallum swung away from the Whin Sill, would it have been necessary to organize separate patrols for the Vallum. Elsewhere, the Wall garrison could adequately perform that duty. It is usually argued that the Vallum was found necessary to mark off the rear of the frontier zone from native intruders and seal off the Brigantes from their potential allies beyond the Wall. This it clearly does, but the demands of military discipline (on which Hadrian had firm ideas) also required that the frontier troops themselves were left in no doubt as to what constituted their proper sphere. Seen in this light, the Vallum is a logical, if very elaborate, solution to a two-fold problem. It defined the rear of the military area for all to see, while allowing peaceful passage through the frontier to natives who could furnish good reason for seeking it. The passage of animal herds and of traders is unlikely to have been normally permitted at the forts and mile castles. More probably special gates which lay well clear of military installations, for example at the Portgate on Dere Street, were designed to fulfil this need, under conditions of strict control.

The Hadrianic garrisons on the Wall are not yet well known. The largest fort, at Stanwix, certainly housed the miliary *ala Petriana*, another pointer to the importance of the western flank in the eyes of the High Command. Elsewhere, the picture is far from clear, but there are signs that *cohortes equitatae* were employed, presumably to give flexibility in the tasks of patrol and interception. Purely infantry cohorts may have been installed at Birdoswald and Great Chesters, but this is not certain. It has often been pointed out that the *praefectus* of the *ala Petriana* outranked all the other auxiliary commanders on the Wall, but it does not follow that Stanwix was therefore the site of Command Headquarters. The *praefectus* will still have taken his orders from the legionary legate at York and ultimately from the provincial governor. The development of separate frontier commands lay far in the future.

Modification to the frontier-works went on until the end of Hadrian's reign. At the eastern end, the Wall was extended, in a gauge of six to eight feet, to a new fort at Wallsend. No stretch of Vallum was provided behind the extension. A fort was added at Carrawburgh, covering the broad gap between Chesters and Housesteads, and in 136 the site at Carvoran was rebuilt as a stone fort. Probably at about this time, or a little later, it was decided to replace the turf Wall in stone. A stretch of some five miles was converted into stone, a new line being adopted for two miles. There are signs of poor quality in the workmanship of this replacement Wall, suggestive either of haste or of a shortage of skilled masons. The purpose and tactical function of Hadrian's Wall have been frequently discussed and the debate continues. The key to its original conception and planning undoubtedly lies in the character and outlook of Hadrian himself. In his provincial policy, Hadrian was a great consolidator. Definition was brought to several frontiers in his reign. In Britain, the demarcation line of the province was to be drawn with exceptional clarity, probably at the direct behest of the emperor himself, a man whose sense of the dramatic was well developed. If this was the origin of the frontier, what was it designed to do? The separation of Romans and barbarians advanced by the biography of Hadrian in the *Scriptores Historiae Augustae* is an entirely plausible explanation of the underlying strategy, whatever the pedigree of that text.[8] But the frontier was to perform that task with flexibility. The linear barrier was clearly designed to permit movement across the frontier under controlled conditions, *via* the gates in the milecastles and the special gates on long-established routeways. This was provided for on other frontiers, notably in Upper Germany and North Africa, but nowhere with such studied elaboration as on Hadrian's Wall. In the conditions of Northern Britain, it might well be thought that such provision was far too lavish.

More intense discussion has centred on the possible military functions of the Wall. Whether or not this was clearly envisaged in the original design, it will have been obvious that this was a frontier that might come under attack. It is less clear as to what tactical deployment was foreseen. The Wall itself was singularly ill-equipped to serve as a defensive barrier. The wall-top could not have provided an effective fighting platform, being too narrow and having access points 300 yards apart. The milecastles offered vulnerable gates at every mile, guarded by no more than a century. The front of the Wall could not be covered by enfilading fire, for there were no projecting towers. The running barrier was thus not conceived as a purely defensive line. The troops stationed on the Wall would only have been fully effective when operating north of the frontier, in gathering intelligence, patrolling and neutralizing military threats at an early stage. The outpost forts played an essential role in this, but the strategy was more generally applied. Hadrian's Wall was more than a political statement on the bounds of Empire. It was not, however, the most important element in the defence of Northern Britain. That role was fulfilled, as elsewhere, by the strength, organization and adaptability of the Roman army.

The building of this exceptionally powerful frontier between Tyne and Solway naturally takes pride of place among the military achievements of Hadrian's reign. But it should not completely overshadow the less spectacular occupation of the Pennines and Wales. A nexus of garrisons was still needed in the upland country of the Brigantes, southward almost to the Trent, and in the greater part of the lands of the Silures, Ordovices and Deceangli. The Flavian conquest of Wales had been thorough and it had been possible to evacuate a number of forts before the end of the first century. But a hold on the main strategic valleys was still necessary as late as Hadrian's reign and even later. The forts at Gelligaer, Carmarthen, Penydarren and Castell Collen were given up in the 120s, and other forts were reduced in size or replaced by fortlets. The army's grip on the main lines of communication was still firm, and the permanence of the legionary fortress at Caerleon is sufficient indication that the inhabitants of the Welsh hills were still considered volatile. The Brigantes, too, had to be kept in check. The western Pennines were still secured by forts at Manchester, Ribchester and Lancaster, and both the Cumbrian mountains and the Derbyshire hills were watched by garrisons. A sizeable army of between fifteen and twenty auxiliary regiments was tied down behind the frontier, and substantial assistance could be raised from the legions at York and Chester if the need arose. On the frontier itself there were twenty auxiliary forts, including the outposts, and a further five on the Cumbrian coast. In Wales, between fifteen and eighteen forts were occupied in Hadrian's reign, giving a total of at least fifty-five for the province as a whole and perhaps as many as sixty-eight. The evidence of military discharge diplomas and inscriptions provides the names of fifteen *alae* and forty-nine cohorts known to be in Britain during Hadrian's reign, a total not far removed from the maximum number of Hadrianic fort-sites at present attested.

Antonine advance and retreat

Hadrian's long reign ended in the summer of 138. His second choice of heir was T. Aurelius Antoninus, an Italian in the Catonian mould. He was already fifty-two years old and had a proven record of public service behind him, including the governorship of Asia. The choice was originally unpopular, for reasons unknown, but the universal respect which Antoninus won from the beginning of his reign was to invest his principate with an almost sacred aura, enabling it to shine as the very pinnacle of the *pax Romana*.

Little that Hadrian did pleased the Senate. His later years were barren of initiative on the frontiers and beyond, precisely as the emperor intended. The policy cannot have been popular with the military, and the extreme dislike of the senatorial order for Hadrian finds one of its true sources here. The tension which had existed between Hadrian and the Senate influenced external policy at the beginning of the new reign, Antoninus being prepared to countenance advance on two frontiers, presumably at the prompting of the *viri militares*. One of the earliest decisions of the reign concerned the northern frontier of Britain. The province was to be enlarged by reoccupying Scotland in strength and by building a frontier wall between the Forth and the Clyde, where Agricola had long before briefly responded to the promptings of geography.[9]

Q. Lollius Urbicus, who had come to prominence in the later reign of Hadrian without incurring that emperor's disfavour, was selected for the northern war, and he was to have time enough to establish the new frontier. He was already in Britain and making active preparations for war in 139, and the war was won by the early months of 143 at the latest. For the only time after success in battle, Antoninus was saluted *Imperator*.

The Turf Wall of Antoninus has never approached the fame of Hadrian's Wall. Its life was short and its visible remains are less than imposing. Knowledge of its component works seemed until recently to be as complete as could reasonably be expected and the outstanding problem for debate appeared to be the date of its final disuse. We are now much closer to a solution of the latter problem, but an intensification of field-work on the Antonine Wall has begun to reveal complexities in its structure of which there was little earlier trace.[10] There is no support here for the view that the Antonine invasion of Scotland was a hollow military achievement, a walkover, and that there was no major fighting. The vivid scenes of conflict which appear on the distance-slabs recording the building of the frontierwork, along with the coin-types proclaiming victory, must refer to serious campaigning, unless the suspension of disbelief among troops who took part was total.

The new frontier extended across the neck of land only forty Roman miles (Roman mile = 1618 yards) wide from Bridgeness on the Forth to Old Kilpatrick on the Clyde. Although having no such topographical feature as the Whin Sill to exploit, the frontier work made full use of what northward-facing ground there is, especially in the central sector from Castlecary to Balmuildy and on the eastern flank. The chosen line involved the crossing of two substantial rivers, the Avon at Inveravon and the Kelvin at Balmuildy. The turf Wall itself, the *Vallum* as it was termed by its builders, had a footing of dry stones at least fourteen feet wide (and occasionally wider) and may have stood nine or ten feet high. A timber parapet may be presumed on the crown of the rampart, thus adding five or six feet to the total height. great care was taken over the drainage of this mass of earth, clay and turf, culverts being placed in the footing to take away the water which seeped through the body of the rampart. In front of the Wall lay a large ditch, up to forty feet wide and twelve feet deep. Its distance from the *Vallum*-front varied from place to place. Usually it lay about twenty feet away, but on Croy Hill the space measures up to 100 feet. In the western sector, the ditch tends to be narrower, between twenty and thirty-six feet wide, and only six to eight feet deep. Much of the upcast from the ditch was dumped on the outer side so that the outer face of the ditch was originally considerably higher than the inner.

The frontier-work was constructed by *Legio II Augusta* and at least vexillations of *Legio VI Victrix* and *Legio XX*, working from east to west. A large number of camps which housed the troops engaged on building are known, and study of their distribution and relationship with the work-sectors assigned to individual legionary

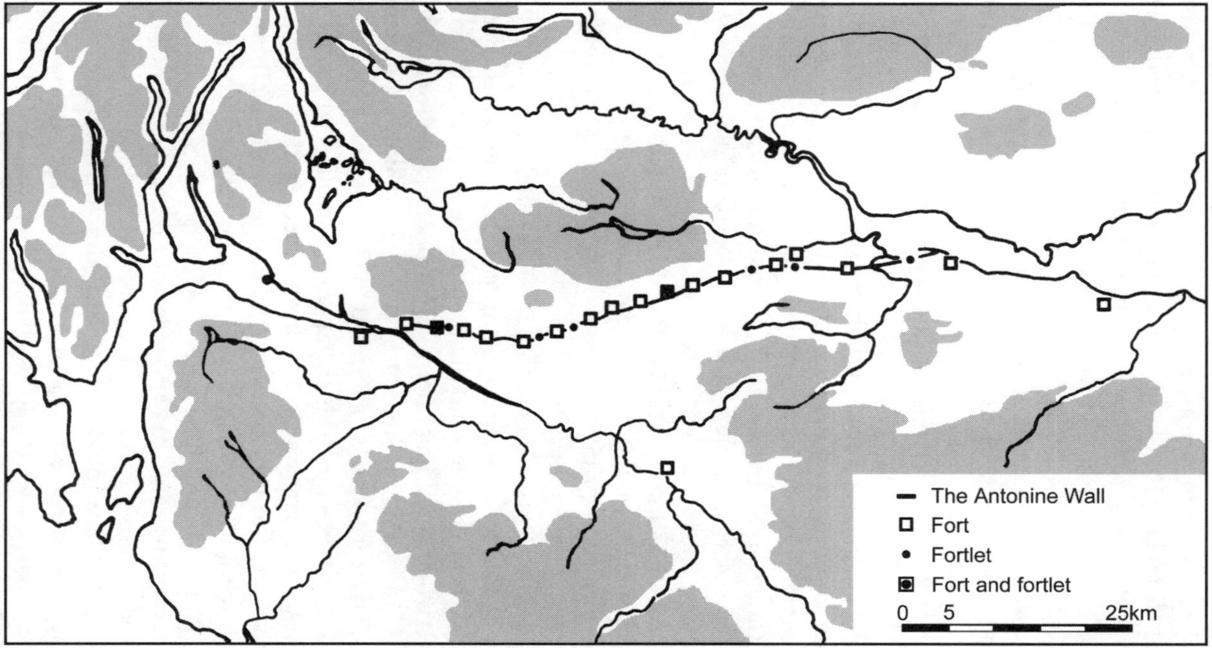

Figure 21 The Antonine Wall.

gangs has suggested that two camps were sited at either end of a sector with the soldiers assigned to a sector working from both ends towards the centre. The lengths generally measured 3, $3^{2/3}$ or $4^{2/3}$ miles, measured in *passus*, a fact superbly recorded for us by the so-called distance-slabs, large and often ornately carved stone tables. Eighteen distance-slabs are known, recording in their texts the building of the frontier and in their sculpted scenes the inevitable victory of Roman arms over the northern tribesmen. Probably four such slabs originally marked off the work-sectors, two at each terminus. At the western end of the frontier, a different *modus operandi* had been adopted, for reasons unknown. The final four miles had been divided into six short lengths, and the record of their completion was recorded in *pedes* not *passus*. There were at least fifteen forts on the Antonine Wall, in varied structural relationships with the running barrier and thus presumably of more than one phase of construction. The interval between each pair of forts was no more than two or three miles, so that where longer gaps occur forts yet to be discovered may be suspected. Their positions were carefully selected to give a wide outlook to the north, and often to all sides. Four large forts, Mumrills, Castlecary, Balmuildy and Old Kilpatrick, are fairly evenly spaced at an interval of seven to nine miles, raising the possibility that these formed a primary series which predated the others; this is, however, mere hypothesis.

The other forts are notable for their small size, ranging from 3.3 acres at Cadder to only 0.6 of an acre at Duntocher. They did not, then, all hold complete auxiliary units. Some, including Croy Hill and Westerwood, may have been garrisoned by small legionary detachments, an exceptional measure on a forward line, presumably reflecting the concern with which the Roman command viewed the north at this date. Others probably held parts of auxiliary units, the remaining centuries and *turmae* being outstationed in the many fortlets and watch-towers to the south. The planning of the Wall forts is extremely varied, in accordance with their heterogeneous garrisons. Only two, Balmuildy and Castlecary, had stone walls and gates, the others possessing turf ramparts and gates of timber. The principal buildings and the granaries had stone foundations, but the barracks were built in timber. Many of the forts had attached annexes, which might provide storage areas to compensate for the lack of space within the fort. Almost all the forts abutted the rear face of the Wall, their north gates piercing the barrier. To the rear of the Wall ran a road, known to modern observers as the Military Way, linking the forts together and forming in most cases their *viae principales*. Bar Hill alone lay detached to the rear of the Wall by a space of about one hundred feet. Camelon lay to the north on the site of a Flavian fort. Like Carriden, close to the eastern terminus, Camelon must be regarded as part of the frontier system, though why it should have been selected for reoccupation is not clear, unless it was intended to guard the Dere Street crossing.

The most important of modern discoveries has been the realization that the Antonine Wall possessed an extensive series of fortlets, resembling in plan the milecastles on Hadrian's Wall.[11] These are now recorded at many points on the Wall – at Wilderness Plantation, Kinneil, Watling Lodge, Glasgow Bridge, Duntocher, Seabegs and Croy Hill – which suggests that they were elements in a comprehensive system; numbers of these may be expected to appear in future field-work. The siting of some of the fortlets in relation to forts, leaving an interval of between one and one and a half Roman miles separating each pair of works, suggests a carefully ordered system. But the redundancy of the fortlet at Duntocher after the fort was built, together with a similar situation at Croy Hill where the fortlet lay only fifty yards west of the fort, suggests that these posts belonged to the primary phase of the frontier and that their occupation had to be modified when the secondary forts were added. If there was a regularly planned series of fortlets, it is reasonable to wonder whether there were not watch-towers between them, as on Hadrian's Wall, but of these there is no sign.

The Antonine Wall holds a special place in the history of Roman frontiers. It was to be the last of the linear frontiers built *de novo* in the confident days of the Principate, and its life was so short that later modification did not rob it of its original cohesion of purpose. Unlike almost all other *limites*, it retained the form given it by its founders, thus allowing unusually precise assessment of its original function. Briefly, it was modelled on the developed form of Hadrian's Wall, though turrets were not provided and there was no equivalent to the Vallum. Its basic strategic purpose was the same as that of its predecessor. It was to be a line of demarcation held in strength, from which troops would patrol and police the areas to north and south, and campaign when this proved necessary.

The great potential weakness of the Antonine Wall lay on its estuarine flanks which in combination double the width of land over which Roman troops would need to maintain a watch. On the western flank a road led down to the Clyde from Old Kilpatrick. This is likely to have been a link with a supply depot and harbour on the estuary at or near Dumbarton. On the south side of the Clyde a fort lay at Whitemoss and a fortlet at Lurg Moor near Greenock. Other elements in this scheme may yet be found. The south shore of the

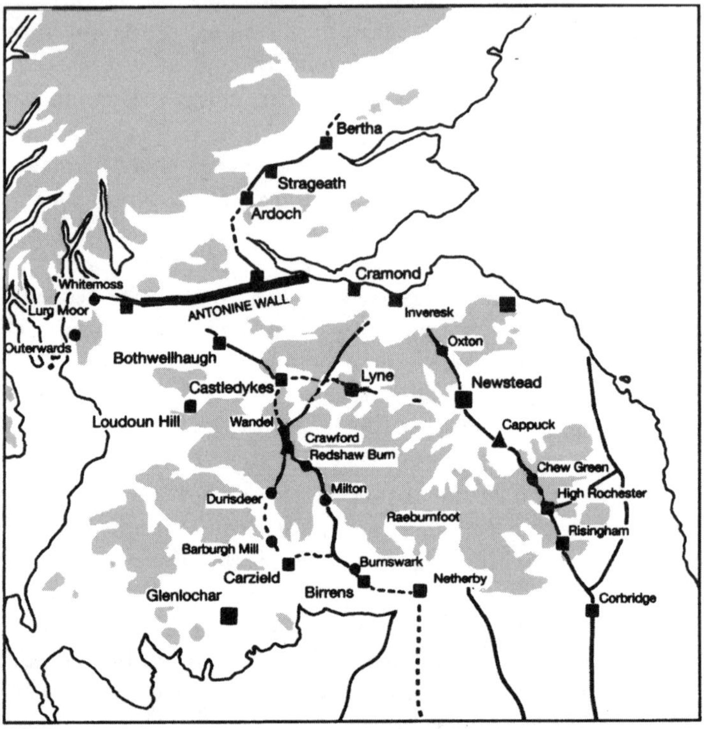

Figure 22 The Antonine occupation of northern Britain, AD 142–58, after D. J. Breeze.

Forth was given protection by forts at Cramond and Inveresk, but, more significantly, on this eastern flank a series of garrisons was outstationed on the road leading north to the Tay, from Camelon through Ardoch, Strageath and Bertha. The greater threat was evidently still expected from this quarter, and it is notable that the garrisoned road ran through the most productive land in eastern Scotland. There is no need to see these Perthshire garrisons as screening off a protectorate. They were a military measure, entirely dictated by the needs of frontier defence.[12]

Behind the isthmus, the military hold on the Lowlands was made more firm by the construction of a network of fortlets and watchtowers. These covered the territory of the Selgovae and Novantae, securing the major routes and enabling supervision of the main concentrations of native settlement. There may have been an especial emphasis upon south-western Scotland, the lands of the Novantae, though Dere Street, too, was guarded by the same kinds of post. The fortlets vary in size, though most seem to have been designed for a century (e.g. Barburgh Mill in Nithsdale) or half a century (e.g. Outerwards in Ayrshire). The watch-towers were square timber structures, probably up to twenty-five feet high, with in some cases their lower storeys encased in dry stone. The type of installation is well known on the Upper German frontier, but the square masonry towers which were being introduced in Antonine Germany are as yet unknown in Scotland. Although often regarded as signal towers, many are not well suited for the purpose and were probably used mainly as look-out posts by patrols.

The province now entered upon four of the most turbulent decades in its history. The first signs of trouble are evident shortly after 150. A legate of *Legio VI* gained success in an engagement *trans vallum*. The officer was L. Iunius Victorinus Flavius Caelianus, and his term in Britain can now be placed in the years 152–5. Which *vallum* was he referring to on his inscription?[13] The find-spot, Kirkandrews-on-Eden, suggests it was Hadrian's Wall, which would imply an insurrection well within the province. The point is of some importance for an understanding of following events. The governor appointed, in 155, to deal with the continuing emergency was Cn. Iulius Verus, yet another example of the transfer to Britain of a legate from Lower Germany. Also from the German provinces, and probably accompanying the new governor, came drafts for all the legions of Britain. These were sent in a body direct to the Tyne, as though all three legions were being employed in the north at the time. The epigraphic records of Iulius Verus' governorship have long pointed to the Pennines and the area immediately north of Hadrian's Wall as his chief concern. No records of his are yet known from Scotland. Several of the Pennine forts abandoned about 140 were brought back into commission by this legate or his immediate successors, surely indicating that the Brigantes and their neighbours were still not willing partners in the Roman peace.

There is another still more remarkable record of these years which must be connected with the suppression of rebellion rather than with an invasion from *Barbaricum*. In 154–5 a large series of bronze coins was struck with a reverse type showing a mourning figure of Britannia.[14] The significance of this issue of coins, which was designed to circulate within Britain, is often missed. The personification of the province is revealed not in the pose of serene triumph adopted by the Britannia of Hadrian's 'Provincial' coinage, but as a dejected and subdued figure such as might be found attending a trophy. This is not the guise of a province which had been conquered long before, unless that province had been the scene of a major insurrection against Roman authority. Although no single piece of evidence yet known proves that there was a major revolt in Northern Britain in the early 150s, the tendency of all the information we do possess is very much in that direction.

The effect on the recently completed frontier in Scotland was profound. The first phase of occupation on the Antonine Wall ended with destruction of the forts, as is attested by abundant evidence from several sites. At some forts, the evidence is for deliberate demolition by their garrisons and not for damage by an enemy. At Bearsden, for example, the internal buildings were taken down and burnt, while at Balmuildy the bathhouse was levelled and carefully buried. Still more clearly the work of Roman hands is the demolition

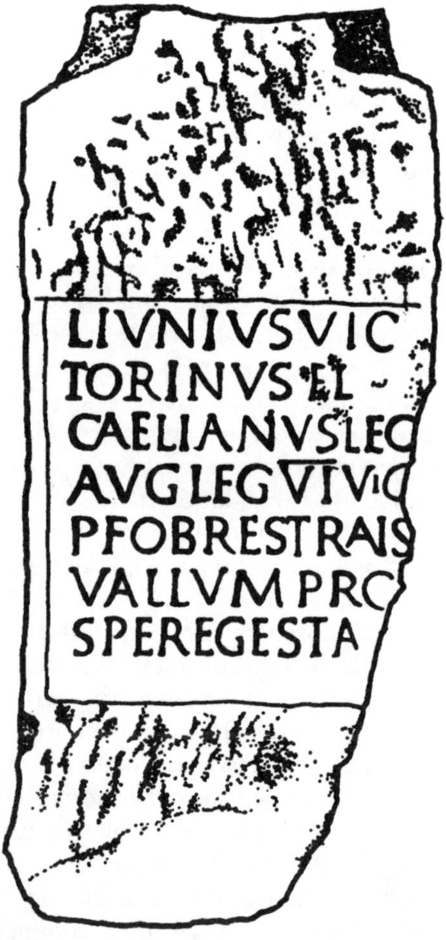

Figure 23 The inscription of L. Iunius Victorinus from Kirksteads (Cumbria) recording a Roman success north of Hadrian's Wall.

of the fort-rampart at Mumrills and the careful burial of the distance-slabs along the line of the Wall itself. There is no room for doubt that the frontier was deliberately abandoned in an orderly fashion in accord with normal practice. All this is in sharp contrast with the evidence suggestive of enemy intrusion south of the Antonine Wall, at Birrens and at Newstead. Precisely when Iulius Verus gave up the Scottish frontier cannot be fixed, but the likely year is 154 or 155.[15] This decision cannot have been lightly taken: the emergency must have been grave.

If the Scottish frontier could not be held, a return to Hadrian's Wall, at least for the time being, was inevitable. Repair work on the Wall was being carried out in 158 by *Legio VI* and there may already have been moves towards the rehabilitation of the milecastles and the Vallum. It is not clear whether Iulius Verus felt that a return to the Antonine frontier would never again be feasible and advised Antoninus accordingly. The legate may simply have temporized, fallen back on the Hadrianic frontier and taken such measures as were required to put it into tolerably efficient order, without restoring it to anything like its pristine state. The abandonment of a considerable part of northern Britain may not have seriously troubled the aged Antoninus, but it would have held no appeal for Marcus Aurelius, who was shortly to assume power. But it was before the death of Antoninus in 161 that Roman forces moved back into Scotland with the intention of refurbishing the Antonine Wall. The decision was to prove premature. The campaigns of Iulius Verus had not brought peace to the north. In 161, the experienced and highly thought of M. Statius Priscus Licinius Italicus was transferred to Britain, after only a few months as legate of Moesia Superior. Statius can only have had time to acquaint himself with the British scene, and perhaps make preparations for war, before he was again transferred, this time to the eastern frontier, where the Parthians had destroyed a legion, possibly *Legio IX Hispana*. To Britain now came S. Calpurnius Agricola, either late in 162 or early in 163. His background is little known, but he can only have earned the command at so critical a time by notable service elsewhere.

Calpurnius Agricola saw his task to be the restoration of forts in the Pennines and in the region of Hadrian's Wall. The building records come from Corbridge, Chesterholm, Carvoran, Ribchester and perhaps Ilkley. Another inscription, from the legionary fortress at Caerleon, may attest work there in this governorship. There is, however, no trace of the work of the governor in Scotland, and it is probable that after an appraisal of the situation in 163 Calpurnius resolved finally to relinquish the Roman hold on the frontier between

Forth and Clyde. The evidence of the samian pottery from the forts on the Antonine Wall does not support occupation later than the early 160s, a conclusion backed by the main body of the numismatic evidence, though this is necessarily less cogent. This does not mean that the occupation of Lowland Scotland was also totally relinquished. There are indications that the fort at Newstead was held later than 165 and the same may be true of Cappuck and Castlecary. These forts, and conceivably others, may have served as the bases of long-range patrols such as probably operated in earlier Antonine Scotland. From the forts on the Antonine Wall itself, however, there is no clear sign that any site played a role in subsequent Roman contact with the Caledonian peoples. There is still uncertainty about when the Antonine Wall was finally given up. A brief occupation after about AD 165 has been mooted but evidence for it is meagre and far from convincing. Given the existing infrastructure of roads and control-points in lowland Scotland, however, it would not be surprising if patrols and even campaigning columns operated there until well after 165.

Antonine policy in Scotland had failed and in a costly manner. From about 165, Hadrian's Wall again became the base for the frontier forces. The Hadrianic view of what could be held in Northern Britain had been vindicated. For the Antonine failure was not least due to a shortfall in manpower. The occupation of this considerable expanse of hilly terrain, in the face of determined resistance from the Britons, required far more troops than the already immense provincial garrison could spare. The advance under Lollius Urbicus was made in days of confidence, when no major threat loomed over any frontier. A decade later, things had changed and by the beginning of the reign of Marcus and Lucius Verus the frontiers against the Parthians and the Danube Germans were giving cause for anxiety. There could, for the time being, be no reinforcement of the army in Britain. How strained Roman resources were in Antonine Scotland is betrayed by the frequent use of fortlets and small forts in the region south of the Antonine Wall, notably in South-western Scotland. The simple fact which bore most heavily upon the army which reoccupied Scotland in the 140s was that the Brigantes and their northern neighbours (excepting perhaps the Votadini) were not so subdued that they could safely be left to their own devices. The Antonine generals recognized as much and substantial forces were left to police the Pennines. But these garrisons were not enough when the rebellious spirit of the Brigantes led them into insurrection. From that time onward the hold on Scotland was doomed.

The next twenty years in Britain are crepuscular, the attention of the High Command being focused on the Danube provinces in particular. But there are clear indications of disturbed conditions, and not only on the northern frontier. The evidence of coin-hoards buried during the reign of Marcus Aurelius is especially revealing, for in the earlier decades of the second century hoarding of the precious metals and bronze alike had not been notably frequent. Between 160 and 170, hoards of silver coins and the larger denominations in bronze become relatively common. In the absence of any known or discernible economic uncertainty, these hoards are to be explained as symptoms of a more general uncertainty affecting wide areas of Britain. A most unusual hoard from Rudchester on Hadrian's Wall, comprising both gold and silver coins, suggests that there was trouble about 168–70, and a second mixed hoard of gold and silver from South Shields is another pointer to this or an earlier emergency. An interesting series of hoards dating from the later reign of Marcus Aurelius occurs in the Pennines, hinting at the continuing volatility of the Brigantian septs. Another, more surprising, group appears in East Anglia and in adjacent parts of Eastern England, perhaps indicating an outbreak of civil commotion. Some of the smaller townships of the Trinovantes were destroyed by fire after 170, though the date or dates at which this happened may be nearer 200. There is similar evidence at this time for hoarding and destruction of sites in Gallia Belgica, though it is usually linked with the incursion of the Chauki in the 170s.

Coin evidence may also help to illumine Roman relations with the Scottish tribes in the years after about 165. Roman silver continued to flow into eastern Scotland in the reigns of Marcus and Commodus, some of it no doubt reflecting commerce between Roman and native. But these coins might also be viewed as a remnant of subsidies paid by Rome to the northerners in the wake of the withdrawal ordered by Calpurnius Agricola. This was already a well established aspect of frontier policy and both Marcus and Commodus practised it elsewhere. The quantity of silver found at this date (i.e. between 165 and 190) in the Caledonian heartland certainly suggests some closer and more official connection with Rome than is easily explained by commerce. Treaties or agreements fortified by cash payments would have been as reasonable an expedient for Calpurnius Agricola as for Ulpius Marcellus. Thus when Virius Lupus later bought off the Maeatae, he may have done no more than follow a procedure already established forty years before (*page 145*).

The later reign of Marcus is almost a complete blank, but for the despatch to Britain of 5500 Sarmatian cavalry, more than half of the troops required by Rome under the terms of the armistice on the Danube in 175. Whether the army of Britain received this force because it was in need of so great a reinforcement of cavalry or because the province offered the best training ground for the immigrant troopers is not clear, nor are the dispositions of the dozen or so new units recorded in any detail. It is most unlikely that the absence of recorded events means that there was any respite from warfare in the 170s. In 180, Ulpius Marcellus was sent to Britain to fight what Dio describes as the most serious war of Commodus' reign. The barbarians 'had crossed the wall which separated them from the Roman forts' – surely Hadrian's Wall – and killed the general (either the unnamed governor or a legionary legate) who led his forces against them. The circumstances of this emergency are shadowy indeed. The war was satisfactorily concluded by 184, when Commodus took the title Britannicus and issued coins commemorating a victory, but where the decisive campaigns had been fought remains uncertain. Was Ulpius Marcellus constrained to carry the war back to the Caledonians and invade Scotland? Was there collusion between the invaders and the Brigantes once the frontier had been breached? Sir George Macdonald believed that Marcellus did return to Scotland and began to rebuild forts on the Antonine Wall, but the evidence on which this claim rested is extremely slight, and capable of more than one interpretation. Recent and larger scale excavation has provided no support for it. On Hadrian's Wall there is more convincing evidence for damage in the early 180s, when the forts at Halton Chesters and Rudchester were involved. Some of the milecastles and turrets which may also have suffered at this time were later repaired. The position at Corbridge still requires clarification, but there is a strong possibility that there was destruction here too, suggesting that the invaders had made their approach along the line of Dere Street. None of the Pennine forts seems to have been damaged. Whether Marcellus needed to carry out an extensive reorganization of Hadrian's Wall is uncertain but not probable: no building inscriptions of his are yet known on the frontier. He does seem to have abandoned all attempts to keep garrisons in station beyond the Wall in the Lowlands and in Northumberland. Newstead and the other forts on Dere Street were now given up, though no doubt some form of surveillance from long range was still maintained.

In the aftermath of Ulpius Marcellus' campaigns there was a serious outbreak of that indiscipline to which the legions of Britain were prone from time to time. The anger of the troops was directed at the governor himself, perhaps because that martinet had been too strict for them or because the donative had been too small. One of the legionary legates, Priscus, was offered the Imperial purple by the army, but prudently refused. Ulpius Marcellus may still have been in Britain at the time, but was shortly recalled to Rome and tried, escaping the death penalty by a narrow margin. The insubordinate mood of the British troops continued despite a rebuke.

The sequel was extraordinary. The British legates chose a delegation of 1500 'javelin-men' and sent them to Italy to demand that the Praetorian Prefect Tigidius Perennis be removed and killed. The *Historia Augusta* offers an explanation for the unpopularity of Perennis with the army in Britain. He had removed the legates who had fought in the earlier *bellum Britannicum* and replaced them with *equites*. Commodus, too, was low in their regard, seemingly because they thought the recent victory in Britain a sham. The British delegation was met by Commodus before it reached Rome and their wish was granted. Perennis was sacrificed. His attempt to employ *equites* instead of senators in the legionary commands had been premature, but it foreshadows the normal practice of the third century. The story of the British 'javelin-men' and their march to Italy is one of the oddest episodes in Romano-British history and defies ready explanation. Dio found the tale remarkable, but could offer no illumination as to how it might have happened. How did this large body of men make their way across Gaul without check? There is no sound reason for linking the deputation with the expedition led by L. Artorius Castus against a rebellion in Armorica. There is no evidence that any of the troops which went to Armorica passed thence to Italy, nor is it even certain that Artorius' expedition dates to 185. A connection with the *bellum desertorum* which broke out in that year seems even less likely, that outbreak being much more restricted than it appears in the colourful pages of Herodian.

The fall of Perennis did not quieten the mutinous mood of the troops in Britain. Helvius Pertinax was recalled from disgrace and went to Britain as legate, in the hope that this upright and trustworthy man could quell what was now taking on the dimensions of a full-scale mutiny. His efforts at restoring discipline were initially successful. Indeed, his personal impression on the troops was so favourable that he was offered the purple. Later, however, there was a major riot in which Pertinax was set upon and left for dead. Shortly afterwards he asked to be relieved of his command, feeling that his relations with the troops could not improve. The spirit of mutiny may still have lived on in the army of Britain, but the minds of troops and officers were very shortly turned in another direction as a crisis arose, in resolving which they were to be put to the most severe test.

Well might the Antonine emperors – and especially Commodus – look to the hero Hercules as the ideal *comes* as they struggled to preserve their Empire.[16] The Antonine peace, it might appear, did not embrace Britain. But such a view is quickly dispelled when we turn from the frontiers to the southern regions of the province. Almost all the cities which have been adequately studied have produced evidence of a burgeoning of civic and commercial life. Many of them, perhaps the majority, reached their greatest physical extent during the second half of the second century and most of the expected public amenities had been provided well before 200. The building industry and its allied crafts were by now fully fledged and increasingly ambitious. Skills gained in the construction of public buildings began to be lavished on private dwellings. At *Camulodunum* well appointed courtyard houses with fine mosaic floors were being built at least by 150, while at Leicester there is further evidence for private indulgence in floor-mosaics and ornate wall-painting. The dating of the many houses at Silchester was not firmly established in the early excavations, but an appreciable number probably belong to the second century and here too mosaicists were at work. Similarly, at Wroxeter an impressive number of substantial houses is known but not yet dated, though there must be a strong presumption in favour of the period following the completion of the forum in 130 and the baths somewhat later. Our most complete information on urban progress comes from *Verulamium*. After a major fire about 155 had destroyed more than fifty acres of the city, opportunity was taken to replan parts of the centre and to add certain new buildings, among them a theatre on the Gaulish pattern. Large dwellings in masonry now appeared for the first time and patronage of painters and mosaicists came into vogue.

Growing communities in a province with so turbulent a history might well have been expected to possess defences. Remarkably, cities and towns with any form of walled protection datable to before 150 are few and are usually explicable by special circumstances of status or history. During the later second century, there is evidence for the construction of simple earthen ramparts, accompanied by one or more ditches, at a wide range of towns and cities. The dating of individual cases is far from precise and some may be placed only approximately in the Antonine period. The earliest date suggested is the reign of Hadrian for Brough-on-Humber, the latest about 185 for Dorchester-on-Thames. None has yet produced evidence for construction after the early years of the third century. It has of late been customary to see in the appearance of these earthworks 'the application of a single policy in a single context', and thus to attribute their building to a single historical occasion, usually between the death of Marcus and the eventual victory of Septimius Severus. Clodius Albinus has his supporters, and the disturbances of the 190s are certainly one plausible context. But there are difficulties. The dates so far available cover a wide range and none points with certainty to the last decade of the century. Earlier periods cannot be excluded from consideration. Furthermore, would there have been time for such a spurt of defensive building, even in earthwork, in 196? That seems unlikely. A more fundamental objection must be raised against the presumption that one date and one occasion must embrace all the known defences. It is true that Imperial sanction was required before a community could construct a defensive wall, but it certainly does not follow that blanket permissions were sent out by emperors to entire provinces. The normal procedure meant that the urban authority made its request to the legate, who then consulted the emperor.

The evidence thus far suggests that these earthen defences date from the final quarter of the second century and the very beginning of the third. Much more excavation is needed before this dating can be refined. One of the most striking features of the British defences is that they were not confined to the cities. Towns of fairly humble degree, such as Alchester, Great Casterton, Mancetter, Godmanchester and *Margidunum*, also received defences in this period. This is all the more remarkable at sites like Mancetter and *Margidunum*, where there can have been little worth defending at this date. But were these works necessarily always designed for the protection of civilian communities? There must be a suspicion that in the case of the smaller settlements on the major routes, it was official installations, such as *mansiones, praetoria*, and *stationes* of the *annona militaris*, which were being guarded and not the modest roadside townships.

Note. I have excluded from consideration in this chapter the much discussed passage of Pausanias, *Description of Greece* viii, 43, believing it to refer not to events in Britain, but to Raetia. See J. G. F. Hind, *Britannia* viii (1977), 229–34.

8

Propagator Imperii

In Rome meanwhile, opposition was mounting against the extravagant follies and waste of the regime of Commodus. Not that the emperor had ever concerned himself to any extent with affairs of state. But now even the policies of his advisors were no longer acceptable to those who had to execute them or to the Roman *plebs*. The fall of Cleander in 190 was followed by a period of blood-letting which accounted for, among others, the lives of more than a dozen consulars and their relatives. How many others perished is unknown, but the purge was almost certainly massive. An outbreak of plague heightened the mood of hysteria in Rome. Cleander's position at the centre of power had not been filled, and in 191 there were signs that Commodus was for the first time turning his attention from his all-engrossing pleasures to the exercise of real power. This new Commodus was less tolerable than the old and the resolve to remove him, which had been alive for some years, grew stronger in certain quarters.

In 191 or 192 a group of conspirators drew together, including a Praetorian Prefect, Aemilius Laetus, and the Prefect of the City, Helvius Pertinax. Laetus was one of a number of Africans now coming to the fore in Imperial government, some of whom were to play vital roles in the melee which followed the extinction of the Antonine dynasty. On the recommendation of Laetus, L. Septimius Severus of Leptis Magna became governor of Pannonia Superior, an unlikely choice for this province of three legions, since his earlier military experience was limited to a legionary command in Syria. Another African, D. Clodius Albinus of Hadrumetum, was appointed to Britain, having earlier perhaps governed Germania Inferior. Both men, together with Septimius' brother Geta, who acquired the two legion province of Moesia Inferior, could be regarded as reliable by Laetus and Pertinax. Between them, these legates held three of the seven northern commands. At least one major province, however, went to someone who owed no allegiance to Laetus and Pertinax. This was Pescennius Niger, who took the Syrian command. The lines were drawn for a struggle which would open a new era.

At the end of 192, the bizarre and costly phantasies of Commodus were brought to an end. On New Year's Eve, the conspirators struck and Pertinax was hailed *imperator*. Although this senior and strict general gave promise of more stable times, his reign was tragically brief. Three months later he was removed by a coup inspired by Laetus and replaced by Didius Julianus. This turn of events was not to the liking of any of the powerful provincial governors. Septimius Severus was best placed for swift reaction. Only twelve days after the death of Pertinax, he was hailed *imperator* at *Carnuntum*, having first ascertained the temper of the Danubian legions. The role which the three British legions under Clodius Albinus might play was potentially of great significance. Septimius promptly sought the support of Albinus by offering him the rank of Caesar,[1] duly accepted by the governor of Britain against the day when he could look for more, either through the death of Septimius or some stroke of his own. Meanwhile, Pescennius Niger had seized control of the ten legions in the east and had himself hailed emperor at Antioch. There lay work for the future, but Septimius knew the importance of securing the city of Rome. He swiftly moved into Italy and within two months of his salutation at *Carnuntum* Rome was his without a battle, and before he himself reached the *Urbs*.

Septimius Severus' position was now secure but not impregnable. The brief reign of Pertinax was honoured, that ruler deified and his name taken by Septimius – an indication that the new emperor wished to be regarded as a perpetuator of the Antonine tradition. Preparations for the inevitable campaign against Pescennius Niger now went forward. The war against the eastern rival and subsequent operations against the Parthians occupied much of 195, although the detailed chronology of events cannot be reconstructed. The successes of Septimius' armies must have given Clodius Albinus due notice of what to expect. The renaming of Septimius' elder son M. Aurelius Antoninus in 195 completed the dynastic manifesto: Septimius would brook no Caesar not of his own family. Albinus was proclaimed an enemy of the State, though he still had supporters in Rome. Already before this, Albinus may have openly renounced the authority of Septimius and begun his preparations for outright war, too late against odds which were now overpowering. Even so, the struggle was to be fiercely contested, and the battle-hardened army of Britain was to give Septimius his stiffest test so far.[2]

As Septimius hastened back to the west, Clodius Albinus crossed to Gaul and established his headquarters at *Lugdunum*. He was not able to take possession of all of the Gaulish provinces. Trier held out against him, assisted by a detachment of *Legio XXII Primigenia* from Mainz. Worse for his cause was the failure to capture the loyalty of the Rhine legions. Success in one engagement, against the governor of Lower Germany, Virius Lupus, was scarce compensation. In the first battle against the army of Septimius at *Tinurtium*, sixty miles north of *Lugdunum*, Albinus' forces were beaten back to regroup at the Gallic capital. On 19 February 196, surprisingly early in the campaigning year, the decisive battle was bitterly fought out near the city. At first, the left wing of Albinus' army was forced back to its camp. Then the left wing of Septimius' army was led into a trap of concealed pits by a pretended retreat and confusion ensued. Septimius himself led his praetorians into the thick of it but only added to the crisis when he was unseated and surrounded. Just as the tide of battle was turning in Albinus' favour, Laetus appeared with fresh cavalry and threw the British forces back. The main body was pursued into *Lugdunum* which was sacked and burnt. Albinus himself committed suicide. The bitterness of the struggle echoed in its aftermath. There were no decent rites for the rival. Albinus' head was despatched to Rome and his body thrown into the Rhone. The corpses of senators who had joined him were mutilated. Executions of prominent adherents of Albinus followed in Gaul and Spain, probably in Britain too. There were confiscations of property, probably involving the samian pottery industries of central Gaul and the production of olive oil in Spain. Although there is no direct evidence for such measures in Britain, it is most likely that a considerable amount of property passed to the *res privata* at this time. Albinus had had many supporters, some in high places. On Septimius' return to Rome, the Senate came in for a drastic purge.

Britain could not be left for long without a governor. The man chosen was Virius Lupus, briefly the legate of Lower Germany, and with him went the British units, presumably after they had been brought up to strength with reliable troops and officers. Valerius Pudens, whose turn in the British command was to come, filled the vacancy in Germany. In 197 the procuratorship of Britain was given to Varius Marcellus, a young relative of the emperor and a man of very little experience of Imperial service. Even in the conditions of the time, this appointment must have been stimulated by exceptional circumstances, perhaps the urgent need to organize the accession of new resources to the *res privata* rather than the hunting down of surviving supporters of Albinus' cause.

What Virius Lupus found on his arrival in Britain is a matter for dispute.[3] A view long entertained, and still with adherents, is that he found the northern parts of the province in a state of chaos and ruin. The removal of garrisons from the frontier and its hinterland had encouraged the Caledonians and the Maeatae (a grouping now mentioned for the first time) to make a concerted attack on the frontier, in which they were joined by the Brigantes, still not thoroughly subdued. The destruction presumed to have been wrought in 196–7 was believed to be in evidence on Hadrian's Wall, in the Pennine forts and even in the legionary base at York. The basis for this view of a major disaster on the northern frontier appeared for long to be as secure as it reasonably could be and seemed to provide a welcome fixed point in the scanty recorded history of Hadrian's Wall. Cassius Dio reports that Virius Lupus was constrained to buy peace from the Maeatae for a large sum, receiving in return some Roman prisoners. Clearly, this attests hostilities before the governor arrived, though we cannot know how long before. Epigraphic discoveries and archaeological investigation provided colouring for the picture. Inscriptions dating from 197 and later recorded restoration of buildings and amenities on Hadrian's Wall and to the rear,[4] this work of reconstruction assumedly occasioned by widespread and severe destruction shortly before. Excavation on the Wall appeared to supply the essential concomitant evidence for disaster, in the form of destruction layers datable to the close of the second century. Almost all the northern fort-sites (and some in Wales) which were examined in the 1930s seemed to their excavators to have suffered damage, if not total destruction, as a result of Clodius Albinus' bid for power.

The case, superficially impressive, is cobbled together from pieces of evidence which can all bear more than one interpretation and it can easily be pulled apart. To begin with, it rests upon the assumption that Clodius Albinus so reduced the northern auxiliary garrisons that they were unable to make any adequate showing against the barbarians when they went back on their earlier agreements. Even if the governor was relying on the Caledonians and Maeatae to honour those arrangements, he would surely have left a sufficient force on the frontier and at strategic points behind it. Probably some of the Pennine garrisons could be spared, and perhaps a greater number from Wales. But the core of his army would be the three legions of Britain, and his best hope of success lay in the prospect of inducing the Rhine legions to defect from Septimius. We have already seen that that gamble failed.

It is worth note that Cassius Dio does not speak of a frontier crossed and a province thrown into utter disarray. We hear only that Virius Lupus had to buy off the Maeatae,[5] presumably because he was in no position to drive them back by force of arms. The scene of operations could as well be the region north of the Wall as the frontier itself. Furthermore, if the frontier had been broken through by a massive barbarian incursion, it seems somewhat strange that Dio makes no mention of the event, either in this context or in his later treatment of Septimius' operations in Northern Britain. A disaster of that magnitude would be known to Dio's readers, and a provincial governor of his experience would not be likely to play it down or belittle the part played by Septimius in restoring the situation. If a disaster had occurred, it was after all due to the actions of Clodius Albinus and not of Septimius Severus.

The epigraphic evidence, too, does not indicate that Virius Lupus was faced by a shattered frontier system. No inscriptions recording reconstruction in his governorship are known from Hadrian's Wall, while those from the Pennines are not suggestive of urgent restorative measures: the fort at Ilkley (not of the first strategic importance), Brough-under-Stainmore (rather more significant), a bath-house and perhaps other buildings at Bowes, and unspecified work at Corbridge. The absence of any sign of rebuilding on the line of the Wall at this date is striking, all the more so in the light of a considerable body of evidence for a spate of activity there about eight years later.

Finally, there is the matter of stratigraphic evidence for destruction on the sites of forts. In considering this question it must be stressed that a destruction brought about by hostile action is in any circumstances extremely difficult to identify with certainty. Deposits containing heavily burnt material and other debris from damaged structures can rarely, of itself, attest the work of an enemy. Further, much of the excavation within the Wall forts before about 1960 was carried out on a comparatively small scale. In such conditions it is very difficult to distinguish between damage to a limited area (whatever the agency) and a comprehensive destruction. That the converse is also true must be allowed. It would be possible for a fort to fall into enemy hands and to suffer damage without there being any archaeologically detectable trace of the event. Not in all cases would the site be sent up in flames. Even if it was, there need have been little effect on the footings of buildings, while subsequent military occupation could remove loose debris and other superficial traces. Discussion of damage to military installations, or its absence, must thus take place within these close constraints.

There is no exaggeration in asserting that the history of the Wall forts has yet to be written in detail, and for many it is not yet known in crude outline. Of the sites which have been examined recently, a striking number have produced no evidence of interruption in occupation, marked by damage and reconstruction.[6] These include Carrawburgh, Rudchester, Halton Chesters, Wallsend, as well as Chesterholm and South Shields. Corbridge, too, may be added to the list. At least three of these, Carrawburgh, Rudchester and Wallsend, show no signs of destruction at any date in the opinion of their excavators. It might be noted that the majority of these forts lie in the eastern sector of the frontier and none lies west of the Irthing. The western sector may still have been the military *Schwerpunkt* and it would thus be a great advantage to know how the western forts and the outposts fared at this time. Unfortunately, the necessary work on the troop accommodation of these sites has yet to be done.

In its sum, our evidence does not suggest that Virius Lupus was confronted by a frontier overturned by its barbarian foes. There may well have been serious threats to Roman authority, from inside the province and without, in the 190s as in the 180s and earlier, but there is no reason to believe that a massive incursion of northerners destroyed the Wall and its works in 196–7. More probably, Virius Lupus found a frontier region in a state of dereliction, particularly in the Pennines. The Pennine forts were half a century old and more. Some may have lain empty for intervals in the period 140–58 and possibly later. Restoring these to usefulness might have been the first task for Virius in 197. The Brigantes may have given him more to do behind the Wall than the Maeatae beyond the frontier. It is at all events interesting that the next governor, Valerius Pudens, was also involved in restoration in the Pennines, as is attested by the only record of his tenure of Britain.[7] A further pointer to unrest among the Brigantes is an altar erected at Greetland, dedicated to Victoria Brigantia. Though undated, this probably records an event in these years.[8]

Little is known about the military occupation of the Welsh hills at this time. The auxiliary garrisons of South Wales had earlier been largely removed, but the inhabitants of the upper Severn valley and the hills of Central Wales were kept under surveillance, as the forts at Forden Gaer, Caersws and possibly Castell Collen were still held. To the east, the large fort at Leintwardine also retained its garrison. In North Wales the forts at Caernarvon and Caerhun remained in commission, but apparently no others. Caernarvon overlooking its harbour might have proved useful as a distribution-centre of supplies from the rich lands of Anglesey and not merely as a garrison-post. In no part of Wales is there evidence for an extensive reoccupation under the governors of Septimius Severus, nor does there appear to have been heavy damage to forts, such as might have been caused by a major insurrection. Such work of restoration as is attested appears to have been similar to that undertaken by Virius Lupus and Valerius Pudens in the Pennines.[9]

The legionary fortresses by now stood in need of repair and improvement. An extensive rebuilding was carried out at Caerleon, beginning between 198 and 209 and probably continuing after the latter date. At Chester, too, there are signs of reconstruction in the early third century. At York, the wall of the fortress was substantially rebuilt at this time and the *principia* renewed, apparently after a fire. The stimulus for the splendid building which now arose may have been the emperor's own residence at York during the final campaign of his life.

Valerius Pudens had succeeded Virius Lupus in 201 or 202 and remained as governor until 205. In that year or very shortly afterwards, L. Alfenus Senecio was appointed to the British command. Little is known about this man, who is not even named by the only source for these years, Herodian. He was yet another African, from Djemila. His early career is unknown. When he first comes into view, he was governor (in 200) of one of the parts of the recently divided Syria, still one of the high peaks of the Imperial service. The despatch to Britain of so distinguished an officer reveals how serious the military situation there still remained, or had become.

Alfenus Senecio had to campaign in the years 205–7, and in the light of subsequent events his armies probably operated north of Hadrian's Wall. He was able to claim a measure of success: at Benwell he dedicated a monument to the Victory of the Emperors (Caracalla had been hailed Augustus in 198). The senior Augustus was impressed and envious.[10] In 207 Alfenus' report from Britain made it plain that Roman control was far from complete. 'The barbarians there were rebelling, overrunning the land, taking booty, and creating destruction.' His recommendation was for 'reinforcements to protect the threatened regions or an Imperial expedition'. Septimius decided on the latter alternative, though he was now sixty-two and suffering from gout or arthritis. Popular report had it that he was also anxious about the deleterious effects that Rome was having on the morals of his sons Caracalla and Geta. However that may be, he was plainly concerned that the young men (Caracalla was nineteen, Geta eighteen) should have first-hand experience of the realities of campaigning and of the administration of a difficult frontier province.

Septimius must have felt that his hold on Rome and the Senate was entirely secure when he embarked on this expedition. In other provinces there are hints of insurrection put down by force. The legate of *Legio I Minervia* stationed at Bonn led an army group against *defectores ac rebelles*.[11] In Pannonia Superior there may have been action by one of the legions of the province against rebels, though the operation could have been against an external enemy. There is further specific evidence from Africa and from Asia.[12] But the promise of the British expedition worked more strongly on the mind of the emperor than any fears he may have had about the security of other provinces. His desire for conquest had not been satisfied by the Parthian campaigns and the venture he now planned offered the prospect of stabilizing the northern regions of Britain, still an outstanding problem of Imperial frontier strategy. Late in 207 or early in 208 he and his sons were in Gaul, in their train a huge army with which the hard-pressed forces of Britain were to be reinforced. The composition of the expeditionary army is not known in detail. It certainly included the recently organized Praetorian Guard under one of its prefects, Papinianus and, one might guess, units from the Rhine. *Legio II Adiutrix* seems to have been missing from its station in Pannonia Inferior in these years and may have gone to Britain.

The army of Britain had meanwhile been rebuilding on the line of Hadrian's Wall and elsewhere, as well as fighting. Fort buildings at Housesteads, Chesters, Birdoswald and probably Corbridge were restored by the troops of Alfenus Senecio, as were the defences of Risingham beyond the Wall. In the Pennines there was still work to be done, as a building record from Bainbridge reveals. This is a remarkable programme of refurbishment. It would seem to imply that Hadrian's Wall was to remain the frontier of the province whatever the outcome of the forthcoming campaign. But another reading of this evidence is possible. Alfenus Senecio may have been ordered to concentrate the efforts of his men on bringing the frontier region into good military order and forget about operations further north. They were to be left to the emperor. The view has its attraction and there is another reason why the army in Britain may not have seemed to Septimius to be ready for strenuous campaigning. Those legions may still not have been restored to the peak of condition after the battle of *Lugdunum* and, further, it was not known how smoothly their loyalty had been transferred to Septimius Severus. That the expeditionary force mustered on the continent was so large suggests that the army in Britain was under strength or under par, and that the emperor had reservations about the present efficiency of the British units may be suspected from another of his unorthodox appointments to a key office.

Inscriptions from Risingham and Chesters[13] indicate that the procurator of the province, Oclatinius Adventus, was associated with the legate in the general oversight of rebuilding. Such a role for a procurator appears to be unique, as was the career of Oclatinius himself. He had not passed through the customary grades of the procuratorial service but had risen from the ranks of the *frumentarii* to become the commander of that body, charged with the duties of secret police and domestic intelligence. His transfer to the British procuratorship must be seen as a special duty assigned to a thoroughly reliable officer who could give the emperor an up-to-date report on the state of the army and, perhaps, a second opinion on what was needed in Northern Britain. Additional duties might have included preparations for the campaign.

The chronology of these, the final, campaigns of Septimius Severus involves considerable difficulties, for Dio's account exists only in fragments, leaving us with the imprecise Herodian. As soon as the emperor had established his headquarters in Britain, Herodian reports that the northern tribes sent envoys seeking peace. But the emperor had come for a victory and perhaps already had set his sights beyond. The preparations made for the expedition against the Caledonians and Maeatae were massive and far-sighted: the commissariat may have outmatched those of the Flavian and Antonine campaigns. The fort at South Shields at the mouth of the Tyne now became a great stores-depot, the barracks being replaced by an additional twenty granaries.[14] This was presumably the main assembly-point for supplies, the store-buildings having the capacity to support some 20,000 men for a six-month campaign. The needs of supply were also catered for elsewhere. At Corbridge one or more granaries were rebuilt and to this time probably belongs the huge and lavishly constructed courtyard building (Site XI), best seen as a depot for military stores like the comparable buildings at Neuss, Vindonissa and Carnuntum.[15] The building was never completed, but in its unfinished state it is one of the most impressive in the entire military zone. Its scale suggests that the intention was to make Corbridge the main supply base for the land-based armies which would use Dere Street as their route into Scotland.

The campaigns beyond the Wall may have begun in 208, certainly by 209. Dio's description of the physical hardships endured by the troops give a vivid picture of a struggle against terrain as much as against a human enemy. The northerners, sensibly, had resorted to guerrilla tactics, with great success, for Roman losses were heavy,[16] and Septimius failed to come to grips with the enemy on a battlefield. But the Roman army pushed northwards, almost to the limits of the

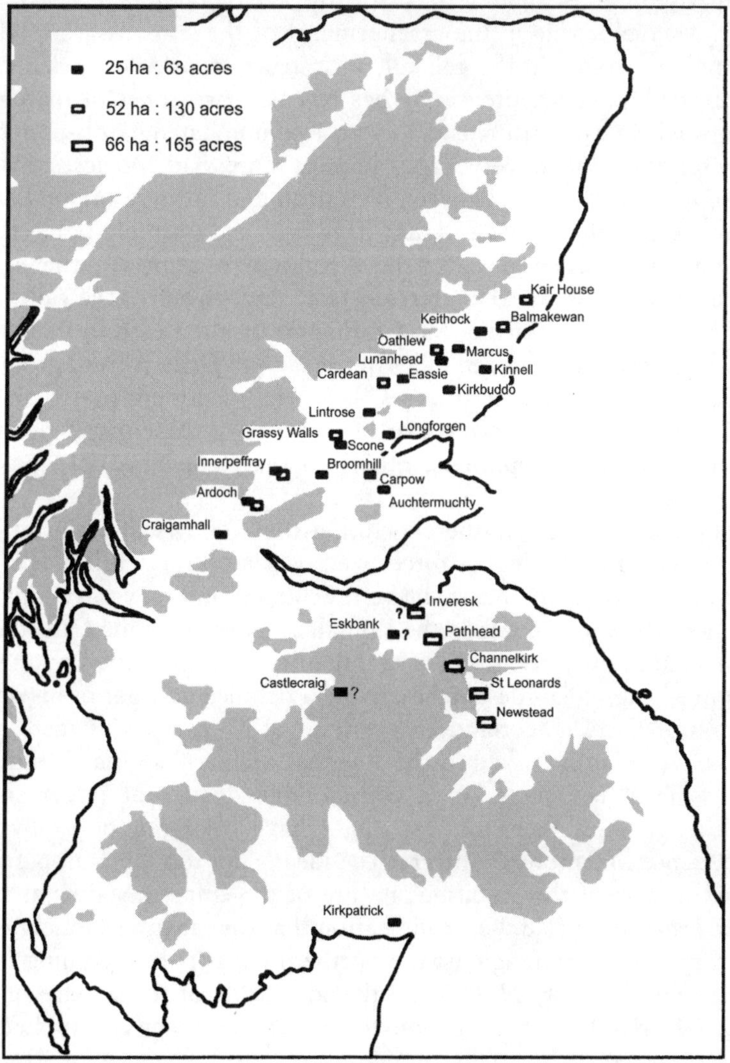

Figure 24 Camps associated with the Severan campaigns in Scotland.

island. At last, the barbarians, themselves worn down by the arduous fighting, were ready to come to terms. When this was achieved is not clear, but late in 209 seems the likely date. The emperor and his sons felt justified in taking the title *Britannicus*. Things had turned out fairly well, but the lull was not to last for long.

The course of the campaign has left some trace of itself on the ground. Dere Street is the obvious route for the bulk of the land-based forces, and it has already been noted that Corbridge played a major role in the arrangements of the commissariat, while Risingham shared in the general reconstruction of Alfenus Senecio's governorship. Air photography has revealed two series of marching camps which can most reasonably be accommodated in this period.[17] One series comprises very large camps of more than 160 acres, five of these lying on the road between Newstead and Inveresk on the Forth. This suggests that Newstead may have been the assembly-point, or at least a major staging-post, for the expeditionary army. Another series of camps extends, at even intervals, from Ardoch across the valleys of the Earn and Tay, skirting the Grampians on their eastern flank and reaching to within a dozen miles of the Moray Firth. A third group of camps, of more than sixty acres, has been identified, partly on the same line and partly to the east of it. Some of these may belong to the expedition of Septimius, others to the campaigns of Antonine generals.

The course taken by the expedition thus follows in main outline that pursued by Agricola's forces well over a century earlier. It is the patent, natural route into Northern Scotland and may have had the further advantage of taking the Roman army through the Caledonian heartland. But there may be another reason why the route was followed. Agricola's despatches giving a detailed account of his occupation of Eastern Scotland and perhaps of his campaigns there may still have been preserved in the Imperial archives, so that Septimius could have had access to a considerable dossier of information, including maps. Some of this might have been reinforced by the experience of Antonine officers. The idea is not too fanciful, particularly in view of the ambitious nature of the emperor's aims as they now began to unfold. Clear indication that they involved much more than punitive action against the northern tribes is forthcoming from the site at Carpow (*Horrea*) on the south side of the estuary of the Tay.[18] Here a large fort of some thirty-two acres was constructed on a site earlier occupied by a temporary base. The new work was intended for a large legionary vexillation, perhaps a mixed force drawn from *Legio VI Victrix* and *Legio II Augusta*. The internal planning, so far as it is known, is similar to that of second-century forts, the central range of administrative buildings including an elaborately planned *praetorium*. But what is most notable about Carpow is that it was designed to be much more than a campaign base. The foundations of the central buildings are massively and well constructed in masonry. This was, then, to be a permanent station for a legionary garrison on the Tay, in such a position as to dominate Caledonian territory.

It appears that there had been a change in the emperor's intentions, for it is difficult to square the siting of a legionary base as far north as the Tay estuary with the thorough-going reconstruction of Hadrian's Wall carried out by Alfenus Senecio. The arduous operations against the northerners may have convinced Septimius that nothing short of occupation of Caledonian territory would preserve the hard-won peace. He may have been swayed by the knowledge of what had happened when Rome's hold on Caledonia had been loosened after the Agricolan conquests. Or it may be that his mind was set on conquest in Northern Britain, as it had been in Mesopotamia, and Alfenus Senecio was given the task of stabilization in the Wall region as the essential preliminary. On balance, it is more likely that the

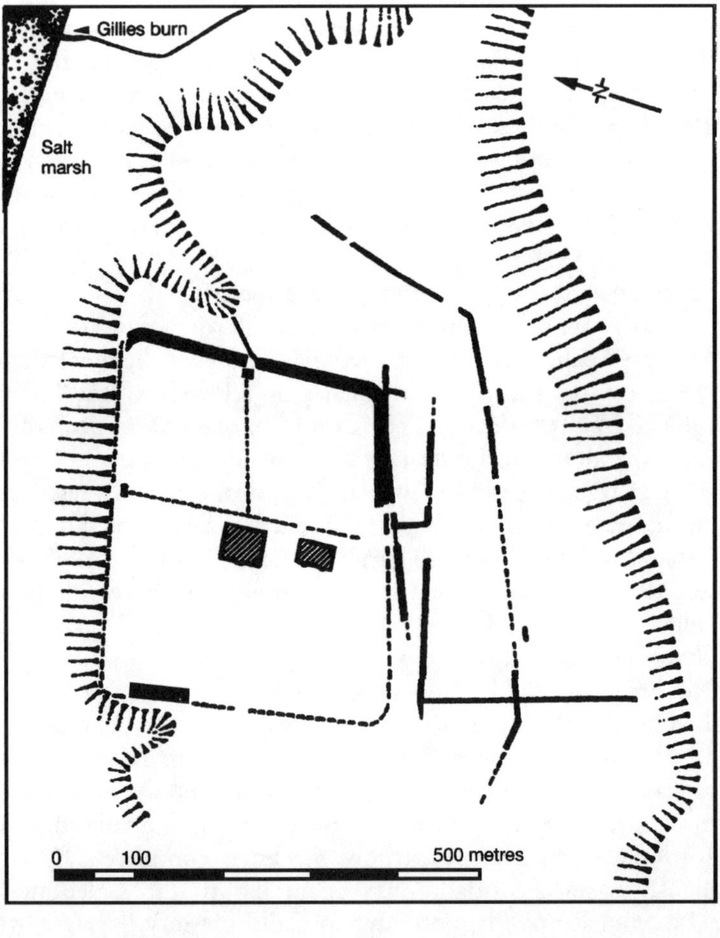

Figure 25 The Severan fortress at Carpow (Perthshire).

emperor altered his strategy in the light of his own experience in the north. The alternative hypothesis requires us to believe that a distinguished general tied down a considerable number of his troops in a reconstruction of the Hadrianic frontier, which would be rendered largely obsolete by subsequent conquests far to the north. That the two elements, reconstruction and advance, were combined in a single strategy seems implausible. It is easier to suppose that the emperor was so impressed by his gains that he decided to hold on to them, in effect to aspire to the total conquest briefly achieved in Domitian's reign.

But the exigencies of manpower were no less pressing than in the late first century. Either the emperor hoped that a limited Roman garrison would suffice to keep the Caledonii quiet or, more probably, was unable to supply as many troops for the north as he would have liked. For other early third century forts in Eastern Scotland are elusive. Apart from Carpow, the fort at Cramond[19] on the Forth was also held, but no others are known in the narrows or to the north of them. There was certainly no attempt to bring the Antonine Wall back into commission or, seemingly, to occupy any of its forts. Further south, Newstead has produced a little pottery of the appropriate date, but as yet no structural remains. Otherwise, the map is blank.

The campaign was over and the treaties signed. The following winter was probably spent at York: the emperor was certainly there in May 210. Such respite as the ageing and now weakening ruler was able to enjoy was shortly interrupted by a rebellion of the Maeatae, later joined by the Caledonii. The campaign of 210 was probably led by Caracalla alone, his father remaining behind at York, still hopeful of taking charge. The senior Augustus was now said to be resolved on a policy of extermination. Whether his elder son attempted to put this into effect cannot be known. Herodian alleges that Caracalla was less interested in prosecuting the war than in gaining the whole-hearted backing of the army. Whether that was true or not, Caracalla knew that his hour had almost arrived. There was probably no need for him to bribe his father's doctors to bring forward the emperor's death. On 4 February 211, Septimius died at York. Caracalla and Geta, joint Augusti, made hurried preparations to leave for Rome. Peace was again made with the northern tribes and the expeditionary force withdrew. Some troops may have remained in Scotland, though not for long.[20] The base at Carpow was never completed. By 215 at the latest, Eastern Scotland was again left to the Caledonii and Maeatae, and Rome's last attempt to claim mastery over the whole of Britain was over.

Virtually nothing is revealed by our sources about the civilian areas of Britain in the reign of Septimius Severus. He can scarcely have had time for any but the most pressing matters of administration during his own sojourn in Britain, and the governors entrusted with the province before the great expedition had been likewise fully occupied. But at least one major innovation was made, the division of Britain into two provinces. In 194, Septimius had divided the powerful and prestigious Syrian command. No one knew better than he how menacing was the challenge of a competent legate with three legions at his back. The date at which Britain became two provinces is debatable. The implication of Herodian's account is that it occurred in 197, not in itself an unreasonable date since restraints on potentially powerful legates were evidently in the emperor's mind in those years. But Herodian is not so precise over chronology that this can be accepted without reserve, and it is true that a division of the province in 197 does provoke problems.[21] Dio's evidence indicates that the legions based at Chester and Caerleon lay in *Britannia Superior* and the York legion in *Inferior*, the implication being that the latter was a praetorian province governed by the legate of *Legio VI Victrix*, while *Superior* had a consular legate. But the men who held the northern command from 197 to 208 were consulars, and it is this apparent anomaly which defies easy explanation. There are several possible solutions. One is to argue that Herodian erred and that the division took place later, perhaps after the death of Septimius, and in the meantime Virius Lupus, Valerius Pudens and Alfenus Senecio served as consular legates of the whole. An alternative view is that Herodian is right and that Dio's evidence on the boundary between the two provinces reflects a later rearrangement, probably in the reign of Caracalla. Dio's passage on the distribution of legions in his day was written, or perhaps updated, after 211, for it records the stationing of *Legio I Adiutrix* in *Pannonia Inferior* which certainly occurred in Caracalla's reign. Perhaps, then, the original division of 197 (to accept Herodian) left only one legion in *Superior*, presumably at Caerleon, while two lay in consular *Inferior*, the arrangement being reversed after 211. This interpretation does not require us to reject anything in our sources out of hand. Herodian's reasonable date of 197 can be accepted, for Septimius would surely have acted swiftly to prevent the emergence of another powerful rival. But it remains true that the large army of Britain remained under the control of individual legates from 197 to 208, so that the gain to the emperor seems slight. Decisive evidence on the entire subject is still awaited.

9

The Long Peace

The northern wars of Septimius Severus did not lead to a permanent occupation of Scotland. In 211 Caracalla and Geta returned to Rome, and almost a century was to pass before an emperor again brought an army to Britain. From Caracalla to Diocletian historical sources are all but silent on Britain, a Dark Age more impenetrable than the fifth century. The first task must be to discover what was the nature of Caracalla's settlement with the northern tribes.

Dio has little to say about the aftermath of the great campaigns, and that grudgingly. Peace was concluded and troops withdrawn, in the months immediately following Severus' death, if we follow Dio closely. The withdrawal may not have been so precipitate. The fortress at Carpow appears to have been held until at least 212 and possibly for a few years longer, though hardly later than about 215. The basis of the treaties struck in 211, it may be surmised, included Roman subsidies, now a common element in diplomacy. These may have been in grain and other useful commodities, though silver may have been an attraction for some chieftains. The continued flow of Roman silver coins into Scotland is particularly well documented by the Falkirk hoard,[1] and this deposit is more easily explicable as an Imperial subsidy than as a commercial venture. Troops could have been demanded from the northerners. The transfer of units of Brittones to Upper Germany followed the campaigns. An inscription of 232 from Walldürn in the Odenwald records a unit of *Brittones dediticii Alexandriani* there, men who were neither volunteers nor conscripts, but who had surrendered to Rome and then been shipped out to another frontier – at an unfortunate time, as things turned out.[2]

There were changes to the very structure of the northern frontier Wall as well as changes in its garrison-force. Many of the turrets seem to have fallen into disuse after the end of the second century, and the Vallum appears to have had no further function to perform. In the peace which followed, indeed, some sectors of the Vallum ditch and the accompanying mounds close to fort *vici* were levelled to make way for civilian buildings of various kinds. It is possible that this slighting of the earthwork had begun in some places before 200. The narrowing of gates in the milecastles (still plainly visible in Milecastle 37, just west of Housesteads), though not firmly dated, would fall into place in the Severan scheme for the Wall. The strength of the Wall garrison was notably augmented in the cavalry arm. Four cavalry units were now in station on the Wall, and the majority of the other known regiments contained a cavalry contingent alongside the infantry. At several forts on the Wall, smaller formations were added in support of the auxiliaries, for example a *cuneus Frisiorum* and *a numerus Hnaudifridi* at Housesteads, another *cuneus Frisiorum* at Burgh-by-Sands, and a unit of *Raeti Gaesati* at Great Chesters. The Frisians from the Lower Rhine brought with them a distinctive type of pottery from their homeland, now identified at Housesteads and elsewhere on the Wall.[3] It may be that entire family groups came in from Lower Germany to be settled in the *vici*.

Some of the Wall forts are too small to have accommodated their attested garrisons with ease, and it is probable that some troops were quartered in the *vici* or perhaps were outstationed in a neighbouring post. It has been calculated that the Wall garrison now comprised some 10,000 men, about 2000 more than in the Hadrianic scheme, and that roughly a third of the total force was cavalry. In the outpost forts the garrison may have been doubled, to about 4000 men in all. Increasingly, emphasis was placed upon patrolling duties carried out by *exploratores*, frontier scouts whose function was to gather intelligence and give early warning of developing problems.

The restoration of the northern forts continued for more than a decade after the campaigns of Severus and Caracalla. The structures rebuilt or repaired between 213 and 225 are various: administrative buildings at Chesters (221–5), gates at Birdoswald (219) and Chesterholm (222–5), *ballistaria* at High Rochester (216, 220 and after 225), granaries at Great Chesters (225), and an exercise-hall at Netherby (222). The completeness of the operation is underlined by the provision (*de novo?*) of aqueducts at South Shields (222–3) and Chester-le-Street (*c.* 216). One of the reasons – perhaps the most important – for this extended programme was the fact that many of the regiments now occupying Northern Britain had apparently newly arrived there. The period of civil war in the 190s, followed by the northern wars in the next decade, had presumably taken their toll. Some of the units in the army of Clodius Albinus may never have returned to Britain. Others may have needed recruitment after the losses at *Lugdunum* and were then sent back to the island, under new officers it may be surmised. The roll of British regiments in the later second and third centuries is far from complete, but at present there are few recorded cases of forts garrisoned by the same unit both before and after the alarms and excursions of the period 196–211.

A number of inscriptions from the northern frontier region (at least eight of them and possibly as many as ten) were set up in the year 213 by various units *pro devotione communi* or *pro pietate ac devotione communi*. Public demonstrations of loyalty and faith on the part of army units are most likely to be made in times when those qualities had been found conspicuously lacking. The wide spread of the inscriptions in the north and their total absence from other provinces certainly suggest that there were special reasons behind this organized display. Perhaps the army in Britain had taken exception to the murder of Geta in February 212 and had made some public gesture which called into question the authority of Caracalla. The inscriptions of 213 reveal no case of a military unit bearing the title *Antoniniana*, as though this honour was only later awarded. It is known that troops in other parts of the Empire, in Italy and perhaps in Dacia, had been upset by the murder of Geta. Possibly the army of Britain too, or at least a part of it, had reacted strongly against it and Caracalla had felt obliged to insist on a clear affirmation of *fides* from the disaffected regiments, or even from the entire army in the north.

The legionary fortress at York probably passed unscathed through the period of the civil wars, though there may have been damage to its *principia* at this time. Evidence for an extensive Severan reconstruction of the fortress, eagerly sought by earlier scholars, has so far proved elusive. The fortress-wall was substantially reconstructed at some point, but this may have been after Severus' day and could have been caused by natural subsidence rather than by hostile action. If there was any extensive rebuilding at York, this is likely to have been carried out before the northern campaigns began in 208 or after Caracalla's withdrawal from Scotland. The excavation evidence, most of it gathered long ago, suggests that the restoration came later in the century.

The military state of Wales in these years is poorly illuminated by our archaeological sources. There was widespread rebuilding inside the legionary fortress at Caerleon before 209, but there is no reason to assume that this was occasioned by damage wrought during a revolt of the Silures in 196–7. Detachments of *Legio II Augusta* had been away from their base for considerable periods in the mid-

and later second century so that refurbishment on some scale may now have been needed to repair the ravages of natural decay. There were repairs to the amphitheatre, too, and possibly to the defences. There was also reconstruction to be carried out in the auxiliary forts, as is attested at Caernarvon in the north and at Caersws and Castell Collen in the central valleys. In the south, the forts at Brecon and Gelligaer seem to have shared in this widespread restoration of the network of garrisons. In no case can it be regarded as certain that any fort had suffered severe damage through hostile action at the end of the second century, though it is true that few of these sites have been extensively examined in recent years. There is thus no warrant for the argument occasionally advanced that the Welsh tribes took advantage of a relaxation of Roman vigilance in 196–7 and attacked the western military installations.

At about the same time as the north and west could be regarded as firmly held, the security of the coasts of Eastern Britain began to give cause for concern. At dates which cannot yet clearly be defined but which most probably are to be set between 196 and about 230, a number of forts were built on the east and south-east coasts of Britain. The earlier bases of the *classis Britannica* appear to have remained in use until the end of the second century. At Dover, probably Lympne and possibly Richborough, the forts were then abandoned and not reused. A reorganization of the units disposed on the coasts brought new forts to Brancaster (Norfolk) and Reculver. In neither case can the construction-date be regarded as firmly established. Little work has been carried out at Brancaster, and the planning of this fort's defences and gates tells us no more than that they should belong to the late second century or the first half of the third. Reculver has produced an interesting building inscription, recording the construction, or reconstruction, of an *aedes principiorum cum basilica*, i.e. the central part of a headquarters building.[4] The stone is not dated by any intrinsic evidence and damage to the inscription denies to us the full name of the provincial governor under whose auspices the building work was done. His *cognomen* was Rufinus and his *nomen* ended in -ius. But that is all we know and it is not enough to enable secure identification of the man. A. Triarius Rufinus (*consul* 210) seems to be excluded by lack of space on the damaged line. Q. Aradius Rufinus (*consul* perhaps *c.* 220) has also been suggested and is often regarded as the strongest candidate. At least his name will fit the spacing. But neither of these consulars had any known connection with Britain, and we are consequently under no obligation to accept either. The lay-out of the inscription and its letter-forms point to the period 150–230, and within this wide bracket the reigns of Severus and Caracalla are the most reasonable context.

That there were other coastal forts established early in the third century must be allowed for. A fort may have been begun at Dover early in the second century but never finished. About AD 130, a base for the *Classis Britannica* was constructed, covering 1 hectare (2.4 acres) and equipped with conventional defences of the period. Within, closely packed buildings may have housed eight sentries. Unfortunately, the area containing the headquarters building and commander's residence was not accessible for excavation. The fine harbour at Dover was flanked by two lighthouses, undated but likely to belong to the second century. The square fortification at Caister-on-Sea, overlooking a broad estuary in Roman times, has many of the characteristics of military planning and is more likely to be a fort than a minor town or port. Excavation within has so far revealed only buildings of later Roman date. If Brancaster, Caister-on-Sea and Reculver all belonged to the same scheme of coastal fortifications, it is tempting to look for at least one other site on the coasts of Essex and Suffolk. Unfortunately, coastal erosion here has

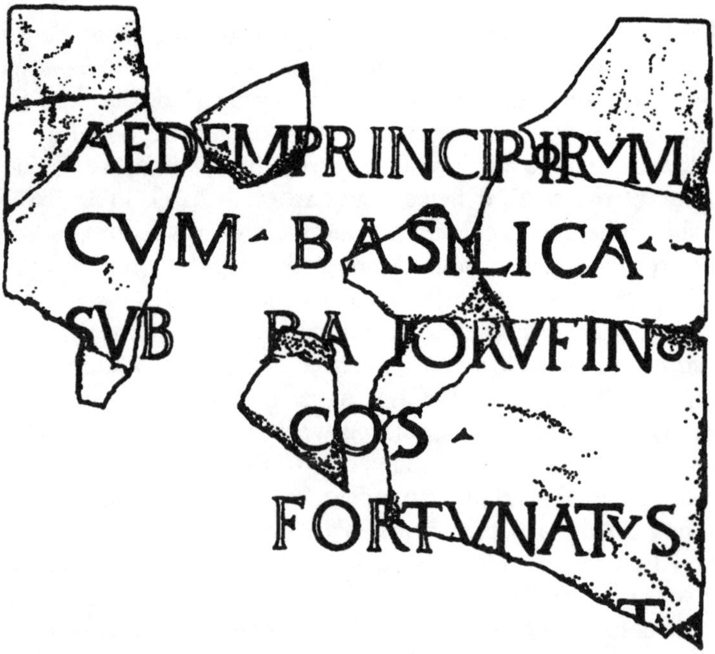

Figure 26 The inscription of ? Q. Aradius Rufinus from Reculver (Kent).

been so severe that the Roman coastline has been engulfed by the sea, and with it several Roman sites, including a settlement at Dunwich and a fort at Walton Castle, have entirely disappeared. The prospects for such a discovery are therefore not very bright, unless an earlier work lies beneath the known fort at Bradwell, now partially destroyed. It is worth noting, too, that a coastal fortification, probably of Roman date, existed on the Lincolnshire coast at Skegness until the sixteenth century. This lost site together with Brancaster could have effectively guarded the approaches to the Wash.

Why were these forts constructed? The security of military supplies passing to and from Britain was no doubt still sufficient reason for maintaining a small number of garrisons on the south-eastern coasts. But it seems as though from the early third century the wider security of the Channel coasts and crossings was increasingly difficult to maintain. Why this was so is not clear. There is very little evidence for a greater degree of mobility on the part of the barbarian peoples of north-western Germania (i.e. North Holland, North-west Germany and the Jutland peninsula) during the third century. There are no contemporary allusions to seaborne attacks on the coasts of Lower Germany, Gallia Belgica and Britain, and no definable archaeological evidence for increased expertise or ambition in seamanship among those same barbarians. About AD 170, the Chauki had invaded Gallia Belgica, but it is not known whether they broke through the Rhine frontier or outflanked it by sea. In the northern coastlands marine transgression was beginning to deprive some of the inhabitants of their lower-lying ground, but this does not seem to have been so drastic as to compel them to seek homes far from their earlier dwellings. For the time being, moreover, there was land enough to accommodate a growing population. Attacks on the Roman provinces were therefore almost certainly piratical rather than indicative of land-hunger. A significant indicator of the reduced importance of Britain in strategic terms after the early third century is the character of the governors appointed to the two provinces. Although the lists for the British commands are not complete, the known holders were not distinguished military men and certainly they could not stand comparison with the commanders of the previous century and a half. The division of Britain does not entirely account for this. The fact is that after the campaigns of Severus and Caracalla Britain was a military backwater for the following seventy years.

Urban life in the middle and later third century appears to have been both stable and prosperous, though there appears to have been very little in the way of ambitious building. Some of the larger private dwellings known at Silchester, Wroxeter and *Verulamium* may have been constructed late in the century but public building was virtually at a standstill, mainly because the principal structures already existed and required only repair and maintenance. It is plain that the cities had reached their greatest physical extent by the earlier third century, for no certain cases of extension beyond the limits of second century earthwork defences have been noted. There was, indeed, at least one instance of contraction – at Caister-by-Norwich. The most significant development in the physical form of cities and towns concerned their defensive circuits. Most of the cities and many of the minor towns had their defences remodelled in stone in the middle and later decades of the century. There has been much debate about when this step of providing stone curtain walls was taken, the tendency over the past half-century being to advance the date from the reigns of Hadrian and Antoninus Pius into the years immediately after the Severi. Very few walled circuits are dated with any precision, but it is increasingly apparent that they were provided at different dates. That at Canterbury was built about or shortly after 270, whereas the *Verulamium* wall was completed by about 230. The walls of London probably also date from the earlier third century in origin, although the riverside wall may not have been added until later. Silchester and Cirencester probably also received their stone circuits in the first half of the century, but the complex building-sequence at the latter city is a reminder of how prolonged an operation defensive building might be. Here, the completion of the walling came after 250 and possibly as late as 300. Delays in construction may be anticipated elsewhere, though they are not directly attested. The colonies of Lincoln, Colchester and perhaps Gloucester already possessed walls (*page 104*) but at Lincoln, at least, there was a major rebuilding of the gates in the earlier third century, while at Gloucester the walls required extensive reconstruction later on.

Minor towns too put up stone defences, in some cases adding them to existing earthworks, in certain others thereby providing their first circuits.[5] The list ranges from sizeable towns like Alchester, Dorchester-on-Thames and *Durobrivae*, to small settlements such as Ancaster, Mancetter and Great Casterton. In all the cases so far examined, the fortifications were conservative in style, there being no discernible impress of the new mode of defensive architecture which began to appear in the 270s. This does not mean that the British urban defences were all built before that decade. Rather, it reflects the kind of work-force which the urban authorities were able to employ and the old tradition in which they worked.

Coinage and inflation in the early third century

When Severus was contending with Niger and then with Albinus, he did not have the advantage of a plentiful supply of money. The extravagance of Commodus had made severe inroads into the reserves of the Imperial treasury. It may indeed by now have been virtually empty. The revenues of the richer provinces of the Empire still lay in the hands of Niger. Like Commodus and Didius Julianus before him, Severus turned to debasement, especially of the *denarius*, which had had its silver content reduced to about two-thirds of what it had been in the 180s. When victory was finally achieved over Albinus, Severus' acute shortage of funds may have led him to confiscate private property in Gaul and probably also in Britain. Dio has a story of 17.5 million *denarii* being seized in Gaul. Subsequently, careful husbandry of the Imperial finances allowed him to give soldiers a substantial increase in pay and still leave behind at his death a healthy surplus. There have been attempts to demonstrate that there were sharp rises in prices in the period 180–210, particularly in Severus' reign, none of them based on a sufficiently wide range of evidence. There are no satisfactory grounds for the argument that the early third century saw the beginning of that inflation which ruined the economy of the Empire half a century later.

The volume of silver coinage in currency probably did rise, and the effects of this would clearly be felt in a province with a large army like Britain. Under Caracalla the troops received another rise in pay, thus giving an already affluent sector of society a greatly enhanced purchasing power. The immediate effects of the issue of Caracalla's new double *denarius* coin in 215, the *antoninianus* as it is generally known to modern scholars, on the quality of the currency have often been exaggerated in the past. Actually the new coin was struck in very small amounts down to 219 and was not thereafter struck again until 238; only then did it begin to dominate the currency.

In Britain, moreover, there are signs of a reluctance to abandon the use of silver *denarii* in favour of the baser new coin. In British hoards of the first half of the third century, *denarii* usually greatly outnumber *antoniniani*; in an appreciable number of cases the hoards consist of *denarii* only. Another indicator of the general preference for *denarii* is the relative frequency with which forgers' moulds for false *denarii* are encountered in Britain. Most of these were produced by impressing official coins into clay discs, from which the forgeries were later cast. Most commonly these moulds were designed to produce forged coins of Severus and Caracalla, but the practice continued as late as the reigns of Severus Alexander and Maximinus. Moulds for false *antoniniani* also occur, but they are much rarer and date, on the whole, from the time when official *denarii* were becoming scarce. It seems, then, that the casting of false *denarii* was an illicit rearguard action, vigorously pursued in Britain and in certain other parts of the West, designed to preserve, at considerable profit to the forgers, the *denarius* in circulation. This was continued until the 240s, by which date official issues of *denarii* had virtually disappeared from circulation, thus removing the final vestige of any credibility which these cast forgeries may formerly have enjoyed.

Interruption in the patterns of trade between Britain and the Continent during the period of the civil wars of the 190s, if it occurred at all, can only have been brief. Earlier assertions that the trade in Baetican oil was interrupted by the civil wars have no real foundation. Baetican amphorae were still reaching Britain after 200 as before that date and they are not merely found in the south of the island. These were probably normally used as containers of olive oil,

Figure 27 The inscription of Gimioga, businessman resident at ? Caister-by-Norwich, from Colijnsplaat, Holland.

wine being transported in wooden casks like those shown on later stone reliefs from the Moselle valley.

Epigraphic evidence for trade between Britain and Gaul in the early third century is impressive and has recently been augmented by important discoveries. Aquitaine had established trade-links with Britain long before 200, but the first clear proof of this traffic comes with the famous altar to Boudiga, the tutelary deity of Bordeaux, set up in that city by M. Aurelius Lunaris in 237.[6] This man was a *sevir Augustalis* of both Lincoln and York, and though his commercial connections with those *coloniae* were no doubt strong, it is most probable that his interests also embraced part of Southern Britain, perhaps including London. Another trader from Aquitaine, M. Verecundius Diogenes, was also a *sevir* of *Eboracum*, his particular business apparently being the provision of vessels for other merchants, if the term *moritex* (shipper?) is correctly read on his funerary inscription.

There were links of trade with other Gaulish ports and harbours. L. Viducius Placidus from Rouen may have been using the Seine estuary as a base for his trading operations, which reached as far as York, but he is also known to have shipped goods by way of the Rhine estuary. The prominence of York in the surviving records is a striking testimony to the growth in importance of the civilian community across the Ouse from the legionary base during the second century. This traffic presumably passed up the Humber and will go some way towards explaining the rise to prominence of Brough-on-Humber in the Antonine period. Although fulfilling perhaps the role of a military supply base, this place never ceded its function as a major civilian *entrepôt* in the north, and a substantial community must have been in existence here by the early third century. By way of contrast, the river-port of London declined markedly after the mid-third century, probably as east coast harbours grew in importance, and continued to decline into the fourth century.

The discovery of the remains of a temple to the Gallo-Germanic deity Nehallenia at Colijnsplaat, on the island of Domburg in the estuary of the Rhine, has yielded up a range of more than eighty altars, many of fine quality, set up to that goddess by the prosperous merchants plying the North Sea crossing in the late second and early third centuries; it has also thrown valuable light on the nature of the trade with Britain.[7] Viducius Placidus is among the merchants who left dedications there, along with others whose main interest was plainly the connection between Britain and the lower Rhine. The commodities traded included at least salt, pottery, wine and *allec*, a kind of Gaulish fish-sauce, but there were no doubt others, such as wool, other agricultural products and metals. Salt was produced in quantity on the lower Rhine, among the Menapii and Morini and in Eastern Britain, so that the Rhine estuary ports may have served as collection points from which this staple commodity was transported up the Rhine and deep into Gaul. The trade in pottery may have carried wares in both directions, samian ware from the east Gaulish factories, especially Rheinzabern, and other table wares from Cologne and the Moselle region passing to Britain, while at least a certain amount of fine slip-coated pottery crossed from Britain to the Rhineland. The abrupt demise of the central Gaulish pottery factories at the end of the second century, quite possibly as a direct result of Severan confiscations in Gaul after the defeat of Albinus, can only have brought benefit to the potters of the Moselle and the Rhine, admirably placed as they were to seize advantage of the river connections with the Channel coast.

The British trade offered enough to attract Gauls from a wide area. There were several representatives of Cologne families with fingers in the pie. Others came from Trier, from Rouen, the territory of the Sequani and perhaps from Lyon. One or two veterans were among them, and of the rest, freedmen appear to be prominent. They clearly prospered, for their votive monuments include some finely carved sculptures.

The countryside in the third century

It is still possible to encounter the view, based to a large extent on the excavation of a number of villas before 1950, that there was a general decline in the prosperity of villas, particularly in those of more than moderately pretentious status, during the middle decades of the third century. This seemed to be proclaimed by the history of the villas at Ditchley, Park Street and Lockleys, which for so long seemed the most reliably excavated and documented sites. The history of villas in the third century can now be seen to be much more complex, partly because the sample of well excavated villa sites has been significantly increased in the past twenty years, especially by the application of area excavation in the place of the earlier method of trenching. Designed to reveal the plan of buildings, it was inadequate as a means of disclosing the full structural history of a villa. Only since 1974 have truly large-scale excavation reports begun to appear, and to date only a few have been published.[8] There is, then, a long way to go before we can claim to have reached a satisfactory stage in our knowledge of the structural history of a reasonable number of villas.

There are, however, other and more severe limitations to the evidence from excavation of villa sites. For long, the chronology of third century pottery has proved, and still proves, very difficult to establish, the material being often difficult to distinguish from late Antonine pottery at one end of the period, and from early fourth century wares at the other. Some progress has been made here, at least in certain regions of Britain, but this is still a subject of the greatest difficulty. A further problem is a more general one, concerning the inability of the foundations and floors of a building, which are usually all that the excavator encounters, to give all the details of the history of the structure. Many substantial changes might be made to the roof and other parts of the superstructure without in any way modifying or even touching the foundations. In a number of earlier villa excavations, the absence of such modifications or additions to the foundation-plan has been taken to mean that the building was in 'decline' or even had been entirely abandoned, whereas nothing of the kind need be indicated except that the structure was in all ways adequate for its occupants and purposes. It would in many cases require a fairly radical modification to the building to involve alteration of its footings.

Taking account of these limitations to our evidence, it is possible to gain a very different picture of the fate of villas in the third century. There are some sixty villa sites which have been reasonably well excavated and published, or whose history can be within limits reconstructed from earlier records and extant finds. Of these at least twenty-five show no trace of abandonment or decay during the century, and this may be true of a further seven. A further fifteen sites have produced evidence for breaks in their occupation, but these are mainly short and are no more remarkable than the interruptions evident in other periods. It is worth note, too, that these interruptions are frequently followed by rebuilding on an ambitious scale, so that they may have been related to a change of ownership caused by death or the sale of the associated estate for other reasons. In only a dozen cases does a lengthy period of abandonment seem to be indicated, but even here there must be doubts about certain of the sites excavated in earlier times. To take only one instance, the villa at Ditchley has been held to have been abandoned after a fire about AD 200 and not thereafter reoccupied until the early fourth century. There are, however, six third-century coins from the site, all of types which did not normally circulate after AD 300 and some of the published pottery may also be of the third century.

A few of the best recorded villas may be briefly examined against this rather sketchy background. A group of well excavated villas in the vicinity of *Verulamium* so far illustrates the varying fortunes of villas most clearly. At Gadebridge Park, steady growth is evinced from the late second century onward. Early in the third century, more rooms were provided by subdivisions within the main house and the baths enlarged by a small swimming-pool. New working quarters were also built, probably including accommodation for the work-force. There is every sign that the prosperity of this estate continued without hindrance down to the end of the century, and beyond. The Boxmoor villa was partially rebuilt in the early third century, while the house at Gorhambury continued in occupation throughout the century and was put into repair at its end. Northchurch was seemingly deserted for a time in the first half of the century, possibly because of flooding, but it was reoccupied by the 250s. Only at Park Street, if we adopt the excavator's chronology, was there a long period of desertion, but even here this came to an end before AD 300. Two villas in the nearby Chilterns, Latimer and High Wycombe, were significantly enlarged early in the century and further embellished by mosaics certainly at Latimer, possibly at High Wycombe.

One of the most extensively examined villas is that at Winterton (Lincolnshire). Here, the main house was erected at the close of the second century and continued without much alteration for about a century, before a substantial rebuilding around AD 300. Taking all the buildings together, the Winterton villa may have reached its greatest extent in the middle decades of the third century, and there is not the least sign of any falling away in later years. The smaller and less ambitious house at Mansfield Woodhouse (Nottinghamshire) was also occupied throughout the third century without break, only minor changes being made to the late Antonine building. This pattern can be matched at several other villas in Coritanian territory.

Elsewhere, there is ample evidence for rebuilding and alteration, especially in the earlier third century. The villa at Ely (Glamorgan) was partly rebuilt in the earlier decades of the century and about AD 300 earthworks were thrown round the dwelling and its associated farm-buildings. Llantwit Major in the same county, however, may have passed through a prolonged phase of dereliction early in the century, ended by extensive rebuilding about 300. At both sites, and at a number of other villas in this period, the baths lost their original function and were perhaps converted to humdrum uses, as workshops or stores. In certain of the Cotswold villas, there are evident signs of growing wealth in the third century, a firm foundation for the impressive development of the many great houses of this region after 300. Chedworth villa in the second century consisted of three separate timber-framed buildings and a stone bath-house. By the middle of the third century, a series of *porticus* had been added, the entire residence now being arranged about two small courtyards.

An area in which the development of villa farming was particularly notable in this period is the heartland of the Brigantes, the Vale of York and the Dales. At both Langton and Rudston in the south of the canton, the first stone buildings of thoroughly Roman style appeared in the mid-third century, though real amenities were yet to arrive. Further north, at Well and possibly Beadlam, further advances were made in material comfort after an initial phase of prosperity in Antonine times. In the valleys to the west there are further signs of pretension to higher standards of housing and perhaps also in farming practice. From the Calder basin come inscriptions set up by Roman citizens whose names suggest that they were veterans. Whether they were exploiting this land within some official scheme of land-settlement or were acting upon private initiative is unknown: both are possibilities, the former perhaps the stronger. There can be no doubt that the enhanced status of York, now a *colonia* as well as a provincial capital, had much to do with this increased pace towards Romanity among the Brigantes. The Vale of York was rich in natural agricultural resources, always liable to appeal to those with money to invest, whether they were veterans, *negotiatores* or landowners who found themselves growing appreciably richer. The land was now peaceful. In this part of Britain the *pax Romana* began only after the early third century. Even the official demands of taxation favoured the productive farmer, so that all conspired to encourage the efficient management of estates.

There has been an understandable tendency to seek further repercussions on Britain of the disasters which overwhelmed Gaul and Germany. Several attempts have been made to trace the transfer of capital from Gaul to Britain in the period 260–80 by identifying Gaulish elements in the architecture of certain villas in Southern Britain.[9] It has been pointed out, for example, that the plan of early fourth-century Ditchley so closely resembles that of the villa at Houdeng-Goegnis in Belgium that it was probably the work of the same architect. The similarity in planning is indeed close, but it is now known that the Gadebridge Park villa possessed an analogous plan, while a simpler form of the same layout also occurs at the early timber house at Boxmoor. It is thus preferable to see this villa-plan as no more than another instance of that dissemination of architectural ideas from Gallia Belgica which had already left its mark on British villas (*page 109*). A group of villas in which the dominant feature of the plan was a central hall, found mainly in

Gloucestershire and Somerset, has also been interpreted as indicating an immigration of landowners, this time from the Rhineland and North-eastern Gaul, where this basic plan is well represented. But the British villas in question cannot all be assigned to the later third century and occasional earlier instances have been noted in areas other than the south-west. It may be, then, that the British hall-villas are yet further instances of the transfer of architectural notions from Gaul, not of the migration of landowners and their capital. It is, moreover, worth asking how easy it would be for a Gallic landowner, first, to dispose of his property in Gaul in the midst of the least propitious circumstances, secondly, to transfer his capital (in what form?) to Britain, and thirdly, to acquire British land. Such procedures may be familiar enough on the modern property market, but in the ancient economy it is most unlikely that the transfer of 'capital' in the form of coined money was ever a normal transaction. 'Capital' in the Roman world meant land, and slaves, and the value of these did not commonly have to be realized. There may indeed have been no machinery to deal with such a case. It remains a strong possibility that some Gauls did seek refuge in Britain in the late third century, but no evidence has yet been adduced to show that an inflow of Gaulish capital played any significant part in the development of the large agricultural estates, which from this time onward are so remarkable a feature of the Romano-British rural scene.

An influx of external capital is not a likely element in the strong growth of prosperity evident in rural Roman Britain. That was due to the productivity of agriculture and the wealth which accrued from secondary products such as wool and leather, in a part of the West which did not suffer the invasions endured by Gaul and Spain. By the later third century it is evident the economic resources of Britain were being increasingly concentrated in fewer hands and the beneficiaries were more and more concerned to display their wealth and status. From this time onward large villas come to prominence, especially in western Britain, at Chedworth, North Leigh, Woodchester, Great Witcombe and Stonesfield, related no doubt to large landed estates which were now delivering substantial profits. It is unlikely that the great landed proprietors of Britain were very numerous, but that does not mean that their influence was negligible.

Developments in Romano-British society

There has in the past been a tendency to attribute to Severus social policies, particularly concerning the soldiers and veterans, of which he was innocent and at which he would have expressed sheer astonishment. It is true that certain measures which were to have far-reaching effects were passed by this emperor, but in no sense can these be regarded as policies rather than responses to the needs of the moment. The measure which has received most attention is that of 197, which permitted serving soldiers to live with their 'wives', an official acknowledgement of an inevitable state of affairs which must have long been evident wherever army units were based for any length of time. There are indications that some centurions, at least, had been allowed to have their families with them inside frontier forts, and it is possible that other ranks may already have been permitted, to a limited extent, to spend some of their lives in the company of their families in the *vici*. It was after all in the interests of the army that there should be a steady supply of recruits from a proper, military background. It is not absolutely certain what Severus' concession amounted to, in particular whether he granted the right of legal marriage or merely allowed men on service to cohabit with women who remained concubines. The bulk of the evidence from the legal codes suggests, but does not prove, that the grant was one of legal marriage.

There must have been, however, complications in legal status, for the women with whom frontier soldiers consorted were usually *peregrinae*. There is no proof that Severus issued an automatic grant of *conubium*, thus allowing a man who was already a citizen to marry a peregrine woman. Technically, therefore, such a marriage would be *ex iure gentium* only. As it turned out, the grant of citizenship to all free inhabitants of the Empire in 212 shortly removed any such distinctions as might have arisen from the measure of 197.

The impact of Severus' legislation on the *vici* of Northern Britain is well known. From the early third century these settlements grew apace so that a century later some of them, such as Chesters, Housesteads, Corbridge, Kirkby Thore, Brough-under-Stainmore, Piercebridge and Binchester, resembled small towns. A few, including at least Housesteads and Chesterholm, possessed not only the outward form of a minor town but also some degree of officially recognized internal organization.[10]

For some commentators, the temptation to link the new family circumstances of the frontier troops with the growth of a soldier-peasantry has proved too strong. To seek in the Severan reorganization of the northern frontier the roots of a system of soldier-peasants is only possible if we ignore the vast bulk of evidence for continuity between the army of the Antonines and of Hadrian with that of the Severi and their immediate successors. The third century

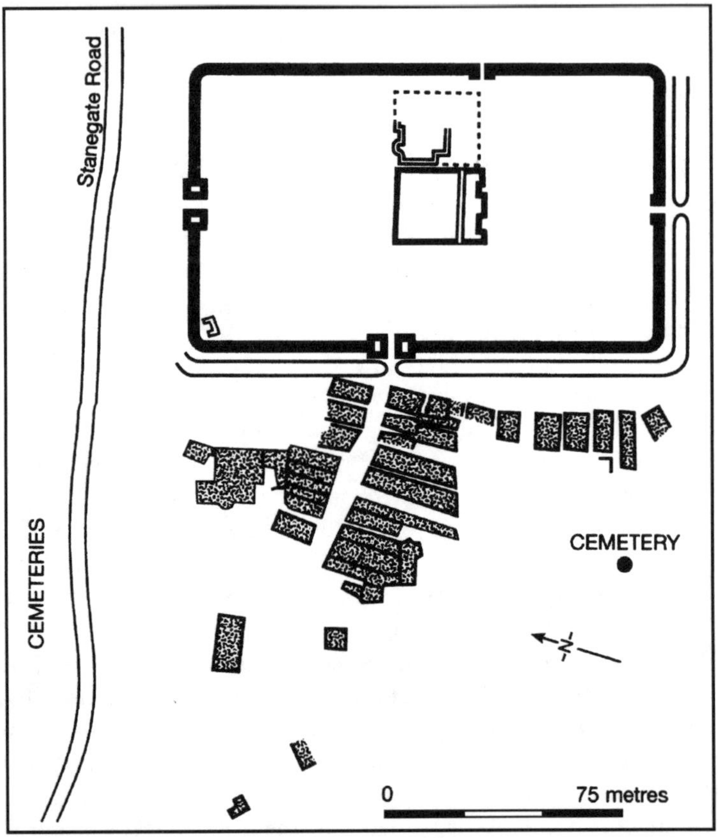

Figure 28 The plan of the *vicus* at Chesterholm (*Vindolanda*).

soldier-peasant is a myth, founded upon a small number of references to land-allotment or land-lease to serving soldiers, some in the law-codes, and one in the highly suspect *Life* of Alexander Severus in the *Scriptores Historiae Augustae*. There is no evidence from Britain to indicate that soldiers were tilling land as a regular practice, their own or anyone else's, at any date. Agricultural implements found in Roman forts (sickles, scythes, billhooks etc.) only show that a general care was exercised over the ground near the fort, that hay was cut for animals and that a certain amount of horticulture was practised. None of this is significant or surprising. The fact that soldiers could inherit land in the province where they eventually settled or might buy land in other provinces proves nothing about soldiers *tilling* land while on active service. Indeed, Aemilius Macer, a jurist of the early third century, states that troops were forbidden to own land in the province in which they served 'lest through their desire to cultivate the land they are distracted from military service'. The evidence for a highly organized form of agriculture from the provinces of Mauretania, Africa and Cyrenaica, firmly under military direction and on paramilitary lines, is evidence of an entirely different order, but it has no bearing on the state of agriculture on the British frontier.

One of the most significant general developments in the northern frontier region during the third century was the steady growth of a frontier society, essentially rural and possessing a material culture which was superficially Roman-provincial, but on which Roman cultural values had made little impression. The characteristic feature of such frontier societies, as known on several sectors of the Rhine and Danube frontiers, and in mediaeval Europe, is their tendency to create social, economic and cultural links between people on both sides of a long-standing frontier and to develop forms of life which were distinct from the core societies at whose limits they lay. Life in a homestead in the Pennines south of Hadrian's Wall was little different in essentials from that in a similar settlement in the Cheviots. Without question upland peasants to either side of the Roman frontier had much more in common with each other than with the inhabitants of Lincoln or Silchester. Intercourse of various kinds across the frontier must have been easier in the third century than ever before. Many of the turrets had been abandoned long before and at least a number of milecastles were given up after the early third century, thus leaving still more passageways through the Wall, though others were maintained and/or repaired late in the century. Long stretches of the Vallum were also out of commission by the early third century, so that many sectors of the frontier lay open to north–south movement.

The effects of the *Constitutio Antoniniana*, enacted probably in 212, are difficult to ascertain, though its impact upon the remaining *peregrini* must have been marked, since the ancient distinction between citizens and *peregrini* now lost most of its significance. Significant rights and privileges no longer derived from being a citizen, but from membership of one of the higher orders of society, namely the senatorial and equestrian orders and the ranks of the decurions. The new constitutional privileges enjoyed by the upper classes, developments of the later second century, were in no way altered, or curtailed, while the mass of the population gained little of real worth from the grant of citizenship. The main gainers were probably peregrine women, for they could now be legally married, with all that that entailed. Citizenship was not entirely devalued. Some who had held it from earlier days could still boast of its possession, but in real terms it can have counted for little, and even this may have been eroded as the third century wore on.

The status of the urban communities was also unchanged in essentials. The legal distinctions between *civitates stipendiariae* and *civitates liberae* remained, as did those between *vici, civitates, municipia* and *coloniae*. But the broad spread of citizenship must have brought about a degree of levelling between the various civic grades. One change which may have been felt in Britain concerned *civitates* or *gentes dediticiae*, which were now presumably granted communal status. It is not known for certain whether any such groupings did exist in Britain, but it is legitimate to wonder whether the Demetae and the Carvetii, for example, fell into this category.

One minor effect of Caracalla's Edict at least is discernible in Britain. There is ample evidence from most parts of the Empire for the adoption by large numbers of former *peregrini* of the name Aurelius from the early decades of the century. In Romano-British nomenclature, Aurelius is by far and away the commonest of the Imperial *nomina* and, although very few instances are dated, it is probable that a high proportion date from after 212. But single peregrine names continue to occur after Caracalla's reign, as they do in other provinces, a reminder that outside the official sphere provincial practice could take time before being assimilated into State procedure. These names thus do not demonstrate that large numbers of *peregrini* still survived in third century Britain, though small groups of non-citizens no doubt persisted in remoter districts until well after 212.[11]

In the higher reaches of provincial society there were major alterations in the role played by men of equestrian rank. After the Severi, centurions and *principales* (soldiers often entrusted with special administrative duties) found it easier to reach the equestrian ranks, and in due course their sons entered the *ordo equester* virtually as of right. Thus the number of equestrians of provincial origin was greatly swollen, augmenting the already numerous equestrian officers and decurions who formed an influential element in Romano-British society. Just how influential such men might be is amply demonstrated by the career of T. Sennius Sollemnis of Gallia Lugdunensis, a municipal magistrate of the Viducassii in Severan times.[12] He was rich enough to afford lavish gladiatorial games and prominent enough to gain the friendship of provincial governors, among them T. Claudius Paulinus of Lower Britain, who offered him an appointment with *Legio VI Victrix*. There were many others of more modest attainments who must have left their mark on local communities, not least through their ownership of land.

The high, and improving, economic status of Roman soldiers in frontier provinces is of major importance for an understanding of developments within Romano-British society in the third century. After Severus, promotion to the centurionate from the ranks became more common as fewer candidates for direct appointment came forward from civilian life. A possible way to social advance was thus opened up for many British provincials. For the more ambitious there were better hopes of aspiring to the ranks of equestrian officers as municipal candidates became fewer and fewer. It is unlikely that many Romano-Britons actually did rise so far. But the opportunity was there, and the entry of men with such names as T. Flavius, M. Ulpius and P. Aelius into the equestrian service demonstrates that provincial families were making their presence felt.

From the middle years of the century and especially from the reign of Gallienus, the role of equestrians in the higher military command was greatly extended. As early as 184, Perennis, the praetorian *praefectus* of Commodus, had tried to replace senatorial *legati* with equestrian *praefecti* as commanders of legions, but had been compelled to abandon the policy. Septimius Severus had appointed equestrians to command his three new legions which were stationed in Italy, but there had been no concerted moves towards the regular advancement of *equites* to legionary commands until Gallienus began to replace the senatorial *legati* with equestrian *praefecti legionum*. His intention was to replenish the thinning ranks of men equipped to hold the major commands by bringing in soldiers of wide and effective experience, and it was thus inevitable that he should turn to the rising *equites*. Henceforward, commanders of the old style legions and of the new vexillations were usually equestrians. The separation of Britain and Gaul from the central Empire from 259 to 274 can only have accentuated this process of equestrian advancement. Commanders of auxiliary units must now have come largely, and perhaps almost wholly, from the ranks of centurions and decurions, no longer from the municipal aristocracy of provinces far from Britain. No doubt the curial families of the British cities also made their contribution to the officer ranks, but this cannot have come near to matching the number of men promoted from the *auxilia*. These developments will inevitably have meant a drawing together of the tribal dignitaries and the ranks of officers in a community of interest which may help to explain the remarkable ease with which all of Britain passed under the rule of Carausius in the 280s. In the military sphere, Britain was a backwater in the middle decades of the third century. After Caracalla's settlement of Scotland no more is heard of disturbance in Britain for half a century or more. The reduced significance of the provinces is reflected in the careers of the men sent to them as governors; none of these figures among the leading commanders of the period.

The year of disaster, 259–60, saw the collapse of the Upper German frontier, the defeat and capture of the emperor Valerian by the Persians in Mesopotamia, revolts in the Danube provinces and the secession of Gaul, Spain and Britain under the usurper Postumus. The brief period of Britain's adherence to the Gallic Empire, from 260 to 273, is barely touched on by the written sources and epigraphy has added very little to the story. The Gallic emperors seem to have had no difficulty in holding on to Britain. No British revolts against their authority are recorded, like that of the city of Autun against Victorinus. Surviving milestones make it clear that Postumus, Victorinus and Tetricus all concerned themselves with the upkeep of main roads in Britain in the civil districts as well as in the frontier lands. The roads of South Wales came in for attention in the reigns of both Postumus and Victorinus, and the main route through Cornwall under the former. Milestones of Victorinus indicate that Ermine Street, the main road north from London, was put into good repair and the frontier area, too, came in for attention at the same time. Three milestones of Tetricus at *Clausentum*, near Southampton, suggest that this place was now increasing in significance as a port of entry, although present evidence for third century occupation here is scarce. Aurelian, on recovering Britain in 273, was also concerned with the restoration of roads in this area, a further indication of official interest in the port of *Clausentum*, perhaps in connection with supplies being shipped from Britain to the Seine estuary and thence to the ravaged areas of Gaul.

The economic state of the Empire, already dangerously weak, was further impaired by desperate measures taken to repair the damage. Chief among these was the tired old expedient of reducing the silver content of the *antoninianus*, this time from some 20% to about 3%. For much of his reign over the western provinces, Postumus tried to keep the quality of his silver coinage as high as he could and no doubt he was aided in this by the silver reserves of both Britain and Spain. But eventually he was forced to admit defeat and in the years 266–8 gave in to debasement. All the base coins were coated with a silver wash, although most now seem to be no more than bronze, the silver wash being either worn off by circulation or made invisible by corrosion. The successors of Postumus went even further on this downward path. Inevitably, the flood of bad coinage drove the remaining silver currency into hoards or the melting-pot. The result is apparent in the hoarding of silver about 268–70: subsequent hoards consist largely (and often entirely) of the base issues of the years 260–74. Even the better coinage of Postumus' early years was steadily driven out of circulation.

This chaotic state of affairs was not remedied when the western provinces were brought back under central control by Aurelian in 274. After this, the issues of the Gallic Empire continued to outnumber by far those of emperors based at Rome, coins of the two Tetrici being overwhelmingly common. Aurelian's new currency was aimed at restoring general confidence in the coinage. He introduced a new, heavier coin which bore the mark XX or XXI – presumably indicating units of account. The earlier, base issues were apparently devalued, but continued to circulate as pieces of low denomination, thus fulfilling a major need which the mints had failed to cater for. The great flood of 'barbarous' copies which now burst forth illustrates the dire need for small change felt by the provincial population of the west and, or so it has been argued, the determined resistance of those provinces, and especially Britain, to the reformed coinage of Aurelian. That coinage did indeed remain rare in the west, the low grade issues of the Gallic Empire forming the great mass of the currency. The relative scarcity of Aurelian's currency, however, may be due to no more remarkable circumstance than that the emperor's recovery of the west was shortly followed by his death, so that there was little time for his issues to penetrate Britain in bulk.

Much has been learnt about the circulation-range of the 'barbarous radiates' in recent years, one of the most significant revelations being that they were not all merely local coinages which did not travel far from their place of origin. The detailed study of die-links and die-identities has shown that coins from the same centre could travel considerable distances within Britain and, further, that some 'barbarous' coins struck in Gaul passed to the island. Thus, coins from hoards buried in Nottinghamshire and Staffordshire were struck from the same dies, while other die-links indicate that coins could travel as far as one hundred miles from their mint centres. The Gaulish evidence indicates that they could circulate even more widely. There are die-linked coins at Mildenhall (Suffolk) from the Seine valley and from central France, while others reached Woodeaton (Oxfordshire) from the valley of the Meuse. The wide distribution of some of these coins in Gaul suggests that more study will reveal many more instances of issues which crossed the Channel, probably in both directions. Though this imitative coinage sprang from local roots, it became much more widespread than has commonly been recognized.

The obverses most commonly imitated by the 'barbarous radiates' are those of Gallienus, Claudius II, all the Gallic emperors and Probus. None are known for certain to copy issues later than the reign of Probus, either in Britain or in Gaul, so that it was presumably this emperor who brought to an enforced end their production. How this was done cannot be guessed at. For a time, circulation of the huge amounts of barbarous coins continued, but large quantities of them were consigned to hoards in Probus' reign never to be recovered. In a few years, the large coinages of Carausius and later of Diocletian ended the life in circulation of the remaining issues, though a few still survived into the fourth century.

10

The Fourth-century Diocese

The later reign of Probus saw a number of insurrections in the western provinces which seem to attest deep-seated dissension between provincials and the central regime. An Italian soldier, Proculus, tried to revive Gallic independence and gained the support of the citizens of *Lugdunum* (Lyon) before he was compelled to flee to the Franks, who promptly handed him over to Probus. Later, Bonosus, commander of the Rhine fleet based at Cologne, rebelled and caused serious trouble before he was brought down. Again, barbarians had been drawn in to the affair. About the same time, an unnamed governor of Britain revolted against Probus and was brought to book by Victorinus the Moor, relying on Vandal and Burgundian troops sent to Britain by Probus after his victory in Gaul in 277. All this implies a more deeply rooted antagonism towards the government of Rome than could be aroused by Aurelian's trenchant reform of the coinage – frequently adduced as a major irritant by modern scholars. The reasons why the Romano-British provincials in particular should have felt disinclined to re-enter the Roman fold are worth attention, after their most successful bid for independence has been discussed.

Carausius

Little more than a decade after Britain had been drawn back to the authority of Roman emperors, the island again parted company with the central Empire, this time on its own. By 284, the Gaulish provinces were so plagued by internal brigandage on the part of the *Bagaudae* that the emperor Diocletian appointed Maximian as leader of a force against the marauders. A major figure in the operations was one M. Aurelius Mausaeus Carausius, a Menapian, who so impressed his superiors with his seamanship that he was given the command of a fleet to drive off the Franks and Saxons infesting the coasts of Belgica and Armorica.[1] This campaign, too, was a success but it was quickly followed by a fall from favour when the report came out that Carausius had been enriching himself by holding on to booty taken from the pirates. Condemned to death by Maximian, he used his naval command to take possession of Britain and declared himself emperor, probably in 286. It is surprising that all of Britain should have fallen to Carausius so easily. Conceivably the rule of the central Empire was rather more exacting than that of the Gallic emperors, and the interwoven Romano-British oligarchy of *curiales* and army officers may by now have become accustomed to arranging matters without much outside intervention. Some motive force stronger than Carausius' own military prestige was surely at work; there is no evidence that he was known in Britain before his usurpation. Evidently Carausius swiftly seized control of a sufficient supply of money to pay the army, and for this his much publicized seizure of booty may have been important. The surviving sources for the episode are all hostile to the usurper. They convey the Roman view of the affair, but they need not have been entirely invention. Carausius was not the first, or the last, naval commander who found loot a useful support in a bid for power.

There was no immediate retaliation against the usurper, for Maximian was faced with emergencies on the Rhine for a further two years. But in 288–9 a fleet was mustered against Carausius and an attempt made to attack his force at sea. The result, not made explicit in the Roman sources, appears to have favoured Carausius, and a grudging peace ensued for the next four years, possibly sealed by recognition of the usurper as *Augustus*.

It has long been accepted that Carausius was able to maintain control over a part of Northern Gaul, the main points for debate being, first, whether he held that continental foothold from 286 or seized it later, and secondly, when his control was finally relinquished. These problems turn on interpretation of the coinages of Carausius from various mint-centres.[2] The most important of these was a mint at London, but there were perhaps four others, one signing itself with a mint-mark C, another with RSR, a third with no mint-mark at all and a fourth generally placed at Rouen. The locations of all of these mints are far from certain. The RSR mint may have been no more than a branch of the London mint. The mint using the mint-mark C has recently been placed at *Camulodunum* on the evidence of find-distributions, though *Calleva* and *Clausentum* have also been proposed. The coins with no mint-mark have been attributed to a continental mint (perhaps Boulogne), but the grounds for

Plate 3 Mosaic floor with bust of Christ in the central roundel, found at Hinton St Mary, Dorset. Photograph RCHME, © Crown Copyright.

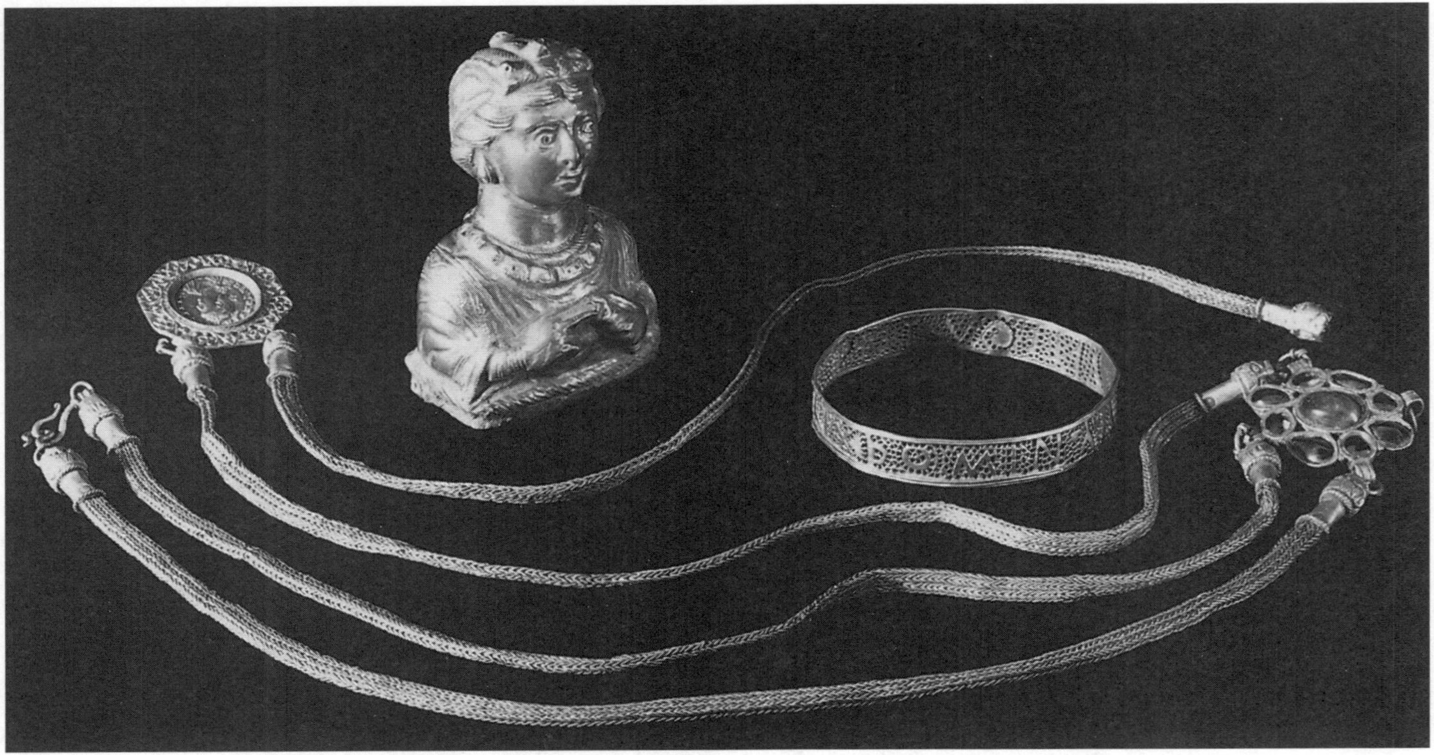

Plate 4 Objects from the early fifth century treasure found at Hoxne, Suffolk. Photograph © British Museum.

doing so have been shown to be non-existent. These coins were issued in Britain, quite possibly at London. Finally, the location of the continental mint at Rouen cannot be substantiated: it might equally well have lain at Boulogne or Amiens. The fact that the coins with no mint-mark now appear to have been struck in Britain is of some importance, for in the past they have been used in support of the idea that Carausius was in control of North-western Gaul from the beginning of his usurpation in 286, the date of the earliest unmarked issues. That numismatic argument is thus now robbed of its power, but the entire case for the Carausian hold on the Gaulish coastal tract from 286 is not thereby destroyed. There is no evidence that Maximian was able to challenge the naval supremacy of Carausius until 288–9, so that in the meantime the usurper had no rival in the Channel. His hold on the coastal ports and their hinterland could thus have begun in 286 and lasted until 293, when the newly appointed Caesar, Constantius, was able to seize Boulogne, the only major setback suffered by Carausius and one which may have led to his downfall at the hands of his own finance officer Allectus.

Virtually nothing is known of changes made to the military dispositions in the north and west in Carausius' reign, and probably there was no need for innovation there. It was, after all, the south-eastern coasts that now bulked large in the minds of military men, not the northern frontier. We cannot arrive at a satisfactory assessment of a man and his policies from the panegyrics delivered in honour of his opponents and from the legends on his own coinage. The usurpation of Carausius must be examined from the standpoint of those who had just observed two decades of tumult and devastation. In 286 the rule of Diocletian and Maximian, themselves usurpers, had not yet been tried and no one could have believed that the respite gained from barbarian invasion and internal disorder would be anything other than brief. Nor did the Carausian revolt come out of the blue; rather it followed a disturbed period in the reign of Probus. We are justified in asking why the provinces of Britain were so intent on following their own path at this time.

It has already been remarked that one of the most interesting features of Carausius' seizure of power is the fact that the whole island apparently passed under his control without disturbance, raising the suspicion that the recent recovery by Rome of the western provinces, and notably of Gaul, was viewed with something less than favour by Romano-British officers and *curiales*. There was one very clear reason why Romano- Britons may have leaned towards separatism in the late third century. Paradoxically, the provinces which lay on the furthest edge of the world were now among the most secure and stable in the west. This had taken more than two centuries to achieve, but Britain was now a productive as well as a peaceful island. Goods were being exported to the continent: grain and wool as well as metals. The agricultural wealth of Britain was shortly to figure in Imperial panegyrics. Private fortunes based on land were being made and palatial villas were beginning to appear. The land-owning interest was entering upon the sort of affluence which its peers in other provinces had known in the Antonine peace, and there are clear signs that in Britain the number of well-to-do landowners, as compared with those who were extremely wealthy, was relatively high. These were the very men on whom the increasing impositions of the State fell: the *annona* and other military requisitions, the full range of taxation, the *aurum coronarium*, and behind all these the municipal *munera* and the strait-jacket of the class into which men were born. Separation from Rome did not mean the abolition of all such burdens, but a largely self-sufficient island could now expect to do much better on its own.

Carausius was brought down in 293 by his own financial officer, Allectus, about whose earlier life and character nothing is known. His reign is no better recorded. In the summer or autumn of 293 he brought about the murder of his master, and the plot may have prospered partly because Carausius' personal standing had been damaged by the loss of Boulogne a little earlier. When we next hear of Allectus in 296, he was facing crisis as the western Caesar, Constantius, mounted a naval expedition against Britain. The attack was skilfully delivered by a fleet organized in two divisions, Constantius himself commanding one squadron based at Boulogne and intended for South- eastern Britain and the Thames estuary, the other sailing under the praetorian prefect, Asclepiodotus, from the Seine estuary and making for a landfall behind the Isle of Wight.

Things went wrong for Allectus from the beginning. He seems to have had intelligence of Asclepiodotus' movements, for his own fleet was waiting for him off the Isle of Wight. But a mist allowed the invader to slip through and land. Allectus, caught unawares, now tried to fall back towards London for which the fleet of Constantius was making. But that fleet had failed to reach its objective and Constantius himself had been forced to return to Boulogne. All depended on the army of Asclepiodotus which advanced, presumably, on London from its landfall, having burnt its ships behind it. Allectus met the invaders, perhaps on the road from Chichester to London and was soundly defeated, losing his life in the battle. He had relied largely upon his Germanic troops who may not have been sufficiently well organized to face the experienced units from Gaul. The survivors of Allectus' forces withdrew towards London but were beaten to it by some of Constantius' vessels which had at last managed to get across the Channel. Shortly, Constantius himself entered the capital, to be received in triumph by a grateful citizenry, as the official sources have it. In the shower of accolades, even the city of London itself may have earned a new title, *Caesarea*. Just as we can form no real view of the character of Allectus' regime, so we cannot know how widely, if at all, Constantius was regarded in Britain as *redditor lucis aeternae*. The recovery of Britain in 296 effectively closed this turbulent chapter in the history of the West.

The defence of Britain from the sea had been an increasing preoccupation in the third century and the usurpation of Carausius had thrown the matter into high relief. Further forts were constructed on the south-eastern coasts,[3] beginning with a small earthwork thrown up around the remains of the triumphal *quadrifons* at Richborough. This dates from shortly after 250. In the following decades, and beginning probably in the 270s, a remarkable series of forts was built, the architecture of which reflects the major changes which were being registered in Roman tactics. Like the new urban defences of Gaul, Spain and Italy, these forts are distinguished by their high and powerful walls, external towers at the angles and on the curtain, and strongly protected gates. A new age of fortification had begun. Among these forts, Richborough has the earliest certain date of foundation: not long after 270. Others at Portchester, Lympne, Dover and Burgh Castle may date from the same decade or shortly afterwards. Bradwell and the lost fort of Walton Castle have produced no reliable evidence of date. Added to the earlier forts at Brancaster, Dover and Reculver, these forts formed a powerful shield for the coasts from the Wash to the harbours sheltered by the Isle of Wight, especially close protection being given to the approaches to the Thames estuary. Attempts to link this series of forts with a single commander or emperor do not carry complete conviction. Carausius' reign is too late for Richborough and probably other forts. Probus (270–82), whose work on the Rhine frontier can be dimly discerned, is a more likely choice on grounds of date, but as someone who developed the scheme of work rather than instigated it. It is most likely that work on the forts continued for several years or even a decade or two. Pevensey may not have been built until after 330, though the evidence is not conclusive.

Many problems surround these fortifications, chiefly concerning their garrisons and how they were intended to operate. Epigraphic evidence for the original garrisons is very slight and excavation within the forts has revealed little in the way of systematic lay-out of buildings; in some cases (e.g. Portchester and Richborough) there were scarcely any late-third century buildings at all. Slight traces of rectangular timber structures which may have served as barracks have been noted at Richborough, Pevensey and Portchester, but they can give no help in determining the character of the units in garrison. To some extent the much looser planning inside these coastal forts reflects the fact that soldiers could now reside *en famille* outside the walls, but even so the lack of administrative buildings and *horrea* is somewhat surprising. Firm evidence for the garrisons is not available until it is provided by the early fifth century *Notitia Dignitatum*, a source which obviously must be taken to include rearrangements of the fourth century, and thus to be no sound guide to dispositions in the late third. Indeed, several of the units listed by the *Notitia* on the south-eastern coasts did not come into being until the fourth century. Only epigraphic evidence will help with this problem.[4]

The development of the *Litus Saxonicum* as a separate and unified command belongs to the fourth century, but already by 280 it will have been obvious that effective defence against Germanic raiders, who took no account of provincial boundaries, could only be maintained by a co-ordinated scheme. Before Diocletian's reorganization of the British provinces at the end of the century, the coastal forts lay within the province of *Britannia Superior* and presumably came under the charge of its governor. There was then no need for the creation of a distinct command. There is no evidence that the coastal command was placed under an independent officer at least before Constantius recovered Britain, and it may have occurred later still.

The relations between the fleet operating in the Channel and the North Sea and the coastal forts were plainly close. Most of the forts lay on excellent harbours or sheltered estuaries and an elementary system of scout-vessels could easily have linked neighbouring forts. The listing of forts in the *Notitia* suggests a system of pairing between adjacent forts, though whether this reveals a late third century expedient is uncertain.

The condition of the northern frontier when Britain was recovered by Constantius can only have been poor. The previous half century or more had seen little in the way of repairs, and the ruinous state of the principal buildings in the fort of Birdoswald[5] may well have been repeated elsewhere. Whether there had been damage due to enemy invasion from the north is something about which there can only be speculation, but it does not appear on present evidence as though there was a major disaster on Hadrian's Wall in 296. The date for long appeared to mark the end of a long period of occupation on the

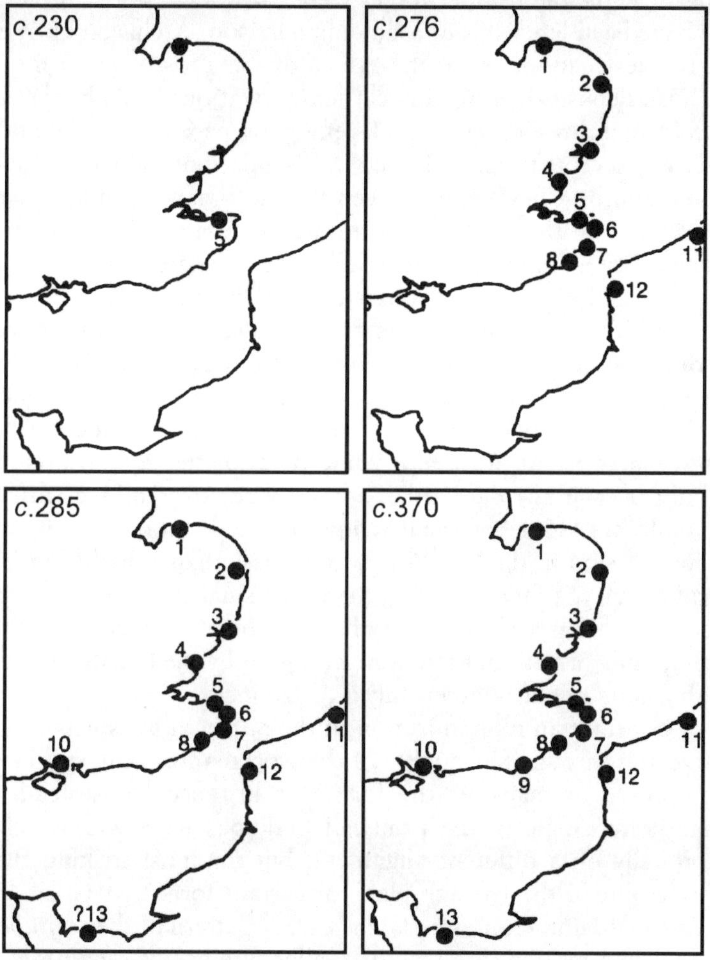

1. Brancaster. 2. Burgh Castle. 3. Walton Castle. 4. Bradwell. 5. Reculver. 6. Richborough. 7. Dover. 8. Lympne. 9. Pevensey. 10. Portchester. 11. Oudenburg. 12. Boulogne. 13. Port-en-Bessin.

Figure 29 The development of coastal defences from the late third century.

Wall, but there is increasing doubt as to whether it is archaeologically detectable. It is quite possible, as has long been argued, that Allectus removed some of the Wall garrison to face the invading forces of Constantius, but it does not necessarily follow that as a result the frontier was swamped by a wave of barbarians. The third century peace in the north had been won as much by diplomacy as by military strength, and appropriate measures will have been taken to maintain the peace while the frontier forces were elsewhere. Nor will the Wall itself have been left without a holding garrison. Archaeological evidence for destruction, as for the events of the 190s, is far from clear cut. Burnt deposits identified in earlier excavations could be the result of accidental fires or even of levelling preparatory to rebuilding. Moreover, several forts, including Wallsend, South Shields, Rudchester and Halton Chesters, have been shown to have been in a state of dilapidation by the 290s as the result of decay rather than wilful damage; they were extensively restored at this date. This restoration also embraced many, perhaps most, of the Pennine forts.

Several Wall forts had their garrisons scaled down in the course of the third century; buildings were abandoned, even taken down. Inscriptions at several refer to rebuilding after a phase of dereliction and this is well supported by excavated evidence at Rudchester and Halton Chesters. At Wallsend, while parts of the central area were not built over at any date, other spaces were covered by a variety of new buildings, some of them temporary. The total area for troop accommodation in the later fort was far less than it had been in the second century, a fact reflecting the much smaller size of later units. Whereas an infantry cohort numbered about 450 men in the early Empire, units of half that size were common by the late third century. Cavalry units might number only 150 troopers.

The Constantian reorganization of the northern forts was comprehensive and careful. The quality of the workmanship can still be seen and admired at many of the forts, for instance Housesteads and Chesterholm. Some of the principal buildings were wholly rebuilt, occasionally on a different alignment, but the most striking change was wrought in the barrack-plans of certain forts.[6] At Great Chesters, Wallsend and Housesteads, the earlier pattern of the *contubernia* was replaced by one in which a smaller number of separate chambers, with narrow alleys between them, occupied the former quarters of the men. This suggests a radical alteration in the internal organization of the centuries, and further study of these early fourth-century barracks should throw more light on fundamental changes to the auxiliary units at this date. So far as our information at present goes, it suggests that the regiment had been reduced in size, perhaps because the supply of recruits was falling off, but possibly also because a somewhat smaller unit could be equally effective in the fairly stable condition of the northern frontier at the time.

Though in the main the work of Constantius Caesar in Northern Britain consisted of restoration, it was not long before campaigning far to the north was required. Constantius had left Britain in 297. When he returned, in 305 or 306, he came as Augustus and was

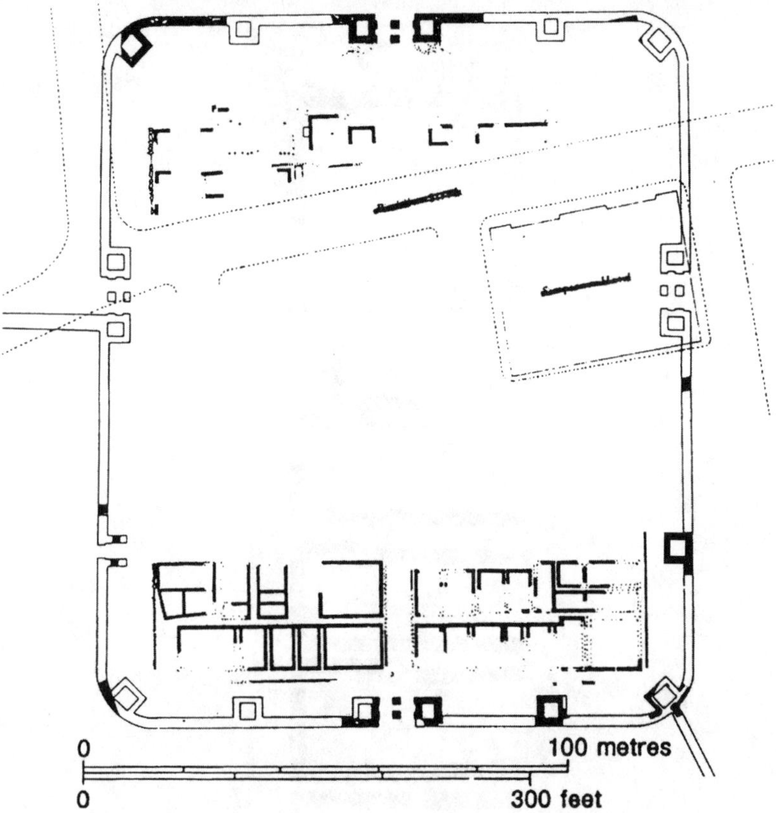

Figure 30 Wallsend in the fourth century.

accompanied by his twenty-year-old son Constantine, who had sped from virtual detention with Galerius to reach his father's expedition just before it left Boulogne. The occasion for a major campaign against the Picts is not recorded, but the fact that the expedition was led by the ailing Augustus himself reveals how serious the threat was felt to be. The federation of the Picts had emerged in the later third century, receiving their first mention in Roman sources in 297. Their territory lay in the fertile area of eastern Scotland north of the isthmus, that same region which had occupied the attentions of earlier Roman commanders, but they may have begun to raid far to the south. By the summer, Constantius had penetrated far into Scotland and won a major victory. Shortly afterwards, he died at York.

A measure commonly attributed to Constantius, though its final form is probably the work of his son, is the siting of mobile forces on the main roads leading from York to Hadrian's Wall. One of these

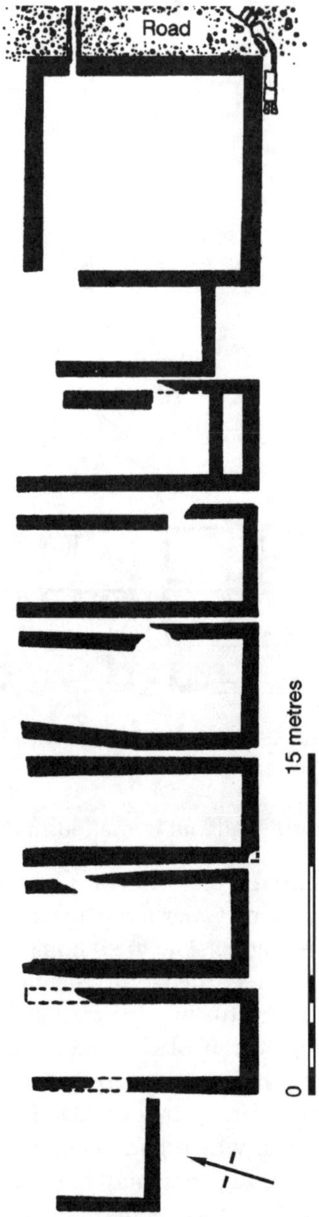

Figure 31 An early fourth century barrack at Housesteads (Northumberland).

units is designated *Crispiani*, derived from the name of Crispus Caesar (317–26). Constantine himself took the title *Britannicus Maximus* in 315, perhaps as a result of further operations beyond the frontier. The new dispositions behind the Wall also involved the removal of many units which had been attested there earlier in the third century, as well as the construction of certain forts, at Newton Kyme, Elslack, and perhaps Piercebridge, probably for large cavalry vexillations which might range widely. The date at which these forts were first built is not certain, but the deployment of mobile forces to the rear of the frontier is fully in keeping with early fourth-century practice, and the introduction of the system may provisionally be dated to the period immediately following 306.

Attention was also paid to the two northern legionary bases at Chester and York, either by Constantine or by his immediate predecessors. The defences at Chester were largely rebuilt, using many inscribed and sculptured stones from nearby cemeteries. But the most dramatic transformation was reserved for the York fortress. The riverside front was embellished with eight massive polygonal towers, giving the fortress a dignity unmatched on other frontiers. The legionary base at Caerleon was occupied with a reduced garrison from the mid-third century. There was restoration of some buildings *c.* 275 but before 300 demolition of certain central structures was taking place. There is no sign of military use after this, though occupation of some kind continued within the walls. The subsequent history of *Legio II Augusta* is obscure but the unit survived. In the *Notitia Dignitatum* it is located at Richborough. Elsewhere in Wales, the earlier relaxation of direct military control was not significantly reversed. The large number of Carausian and Allectan coinhoards in Wales may point to unrest in the period 286–96, though they might also be explained as an uncertain reaction to the Constantian victory. A fort of the new type was sited at Cardiff, probably to serve as a stores-base for a fleet in the Bristol Channel; but no other new measures are known to have been taken. The forts at Caernarvon, Forden Gaer, and possibly Leintwardine retained garrisons and there are traces of unspecified occupation at Caersws, Castell Collen and Brecon. At Caernarvon the garrison was increased at the end of the third century, possibly in connection with an enhanced administrative role for the fort.

Constantine and later

On the death of Constantius, the military units at York hailed Constantine as Augustus, and such was the power of the army then in

Britain that Galerius was compelled to recognize him, though for the moment as Caesar only. The role played in the affair at York by the Alamannic chieftain Crocus, who had come to Britain in the entourage of Constantius, was of major importance – one of the earliest cases of decisive intervention in affairs of state by a barbarian leader. Crocus and his men formed part of the army which had just taken part in the campaign against the Picts, and we may not assume that the chieftain was awarded land on which to settle in Britain. That kind of treatment belongs to a much later time in the relations between Rome and the barbarians. The incident is of some historical importance in revealing the growing importance of barbarian leaders in the politics of power at the same time as barbarian troops were coming to form a larger proportion of the Roman army.

Constantine could not remain long in Britain after his elevation, no more than a few months, and there was little time for anything other than the consolidation of Constantius' measures in the north and the repair of major roads. Coins struck by the London mint with the reverse type ADVENTUS AVG have been taken to suggest that the emperor returned to Britain between 310 and 312 and again in 314 but the point is not proven.[7] A salutation as *Britannicus Maximus* in 315 implies that some military success had been won but no details are known. The victory could easily have been achieved by one of the British *praesides*. History records nothing for the next quarter of a century; to discover how the provinces as a whole were faring we must turn to archaeology and numismatics.

After Diocletian's currency reform, the coinage was based principally upon a fine gold coin and silvered bronze *folles*. Little silver was actually issued for the following thirty years, though the denomination theoretically still existed. The *follis* coinage was readily accepted in Britain, and the coin is well represented in British hoards and site-finds. In the virtual absence of silver, the *follis* was directly related to the gold at a value far above its worth, inevitably leading to inflation of prices and a consequent devaluation of the silvered bronze currency. Hence the fairly common hoards of *folles* dating from the early fourth century and the steady fall in weight and silver content of these coins from about 10gm to only about 2.5gm by the 320s. Thereafter the deterioration was still more rapid. In such a situation it was inevitable that small coins of the late third century should continue to circulate in some numbers.

Inflation was one of the most serious evils which faced the Romano-Britons in the first decades of the fourth century. More and more evidence of hoarding during Constantine's reign testifies to a remorseless spiral as an increasingly base coinage was continually augmented by still more from the mint, issued initially as pay, without any systematic withdrawals from circulation or other controls, save a periodic reform of the coinage. Nothing illustrates more clearly the almost total lack of official direction in financial affairs.

At the beginning of his reign, Constantine issued a new gold coin, the *solidus*, at 72 to the pound of gold, and this denomination (and its subdivisions) remained in being throughout the century. This was the only stable element in the currency. Silver played a minor role until mid-century, and the bulk of the coinage consisted of small copper pieces tariffed in *denarii*. It is in these that the pace of inflation can be measured, both in the abundant site-finds and in the Egyptian papyri: in 324, 4500 *denarii* to the *solidus*, in 337, 275,000. The mint of London which had been established by Carausius continued to operate until 326. Thereafter, the bulk of Romano-British coinage came from Trier, Lyon and the other western mints.

That British landowners were able to bear the brunt of economic ills fairly well is evident from the large number of villas which entered their most comfortable days at this time. The geographical spread is wide, from the Vale of York to the Devon coast, from the Welsh borders to Kent, and the list includes sites founded anew as well as long-established estates. For reasons that are still obscure, many landowners in the Cotswolds were able to build magnificent houses, no doubt set within spacious grounds, and adorn their interiors with fine mosaics and wall paintings. In all parts of Southern Britain the vogue was for figured mosaics, often alive with scenes from Graeco-Roman mythology but occasionally hinting at more serious or more sophisticated tastes, as in the Christian pavements at Hinton St Mary and Frampton, and in the Gnostic symbolism of the Brading mosaics. Britain's fourth-century wealth was no sudden flowering but followed the steady growth of the previous hundred years. Those responsible, the estate proprietors, were more like fifteenth-century squires than eighteenth-century nobles, but their contribution to the *apogee* of Romano-British culture is not the less profound for that.

It would be remarkable if this prosperity on the land were not reflected in the cities and towns, though the evidence here is not as clear as one could wish, not least because the later levels of Roman towns have rarely been studied with the attention they deserve. The major public buildings in the cities were now two centuries old, so that substantial repair, or even radical rebuilding, would not be surprising. The baths at Silchester were extensively repaired in the 320s, while at Cirencester the forum and basilica underwent alteration, perhaps in connection with the elevation of the place to the rank of a provincial capital. The forum at Caister-by-Norwich was rebuilt about 300 after a century of ruin. No cases of new public buildings are known to date from these years. The expansive age of private benefaction was over.

In the other side of the balance, there are cases of decrepitude and ruin. The great basilica at London was deliberately demolished in the early fourth century. The Wroxeter forum, initially destroyed before 300 by a major fire, was never rebuilt, its site being thereafter used for domestic and commercial purposes. A nearby temple was also demolished at this date and by the mid-fourth century the market-hall and the public baths were also out of use. At Winchester the forum area and adjacent buildings seem to have been run down, if not become actually derelict, during the fourth century and some of the major streets went out of use. Whichever particular causes may lie behind these instances of decay, there is a general reason why leading members of the civil order should be reluctant to spend money on public amenities. Their enforced obligations to the State were now pressing as never before and, provided the commercial and administrative functions of the urban communities were adequately maintained, it is unlikely that anyone was much troubled about the level of civic culture. The public good was not a major preoccupation of the late Roman Empire.

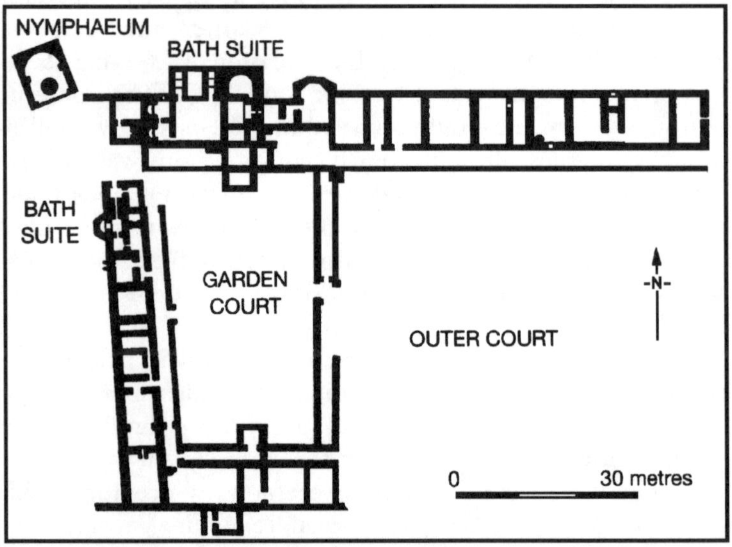

Figure 32 The early fourth century villa at Chedworth (Gloucestershire).

Moreover, the *curiales* had other outlets for their spare capital, a considerable number of them choosing to build large town-houses as well as enlarging their rural homes. Most of the larger houses at Silchester, Cirencester, *Verulamium* and Caerwent date from after 300, and the standard of comfort in the best of these compares well with those of the villas. Though bath-suites were rare, the crafts of the painter and the mosaicist were again given scope. It is unfortunate that so little is known of urban housing at all levels and in all aspects. Study of ancillary buildings would be particularly rewarding as it would throw light on the, presumably close, relations between the owners of these dwellings and the agricultural economy of the surrounding region, and on the activity of craftsmen in many trades. There are clear indications that the earlier fourth century saw a marked advance in growth of many trades, stimulated no doubt by the burgeoning of agriculture, and in this the cities and the lesser towns took a major part. Shops and workshops continued to figure prominently in fourth-century cities, in many cases, one may suspect, thereby augmenting the wealth of individual landowners either through rents or through direct ownership. The crafts and minor industries were especially vigorous in the minor towns, which, being closely linked with their agricultural hinterland, now enjoyed their heyday, the majority reaching their greatest extent. The larger houses in these townships appear to date from these decades, and it is a reasonable inference that the growth of the settlements owed more to the influence of men of substance dwelling close by than to the operation of 'natural' economic causes. Apart from the customary range of crafts, a smaller number of towns had now developed into major centres of industry. *Durobrivae* had grown steadily during the previous century partly through its pottery industry, partly through metal- working. It is probable that by this date it had become the *chef-lieu* of a new *civitas* in the Nene valley. Weston-under-Penyard had long been connected with iron-extraction in the Forest of Dean, Charterhouse with the lead and silver of the Mendips. The salt-deposits of Droitwich remained important throughout the Roman period and later passed into Anglo-Saxon royal possession. At many other towns craftsmen in metal and pottery flourished as never before. When *vici* prospered in this way it is probable that they achieved a measure of independence from the parent *civitas*. This meant that the old cities lost control of some of their land and other property, and there might be further alienation of land from the administration of cities due to the patronage of private landowners. A law of Aurelian had made the entire civil order responsible for the taxes due on estates which had been abandoned by their members. If an *ordo* would not, or could not, resume the burden, the land was to be distributed among the neighbouring *vici* and private estates.

The life enjoyed by the landowning society of fourth- century Britain did not differ in its essential tenor from that of fifth-century Gaul, so vividly recreated in the correspondence of Sidonius. It was easy, outwardly secure, somewhat artificial and based upon a relatively small number of families. In that sense it was precarious, and in another and more profound sense it was also far from stable. So far as can be judged from its art and its buildings, the intellectual inspiration of this society was derived from far-off lands and days. The imagery and symbolism which confronted the Romano-Briton in daily life were largely those of pagan mythology. There seems to have been little that was British, or even more generally Celtic, in the intellectual and spiritual life of the ruling oligarchy. How deeply men's minds were affected by that ancient mythology is not to be measured against an objective standard, but little intellectual satisfaction was generated by the deeds of gods and heroes. There was a fundamental weakness here which may have helped to undermine the most significant group in society in later days. Not only was the oligarchy narrowly based, it had few links with the ranks below it: the dependent peasantry, the craftsmen and the *coloni*. The real void in Romano-British society continued to be the absence of educated and independent townsmen who might have provided a secure base for the social order against the shocks of the next century. In other provinces, the Christian Church provided a focal point for such a social group.

From Constantine's reign Britain was part of a Christian Empire, but even until well after the Peace of the Church the progress of Christianity in the provinces can be measured only very imprecisely. An episcopate based on cities had certainly evolved by the time of the Council of Arles in 314, at which three British bishops, a priest and a deacon were present. Whether or not the organization of an episcopate had long preceded that event is quite unknown. Though small Christian communities were probably in existence somewhat earlier, it is unlikely that a fully developed episcopate came into being much before the fourth century. It is unknown how and when Christianity was introduced into Britain. The Faith may have been spread along similar routes and by similar means to those followed by such eastern cults as Jupiter Dolichenus, Isis and Mithras, and we should thus expect Christian adherents to be discovered in the larger ports, the cities, legionary bases and on the frontiers. As yet this is not the case, but it must be remembered that before Constantine's reign traces of their presence are bound to be scarce and often discreetly veiled. The

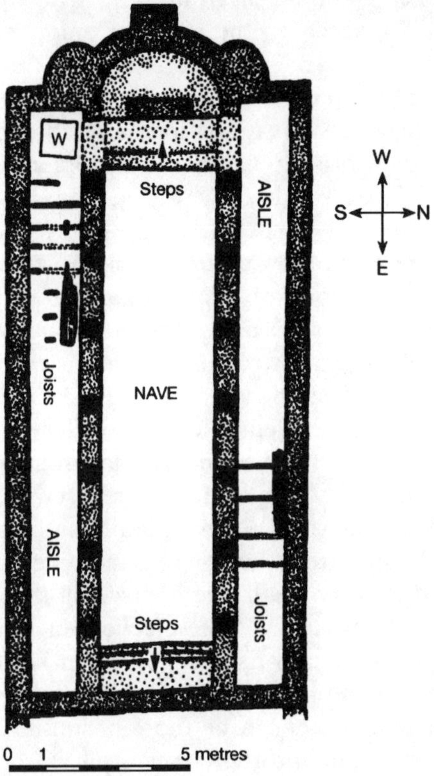

Figure 33 The temple of Mithras at London, late third/early fourth century.

siting of Jewish communities was often an important influence on the distribution of early Christian groups and such Jewish communities were scarce in the north-western provinces. The presence of an early Romano-British martyr with a Jewish name, Aaron of Caerleon, is an interesting hint, though no more, of a Jewish element among early fourth century Christians in the island.

The earliest literary references to Christianity in Britain, by Tertullian and Origen in the early third century, carry more than a hint of optimistic exaggeration and the remainder of the century produces no testimony to a highly organized and vigorous Church in the island. The martyrdom of the soldier Alban probably did occur before the persecution of the years 303–12, since Constantius was exonerated by his contemporaries from any share in that episode. But ingenious arguments advanced for dating the death of Alban to the years 208–9 are without substantive support. The persecutions in mid-century under Trajan Decius and Valerian are equally plausible occasions. Archaeology adds nothing to the virtually empty canvas. Even the much-quoted word-square from Cirencester (now matched by another from Manchester) is more likely to belong to the world of magic than to the Christian faith. In the third century, then, it is improbable that the Christian Church was more influential in Britain than the eastern mystery cults. Away from the major cosmopolitan centres it may have left no mark at all.[8]

Not until the reign of Constantine was Christian influence more widely spread. From about 330, large churches began to appear in the western provinces in response to the marked growth in Christian communities. In Britain, no structure has yet been revealed which is comparable with the fine churches of Trier, Aquileia, Bordeaux or Cologne. A large basilica recently located on Tower Hill in the eastern area of *Londinium* is most probably a late fourth century church, possibly of the time of Magnus Maximus. Elsewhere, certain intramural churches are elusive. A small building near the forum at Silchester has its supporters, but there is nothing specifically Christian about it and its very small size is puzzling if this was the main church in the city.[9] It could well be a *schola* or other meeting-hall. The site of a Roman church has been claimed within the forum at Lincoln, though this is unproven. Extra-mural churches, associated with cemeteries, would seem to be more promising, given their frequency in northern Gaul and the German provinces. The most convincing example in Britain has been identified outside the walls of *Camulodunum* amid late Roman graves, while others have been suggested at *Verulamium* and Canterbury. As for shrines associated with martyrs and other distinguished dead, Britain has little to show. The shrine of St Alban, on the hill above *Verulamium*, is usually taken to be a late Roman foundation and this is at least highly likely. But if this was so, why did the medieval abbey not claim continuous descent from the most famous British martyr? Not only in cities are traces of Christian structures scarce. Military sites too have produced little evidence for Christian observance. The most convincing installations are a stone baptistery and associated timber building within the fort of Richborough. An apsed stone platform at Housesteads has been proposed as the base of a church, but without supporting evidence. The scarcity of intra- mural churches is probably more apparent than real. Existing public buildings could well have been utilized as churches without necessarily leaving behind any trace that they had been so used.

That some Christian communities of Constantine's day were reasonably wealthy was startlingly demonstrated in 1975 by the discovery of a cache of silver liturgical vessels at *Durobrivae*, a find which throws unexpected light on the connections and outlook of Romano-British Christians in the earlier fourth century. The treasure is the earliest collection of early Christian silver so far known from any part of the Roman Empire, having been buried before 350.[10] Though it does not demonstrate the existence of a church at *Durobrivae*, it does reveal the possibility of contacts between the Church in Britain and the wider Christian world. For the treasure contains vessels which are inscribed with phrases and lines of verse which are reminiscent of eastern usage, along with other objects which bear Chi-Rho monograms of an eastern type. How these found their way to Britain remains a matter for conjecture and their presence is a reminder of how imperfect our knowledge is. The discovery of the *Durobrivae* treasure is probably the most important yet made for Romano-British Christianity. The three British bishops who were compelled by poverty to accept Constantius II's offer of travelling expenses to cover their journey home after the Council of Ariminum in 359 were perhaps not true representatives of all the Christian communities in Britain.

That some members of the landed class were devout Christians has been shown in the most spectacular fashion on certain of their country estates. At the Lullingstone villa, part of the house was adapted into a private chapel or house-church in the mid-fourth century, its walls being adorned with splendid frescoes showing worshippers in the 'orans' attitude of prayer.[11] At about the same time, the Hinton St Mary villa was provided with a two-roomed chapel floored by magnificent mosaics depicting Bellerophon and the chimaera (in the antechamber) and a portrait of Christ in serene majesty (in the main room) – the earliest representation of Christ so far known in Britain.[12] Nearby, the villas at Frampton and Fifehead Neville possessed mosaics which may have been produced by the same craftsmen responsible for the Hinton St Mary mosaics, and that at Frampton at least may also have lain within a devotional chamber. Rather lower in the social scale, there are other indications of the rural faithful in a series of leaden tanks ornamented with the Chi-Rho monogram and plainly intended for ritual use, probably in baptism.

It is steadily becoming easier to appreciate the character of Romano-British Christianity, at least in the educated circles where it made its most significant impact. The discoveries at Lullingstone, Hinton St Mary and *Durobrivae* reveal that British Christians were tapping the mainstream of western art and ideas in the fourth century. There is nothing of the backwoods about the figures in the

Figure 34 The possible church at Silchester.

Lullingstone frieze, or in the grave and moving portrait of Christ at Hinton St Mary. In few works of art did Roman Britain come closer to the best in the intellectual life of the western Empire and though the experience was brief it must be counted as the highest point attained by Roman culture in Britain.

As in many other parts of the Empire, the attractions of paganism were still potent, especially in the remoter countryside. A considerable number of rural shrines continued to attract devotees in the fourth century, and later, in certain cases perhaps because they were the sites of fairs or folk-moots. Some pagan temples were substantially rebuilt well after 300 and a small number were constructed *de novo* in the later decades of the century, including the remarkable shrine at Lydney and the hill-top temple at Maiden Castle. Some rural shrines continued in use into the fifth century and beyond, as at Pagan's Hill (Somerset) and Uley (Gloucestershire). At Uley it may be that the site was turned over to Christian worship in or after the fifth century.[13] In vain had Constans and Constantius II decreed the closure of all pagan shrines. Less is known about urban temples in the fourth century. That of Mithras in London was forced to close early in the century, but it came back into use later. The theatre and temple at *Verulamium* fell into decay after 350 and a similar fate may have accounted for many other urban shrines. Now and again, a prominent official might give support to the old gods, as did L. Septimius, a governor of *Britannia Prima*, when he restored a Jupiter column at Cirencester and lauded the ancient religion.[14] But by and large, rural Celtic paganism seems to have been much more tenacious than its urban counterpart. Britain was a Christian diocese but we can never measure with any precision what proportion of her population accepted the faith of Christ or appreciated what it entailed. No doubt there were many families, like that of St Augustine, which were divided in their religious loyalties.

No single find illustrates better the religious and cultural mix of Britain in the late fourth century than the hoard of jewellery and silver objects found at Thetford (Norfolk).[15] This unusual collection was associated with the cult of the minor Italian nature deity Faunus and was possibly specially commissioned for a shrine to him. Precisely how this obscure cult was transported to Britain is beyond knowing, but the private devotion of an official is the likeliest medium. Finds like the Thetford and *Durobrivae* hoards are salutary reminders of how imperfect is our knowledge of the religious life of Britain in the spiritual turbulence of the late Roman world. They may not tell us much about the religious experience and preferences of the mass of the population, but they do reveal the many and various strands in the religious life of the provinces. Not for nothing did the inscriber of a fourth century curse-tablet at Bath ensure comprehensive coverage by including Christian and pagan in the categories of those he cursed.

It was not until the middle of the century that the threat of serious warfare is again reported to have disturbed the peace. Early in 343 the western Augustus, Constans, paid an exceptional winter visit to Britain. A part of the field army seems to have accompanied the emperor under the command of the *comes* Gratian, so that serious campaigning was in prospect. The details are entirely lost to us and we cannot be certain whether it was against Saxon sea-raiders or northern Picts and Scotti that Constans made his name.[16]

The seizure of power by Magnentius in 350 and its aftermath again brought Britain to the attention of Ammianus Marcellinus, our only source for these decades. The usurper may himself have been of British descent. The island was not directly involved in the events of Magnentius' short rule, except that it probably supplied troops for the usurper's army which fought and suffered heavy defeat at Mursa in 351. Magnentius was able to hold on to power in the west until 353, and it was immediately following his death that Britain suffered the full effects of the episode. Severe reprisals were taken against Magnentian supporters, under the direction of an agent of Constantius II, a certain Paul, and his soubriquet *Catena* – 'the chain' – was entirely appropriate for one who dragged men down to destruction. Martinus, the *Vicarius* of Britain, did what he could to ward off the worst excesses of Paul but the position was hopeless. Finding himself accused, Martinus attempted to kill Paul with his own hands but, failing, had no choice but to turn his sword against himself. The career of Paul brought down not only British officers who had backed Magnentius but many others. Many were hailed off to Constantius' court, there to face torture from which the only release was either exile or death. This is reported by a sober historian, and there is no reason to suspect that Ammianus has exaggerated in describing these miserable events. The impact on Britain must have been serious, though there are few outward signs of tumult in our archaeological sources.

Magnentius' monetary policy seems fairly well suited to the currency problems of the day. About mid-century the volume of currency in circulation seems to have been falling, now that the massive coinages of the late reign of Constantine were ageing and had not been replaced by issues of anything like comparable volume. Magnentius issued a substantial series of large *folles* from the Gaulish mints, much heavier than those of his immediate predecessors, and these entered Britain in considerable numbers. But the increase in the common currency did not satisfy the need for small denominations and locally produced copies abounded in the years after 350. Among these local issues is a small group, struck between 355 and 358, which bears the legend CARAUSIUS; this seemingly attests either continuing admiration for the earlier usurper or some obscure and local pretender. The coins are very scarce and no other source throws light on the matter, whether it be a case of commemoration or usurpation.

The barbarian enemies of Roman Britain were steadily growing in strength and ambition.[17] The northern peoples, Picti and Scotti, struck a serious blow in 360 when they abandoned agreements made earlier and began to ravage the lands close to the frontier. The Caesar Julian felt he could not himself lead an army into Britain, as the Alamanni at that time were threatening Gaul, and the *magister militum* Lupicinus was sent to the island in his place, together with a strong force of four units of the field army. Lupicinus was an arrogant and cruel man, but a competent soldier. The outcome of his activities is not known, but as he was soon back in Gaul some success was clearly gained. The respite for the British garrison was brief. Five years later we hear ominously of attacks by all the barbarian peoples: Picti, Scotti, Attacotti and Saxons. In 367 the main blow fell. For the first time, the separate barbarian groups combined in a brief alliance and attacked the island from all quarters; the confusion they caused was compounded by the treachery of the *arcani* on the northern frontier. The *Comes Litoris Saxonici* was killed and the *dux Britanniarum* cut off: the army in Britain was indeed at its lowest ebb. For several decades, whenever really serious campaigning was in prospect, field army units were transferred from Gaul, usually under a senior commander. Now in 367, the *arcani* supplied military intelligence to the barbarians in exchange for bribes, while behind the frontier indiscipline was rife as bands of deserters roamed the countryside at will. Such a breakdown in authority had probably never before occurred in Roman Britain, and the storm broke as the emperor, Valentinian, was preparing to deal with the Alamanni in North-eastern Gaul. Choice of a commander for the emergency in Britain fell first on Severus, the *comes domesticorum* and later on Jovinus, the *magister equitum*. Each made little headway, perhaps because of a shortage of high grade troops. Late in 367, with Britain still in confusion, the command was given to the *comes rei militaris*, Theodosius, father of the later emperor of the same name, and once again a strong contingent of the field army was put at his disposal.

When we come to assess Theodosius' success in Britain, we are bound to take into account one important fact relating to our source for the period. Ammianus wrote his history in the reign of the son of this man and it is no coincidence that of all the public men of the period the elder Theodosius is the only one to enjoy the historian's unstinted praise, even to the extent of being classed with Pompey, Camillus and Corbulo. Although Theodosius certainly was an able general, one may doubt whether he can take his place in such company; there is some evidence from his conduct of earlier campaigns in Africa that his strategic sense was less than sound and that his discipline was exceptionally fierce. Unfortunately, Ammianus gives only a brief account of the British campaigns of 367–8 which is dominated by the figure of the general, with the conduct of affairs related in the sketchiest way.

Theodosius first had to clear raiding groups from the south-east and secure London. The campaign season was already advanced and there was no time for anything more ambitious. The following winter could be devoted to recovering deserters and making plans for the main operation which still faced him, the enemy armies being still undefeated in the field.[18] The campaign of 368 was not an easy one, and Theodosius felt the need for new officers of proven skill at the highest level. Dulcitius was sent to him as the new *dux Britanniarum*, and the steady and dependable Civilis took over as the *Vicarius* of the praetorian prefect of Gaul. But we hear nothing of any part taken in the proceedings by these men. It was Theodosius who gathered the army together, led it forth from London, laid ambushes for the, by now, unwary barbarian bands, and himself shared in the danger of fighting off the various invading forces. Ammianus' account is brief and infuriatingly vague. Cities and military posts had been attacked, seemingly after a long period of peace, but no indication is given of where these lay. The impression conveyed by the historian is of widespread damage to the major settlements of the province, calling for a large-scale programme of restoration. Theodosius thus appears in the pages of Ammianus as both soldier and saviour, the man who built as well as the man who conquered.

There must be a suspicion that the picture has been painted so as to flatter the *comes*. We must accept that the disaster in Britain was severe. But if there had been serious damage to cities and towns, there should be some trace in the archaeological record. And yet there is virtually nothing of this, despite fairly extensive examination of the late levels of urban sites. Certain convincing signs of destruction have been recovered from a number of villa sites in the South-west and in the West country,[19] though not all of these need date from 367–8 or be the result of barbarian invasion. Odder still, there is no notable concentration of coin-hoarding late in the 360s compared with the years immediately before and after. It is then no exaggeration to say that, without the text of Ammianus, archaeology on its own would not have pointed to the late 360s as a time of upheaval and destruction in the provinces at large. Even on the northern frontier the evidence for a major barbarian break-through attended by destruction of forts is very meagre. Several Wall forts recently excavated show no sign of damage, and earlier observations of shattered buildings later extensively repaired are explicable in terms of a radical rebuilding under Theodosius rather than hostile action. That there was a drastic rebuilding of the frontier and its hinterland after 368 is beyond question. Most, if not all, of the Wall forts were substantially repaired or reconstructed at this time and two forts which had lain unused for many years, Halton Chesters and Rudchester, were brought back into commission. Forts in the hinterland on both sides of the Pennines were included in the reorganization but the remaining outpost-forts on Dere Street seem now to have been finally given up. Behind the latter measure lies Theodosius' removal of the *arcani* after their dismal showing in 367. Whether or not all control was now exercised from the Wall itself is not certain, but it is striking that Roman objects of trade ceased to cross the frontier at about this time, as though the worlds of Roman and barbarian were parting company.

In the midst of his work in Britain, Theodosius had to deal with a plot against himself.[20] Among several notable figures who had been exiled to Britain in the period, one Valentinus, a Pannonian, tried to persuade some of his fellow-exiles and soldiers to overthrow Theodosius and thus seize power in the island. The *comes* got wind of the plot shortly before it was due to be put into effect, and Valentinus and his immediate adherents were handed over to Dulcitius and sentenced to death without further investigations. Illustrating as it does the fact that Britain was considered remote enough to serve as a place of exile and that the propensity of the island to produce usurpers was as strong as ever, the episode is an interesting harbinger of the last years of Roman Britain.

11

Nostro Diducta Britannia Mundo

The restorative work of Theodosius left the British diocese in a reasonably good condition to face its enemies, whose attacks, though increasingly frequent, were generally confined to small-scale raiding. Britain was by and large better equipped to fend off such dangers than the provinces of Gaul and Germany with long land frontiers which were now under constant pressure. The weakness of the western Empire in the late fourth century lay not wholly in its inability to keep the barbarians at bay – serious though that was – but in the competing ambitions of leading commanders and courtiers and the resultant tendency for troops to be drawn away from the defence of frontier provinces in the pursuit of private aims. This was the nature of the next crisis which Britain faced.

In 383, Magnus Maximus revolted against the central authority from his base in Britain, of which he was perhaps the *dux*. Disappointed by the progress of his own career, Maximus found it easy to gain the backing of the army in Britain. He had earlier served with *comes* Theodosius and was well known to the senior officers in the diocese, whereas Gratian, the western emperor, was out of favour with much of his army. Maximus, moreover, had a victory to his credit, over Picti and Scotti in 382. His fame in later British history as Maxen Wledig is sufficient indication of his popularity in the island. His immediate aim, which was quickly achieved, was the seizure of Northern Gaul and the lower Rhine. Gratian's army crossed to Maximus' side after only minor skirmishings, and the emperor panicked and fled, leaving most of the west to the usurper.[1]

The forces which Maximus led to Gaul must have included a considerable proportion of the *limitanei* from the north and the west, together with whatever troops were now stationed at York. Although some of these units presumably returned to Britain after the collapse of Gratian's opposition, the expedition must have occasioned a redisposition of the frontier forces in the north and in Wales.

Theodosius is usually credited with the construction of a series of watch-towers on the north-eastern coast, though the opening date is far from certain. This watch on the coastal approaches may have been instituted a few years later by Magnus Maximus. The known towers run from Filey to Huntcliff on the Yorkshire coast, but they may once have extended south to the Humber and north to the Tyne. A late Roman stone structure stood on an eminence at Seaham on the Durham coast and this may have formed part of a tower. Both the east Yorkshire and the Durham coasts have suffered heavy erosion and other sites could easily have been lost. The headland at Hartlepool, for instance, commands long lines of coast to north and south, and late Roman material is recorded here.

The adventure of Magnus Maximus was short-lived. In 388 his downfall was accomplished by Theodosius I. For almost a decade after his fall, our sources report nothing of Britain. It is not even certain that the island was immediately recovered by Rome. We know that from 388 to 391 Theodosius devoted considerable care to the rehabilitation of the western provinces, appointing to the main offices men with proven records of services in the east. It is just possible that when we next hear of a Roman army operating in Britain, it had been sent in to bring the island back to the Roman fold.

Towards the end of the century attacks by Picti and Scotti were so troublesome that an expedition was sent out to Britain at the behest of the most powerful western general of the day, Stilicho, and possibly under his personal command.[2] The chronology of the operations which followed can be fixed only in the most general way and no clarifying detail has so far been added by archaeology. A major campaign in the north was fought in 398, and in the next year Stilicho ordered various measures to strengthen the defences of the diocese. We do not know if it was the northern frontier which came in for attention in 399, or the coastal forts, or both. The work of Stilicho or his commander need not have been very extensive to find record in Claudian's verses, and in any event it was not long before troops were being summoned from Britain for the defence of Italy against Alaric's Goths. After 401, the effective military strength of Britain had been drained away.

The final phase of the northern frontier is still very shadowy. Occupation continued in the forts for which there is reliable evidence (South Shields, Chesters, Housesteads, Vindolanda, Birdoswald) down to the end of the fourth century at least and probably a little later. The outpost forts, however, had been given up by the 340s or even earlier. Unfortunately, coins of the house of Theodosius are rare in northern Britain and therefore their scarcity on and near Hadrian's Wall may not be taken to mean that the frontier was denuded of troops. The large coin-series at Corbridge ends with nine coins of Arcadius and Honorius, thus taking use of the site into the early fifth century, but how far and by whom? From the Wall forts themselves the latest issues are of Arcadius (395–408), but only two have certainly been recorded. At Carrawburgh a hoard of worn bronze coins was probably buried about or shortly after 400. Along the entire frontier, the old standby of a datable pottery series cannot be identified after the close of the fourth century. Most, if not all, of the production centres in the north had ceased manufacture by the early fifth century at the latest. There is thus no basis for any orderly military occupation of Wall forts after the first decade of the fifth century, much less for a co-ordinated frontier system. Aside from other considerations, it is difficult to imagine which authority could have been paying troops after this date. Strategically and tactically Hadrian's Wall had ceased to exist in the years immediately following AD 400.

The demise of the frontier, however it occurred, was not accompanied or followed by a southward movement of the northern peoples. Some of these groups may have been neutralized by their long contact with the frontier, while some may even have enjoyed allied status, though this is no more than surmise. But it might have been expected that those enemies who had threatened the frontier in the later fourth century would have attempted to strike south in search of land and portable wealth. If any of them did, there is no sign of it. Some degree of stability may have been brought to the areas immediately north of the old frontier by the spread of Christianity in the fifth century. The establishment of a church and community at Whithorn, traditionally the work of Ninian, or Ninias, had been achieved by the early fifth century on the evidence of recent excavation; to this date also belongs a fine memorial inscription in good Roman lettering. Also in south-western Scotland the evidence is as clear from Kirkmadrine, where fifth century inscriptions commemorate priests or bishops, Ides, Viventius and Mavorius, implying a fair degree of ecclesiastical organization in the region. The origins of this order are unknown, but the continued occupation of the city of Carlisle into the fifth century and later surely cannot be ignored.

The end of the military frontier may thus have given rise to other social structures, based on the frontier society in the region, now some two centuries old. Some of the forts may have become local centres of power; a few have produced significant evidence of occupation in the fifth and sixth centuries. At Birdoswald, a large timber hall was built within the fort in the fifth century and there are other indications of occupation at this date. At Vindolanda, a substantial apsed stone building went up near the centre of the fort late in the fourth century or soon after 400, possibly a church, and a memorial inscription for one Brigomaglos presumably points to a local lord here then or later. Other forts survived in such condition as to attract occupiers, as Housesteads was to do as late as the sixteenth century, though the archaeological levels relating to the fifth and sixth centuries have rarely been recovered. On some sites they may not exist at all, though work at places like Carvoran, Great Chesters and Carrawburgh might be productive in this regard.

The final military phase is no clearer. By the late 360s probably only five military bases were held in Wales, aside from the fortress at Caerleon: Caernarvon and Caerhun in the north, Forden Gaer in the centre, Brecon and Cardiff in the south. Forden Gaer and Caerhun may have been given up shortly afterwards. Attention was then focused on the north where Caernarvon was held until at least 395 and where a watch on movements by sea may have been effected from the small coastal fort at Caer Gybi on Anglesey. The absence of any garrison in Wales from the *Notitia Dignitatum* may not mean that all forces had been withdrawn by AD 400, but the sum of the archaeological evidence indicates at present that a military presence did not continue much beyond that date.

At the very time when the security of Britain came under increasing threat, the Church in the island was plunged into dispute. Victricius, Bishop of Rouen, paid a visit to Britain, probably between 395 and 397, apparently to settle some serious argument. Whether its nature was theological or administrative is quite unknown. Some, however, have seen the mission as a precursor of the more famous visitation by Germanus of Auxerre in 429, and have linked it with the great controversy which bears the name of the British monk Pelagius and which came to a head in the first years of the fifth century.[3] The early Church had, as a whole, preferred to 'consider the riches and rewards of the adopted sons of God rather than the fate and problems of individuals,' as Dom David Knowles put it, until Pelagius, who had arrived in Italy towards the end of the fourth century, began to insist that man should by his own efforts aspire to grace by keeping the law of God. This ran clearly counter to the teaching of the *Confessions* of Augustine, and their author took up the cudgels in reply. The succeeding debate was stormy and long outlived both Pelagius and Augustine.

It is not clear how and when Pelagian views reached Britain, nor how widespread and influential they were in the island. There have been determined attempts to interpret the Pelagian debate in terms of the social and political tensions of the late Roman west. The debate, however, like the concepts at its centre, was complex and cannot be reduced to a simple pattern of antagonism between bureaucracy and the governed, between hapless provincials and their oppressors. If Pelagius' ideas are to be related to political events, it must first be explained why an essentially religious movement should possess political and social aims. The argument does not clear the first hurdle. The main aim of the Pelagians was to be *integri Christiani*, to rise above their fellows and their own pasts. Political power and public office are specifically condemned in Pelagian treatises. It is true that exhortation towards the acceptance of social duties does also appear, but, as the basis of a Roman way of life disintegrated around them, bishops and priests did not really need to be told by Pelagians where their Christian duty lay.

On the last day of 406 a vast army of Suebi, Vandals and Alans crossed the Rhine and began to move towards the Channel.[4] During the following months their bands steadily approached the coast of Gaul and it began to appear as though Britain itself might be invaded. Earlier in 406 the army in Britain had raised an otherwise unknown soldier, Marcus, to the purple – for reasons of which we know nothing. During the barbarian advance across Gaul, Marcus was overthrown and killed, his place being given, again by the army, to Gratian, a *municeps* or urban councillor. He survived for only four months, the next choice of the soldiery falling on Constantine, one of their own number. The outline of events is clear, though the moving forces behind the three elevations are not revealed. What lay behind the election of Marcus and Gratian can only be guessed at. Constantine was presumably chosen to provide better defences for Britain against the barbarian threat.

No sooner had Constantine taken over than he crossed to Gaul, taking a large proportion of the army with him. The threat to Britain receded as the barbarians turned to the south, and for the next eighteen months Constantine was able to consolidate his hold on Gaul and to extend his control to Spain. But very soon his power was shaken by his own commander in Spain, the Briton Gerontius, and by a rising of the barbarians in Gaul. Constantine was now left with virtually no army to command. The sequel to these events in Gaul was the end of Roman rule in Britain.

The only source for the British response to Constantine's difficulties is Zosimus,[5] whose deficiencies as a historian need no further comment. But for these events he was drawing upon a vastly more reliable writer, Olympiodorus, so that what Zosimus has to say must be taken seriously, however difficult interpretation of the relevant passage may be. Realizing that they could expect no assistance from Constantine, the Britons looked to their own defence, took up arms, and freed their cities from barbarian attacks. The source is quite explicit about what the Britons did. They rebelled against Rome (not against Constantine) and removed themselves from Roman jurisdiction. This, then, was a separatist movement and not a vote of no-confidence in a usurper. The British lead was followed by the inhabitants of Armorica and other parts of Gaul, who expelled the Roman officials and set up their own constitution. These events took place in 409, and the anonymous Gaulish chronicler adds the important detail that Britain had been visited by a Saxon invasion in the previous year, thus explaining why the Britons had to rescue their cities from attack. The sequence of events described by Zosimus is convincing and appears not to be infected by invention. What lay behind it all is of prime importance, for what is being discussed is how Britain was severed from the Roman world. Unfortunately, on one vital matter Zosimus throws no light: who were the prime movers towards separation?

When the Armoricans revolted against Rome in 417, we know that it was a revolt of the poor and landless against their masters. But we cannot assume that the British rebellion had the same roots. Indeed, one piece of evidence suggests that it did not. After they had seized control, as Zosimus reports, the Britons rescued the cities from barbarian attackers. Why the rebels should do this is inexplicable if they were landless peasantry. Such an action is entirely understandable if the rebellion was led by the curial class and other landowners whose interests were centred on the towns. For these men, there was no longer any reason why they should give support to Rome. What Zosimus describes was the natural reaction of a landowning group to the Roman failure to protect its interests, or even to guarantee the security of Britain. If this reading of our source is correct then Rome did not withdraw from Britain: she was ejected.

It remains to ask whether these events can be squared with the action of Honorius in 410, when he wrote to the *civitates* of Britain – there being no other recognizable authority – instructing them to look to their own defence.[6] Sense can be made of this if the emperor's letter is seen as an attempt to draw a discreet veil over the real course of events in the previous year and to conceal the shameful fact that Britain had rebelled. This brave face can have deceived no one in Italy, assuming that anyone in the peninsula was interested in anything other than the presence of Alaric's army. The context of Honorius' letter has for long been obscured by the common assumption that the emperor was replying to an appeal for aid or protestation of loyalty from Britain.[7] Not only is there no evidence for any such initiative from Britain: if Zosimus' account is accepted, the supposition becomes nonsensical. Why should the Britons appeal for assistance to the very authority they had overthrown only months before? What aid could they expect in any case? There was no appeal from Britain; the weakest of emperors formally announced the severance of Britain from the Roman world – without admitting that the Britons had cut the cord themselves.

The ruin of Britain

Occupation of some kind can now be more confidently demonstrated in cities than was possible twenty years ago.[8] But what was the nature of this occupation? To what extent was it urban? Who were the agents of continuity and how long were they able to maintain themselves? What did this phase owe to Roman traditions and what was British? Large-scale excavation within a number of late Roman cities notably Verulamium, London, Cirencester, Winchester, Colchester among others has illumined several facets of life in Romano-British cities, while leaving many of these central questions unanswered. What is clear is that the experience of urban communities in Britain from the late fourth century onward was varied and the application of any single model is pointless and misleading. Some urban centres survived more strongly into the fifth century than others. The underlying causes cannot be easily established in all cases.

Many of the cities still contained flourishing communities in the late fourth century. Within the walls of *Verulamium*, Cirencester and elsewhere new buildings were going up and older structures at many other centres, including Colchester, Lincoln, York and Exeter, were still in use, though not necessarily for their original purposes. The continued resilience of urban culture into the first half of the fifth century in other exposed parts of the Roman Empire is an important reminder of the strength of urban habits. The links between town and country may have been weakened by the decay of Roman administration, and urban centres probably lost virtually all significance as centres of craftsmanship and trade. Urban population may have begun to fall as a result, with the level of cultural life approaching more nearly that of the countryside. But the tendency of recently acquired evidence points increasingly to the continuing significance of cities and towns in their territories, not only for their Romano-British inhabitants, but also to some extent for Germanic immigrants.

None of this puts a strain on credibility. As safe places which still offered many amenities, walled towns would continue to be occupied unless there were powerful reasons to the contrary. Desertions like that which Bede records for Cambridge[9] are more likely to have occurred from the late fifth century onwards than earlier.

It is a striking fact that many, probably most, of the cities of Britain were active and viable communities in the late fourth century; yet half a century later they were bereft of most of their populations, their buildings in ruins, their social and economic cohesion destroyed. Even so, the ruin and abandonment which is evident in the archaeological evidence does not necessarily mean that all significance was lost. Walled centres could still retain their attraction as centres of authority, even in decay. This may help to explain the survival of structures and some degree of organized life at a number of cities. At Lincoln several buildings are known to have survived for some time after AD 400, perhaps throughout the fifth century. By the early seventh century an Anglian occupation had begun in the lower part of the town. At about the same time, actually in 627, Paulinus converted the Anglian leader Blaecca, whom Bede calls *praefectus Lindocolinae civitatis*, and built a stone church in the city.[10] The sequence here is easy to accept as unbroken, but it need not have involved a large population or a complex social structure. There is a further suggestion of the survival of a British community at Lincoln in the striking scarcity of Germanic material in the city and its immediate environs, while there is another possible echo of a British enclave in the Celtic name of the third king, Caedbad, in the king-list of Lindsey.

On one point there is general agreement among archaeologists. There is little evidence for widespread destruction in those levels of Roman towns and cities which relate to the late fourth and early fifth centuries. It does not seem that the barbarian attacks of the period were successfully directed against the cities. Either the invaders avoided the walled centres altogether (as well they might) or their attempts to take them by storm generally came to naught. Germanic tribes were not well practised in siege warfare and these raiders of late Roman Britain came in such small bands that protracted sieges were not practicable. There are a few cities in which destruction layers of the period have been identified, though in no case is the date beyond question. The evidence from Silchester suggests that the public buildings had fallen slowly into decay. The latest levels in the basilica, however, contained a thick layer of ash and further intense burning was in evidence in the forum. At Caerwent the basilica had suffered damage by fire at the end of its life – whenever that was – and shops and houses on the main street may have fallen victim to the same conflagration. It has long been known that the central area of Wroxeter has produced evidence of severe burning, and a number of bodies in the hypocausts of the public baths – one of them with a late fourth-century coin-hoard – cannot easily be explained away as later burials. The presence of other burials within the walls at Wroxeter indicates the abandonment of normal Roman custom. But the problem remains: when did this occur? We encounter the same difficulty at Caister-by-Norwich, where a large dwelling was found to contain the skeletons of no less than thirty-five individuals, men, women and children. The house itself was destroyed by fire in about 400, and it is tempting to link the human remains with that violent episode. But that is to assume too much. Deposition of the bodies may have occurred much later than the fire and long after the Roman community had ceased to exist.

At several cities at least the possibility of continuous settlement from Roman Britain to the Anglo-Saxon kingdoms seemed highly likely. London seemed to hold out the strong prospect of continued occupation, guaranteed by its location and by its standing as the premier city of the Romans in Britain. The long series of excavations in *Londinium* since the 1960s, however, has produced a consistently negative record of occupation after the fourth century in any part of the city; in several areas there is little sign of activity after AD 200. The waterfront which had been so vital a part of the early city was moribund by the late fourth century, if not before. Fifth century material of any kind is rare in London and there is no indication of an ordered community within the walls after AD 400. There is, however, evidence of a shift in focus to a site outside the walled area, west of the city in the area of the Aldwych, itself an evocative name ('old *vicus*'). But when this shift was made is uncertain.

London, like a number of other cities in southern Britain, has revealed deep deposits (over a metre in some cases) of black humic earth in its later phases. These deposits began to form as early as the third century, implying significant change in the use and character of the city. The nature of 'black earth' and what it indicates about urbanism in late Roman Britain have been much debated subjects. Was it due to the natural growth of humus on abandoned plots of land or did it build up as the result of the dumping of organic rubbish, perhaps with subsequent working of the soil for cultivation? The evidence from London suggests that the dumping of refuse did take place but that cultivation was not pursued. The picture is of an urban wasteland, not a horticultural pleasance, following abandonment of sizeable areas of the city on both sides of the Thames. This period of disuse continued for long after AD 400. This may appear to be clear evidence for a city in steep decline, but it is not dissimilar from the state of affairs increasingly revealed in several cities in the western provinces, including Italy. It does not imply the abandonment of all urban functions, merely that these were exercised within a different framework.

No uniform pattern emerges overall. The decay of urban structures and the functions which they represented are well displayed at Winchester, Canterbury and Silchester. The urban plan of Winchester was being eroded by the early fifth century and major buildings were going out of commission. Canterbury presents an even more dramatic picture of urban decline, with many small timber buildings being erected in the centre of the city, in some cases over the lines of Roman streets and within the remains of stone structures. By AD 500, any resemblance to a Roman city was completely lost, aside from its defensive circuit. At Silchester, steady decay is evident from the later fourth century, occupation becoming progressively limited in the fifth and ended by about 500. In several other cities, there was an evident tendency towards the creation of smaller nuclei within the Roman defences, the areas between being left empty. This is so at Exeter, Gloucester and Leicester. It may suggest a significant change in the social groups occupying these places: no longer coherent urban populations but familial or other bonded groups under local masters.

It is noteworthy that not only in those areas of Eastern and Southern Britain exposed to Saxon raiding is there evidence of fairly rapid urban decline after the early fifth century. Exeter lay too far to the west to be troubled by Germanic invaders, and there is no certain evidence for Irish attacks on the south-western peninsula as early as 400. Yet here, too, the centre of the city was undergoing profound change, as the public buildings lost their original functions and were partially rebuilt. The forum courtyard was abandoned to natural processes and lay deep in black earth. The survival of some form of urban community here, however, as elsewhere in the west, at Cirencester and Gloucester for example, is reasonably certain. Both Cirencester and Gloucester later figure as recognizable centres of the Britons in the sixth century, while Cirencester, at the heart of a landscape dotted with large villa-estates, has further yielded evidence of organized, corporate life in the fifth century.

Archaeological investigation will continue to give greater definition to the material life of cities and towns in the fifth century, and as a result our views on the survival of urban communities should be much firmer in twenty years' time. At present, although continuance of occupation until well into the fifth century has been attested in several cities, in very few cases does this take the form of an orderly urban society. The evidence for a more ordered community is clearest at *Verulamium* (where Germanus of Auxerre in 429 encountered civic leaders who still had the means to afford fine garments and the leisure to indulge in theological debate, and where archaeology attests certain amenities inside the walls and control of the territory outside them until after the middle of the century) and Wroxeter, where the site of the baths basilica was carefully replanned and covered by a series of timber buildings at the beginning of the fifth century.[11] The impression conveyed at both places is of sizeable communities able to act effectively in concert and still possessing an elementary internal structure. How many of the elements of Romano-British society continued to survive after the separation from Rome is, of course, unknown. From the little we know of Romano-British society after 400, it seems unlikely in the extreme that the curial class continued to exercise control of the cities for long after the end of Roman administration. Although the *curiales* may have taken a decisive role in the events of 409, their influence thereafter seems negligible. The men who greeted Germanus at *Verulamium* are virtually the last representatives of the curial class of whom we catch any glimpse. The removal of the machinery of Roman administration with all its manifold obligations for the raising of taxation and other dues inevitably meant the end of the *curiales* as a clearly defined social group. The effects of this on the life of cities can only have been profound, for this was the very social group which had contributed most to the government of cities for more than three centuries. Without a curial *ordo*, able and willing to keep things moving, a Romano-British city had no chance of continuing as before. Willing, the *curiales* had not been for a long time: able, they could not long remain in the circumstances which enveloped Britain after 409.

After the end of formal Roman control, whenever that is placed, who filled the power vacuum? We can review the possibilities, but no certainties emerge. The succession of usurpers thrown up in Britain from Magnus Maximus to Constantine III could well have been extended on a local basis after 410. Such rulers could have been the 'tyrants' who, according to Procopius, seized power in Britain after the severance from Rome. The leading families in the civitates also had an interest in preserving some elements of the *status quo ante*, at least within their own territories, but there is no evidence that any member of an urban elite made a bid for wider power. A more credible development is the emergence of a mosaic of local powers

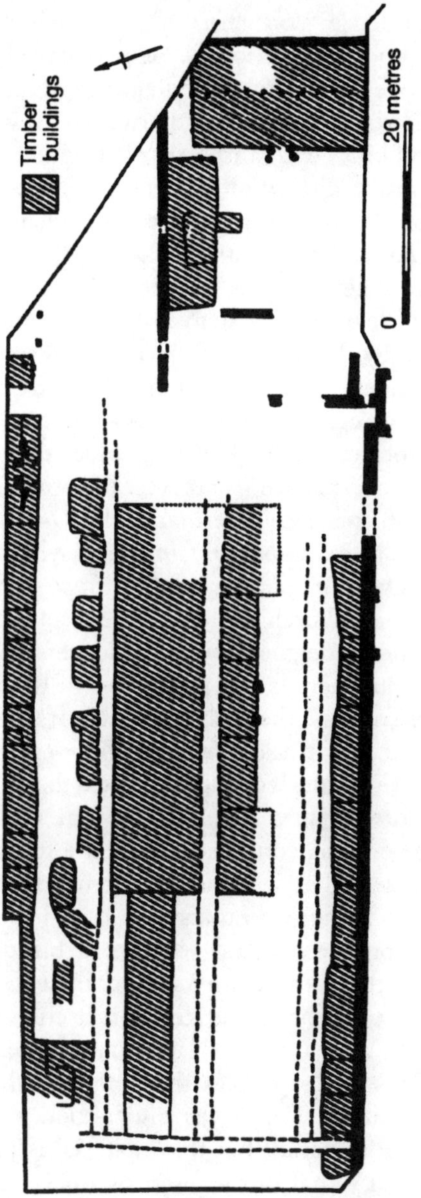

Figure 35 Late Roman timber structures within the baths basilica at Wroxeter, after P. A. Barker.

in which at least some cities still played a part. To this shadowy period between 410 and 450 belongs one leader in whose existence we can have confidence: Vortigern. Whatever manner of ruler Vortigern was, he must be taken seriously. He may have been an independent figure who none the less possessed enough authority to invite and deploy federate barbarians from northern Europe. It is less likely that he was a powerful king, with authority over wide areas of Britain. To attempt to present the history of fifth century Britain without leaders is obviously nonsensical and this has been evident from the time of Bede. Vortigern has more substance than most, but when and where did he operate? As he was able to establish Germanic federates on British soil, he must have held sway over a part of eastern England. The victories won by the rebellious warrior-bands he based in Britain included engagements at Aylesford and Crayford, both in Kent, which is as likely a region as any for settlement of barbarian forces. Later sources associate him with Wales, under the name Gwrtheyrn, though his historical presence so far west is not well supported. Bede places the revolt of Vortigern's Germanic allies between 449 and 456, later followed by the *Anglo-Saxon Chronicle*, which gives a plausible context shortly before mid-century for a British war-leader.

A strong Christian church with a resilient episcopal organization might have provided a degree of political leadership and social cohesion, as in Gaul. But there is no sign of this in Britain. Although the mere fact that Germanus, the Bishop of Auxerre, made two visits to Britain in 429 and about 440 is of great interest, it must be recognized that what he witnessed and achieved there is presented in a laudatory text written half a century later. The *Life* of Germanus by Constantius of Lyon was compiled between 480 and 494, probably between 480 and 490. The work was written from the perspective of a Christian author living in Frankish Gaul and thus contains much interesting detail on the life and work of a bishop in Gaul in the second quarter of the fifth century. By contrast, what it says about Britain in this period is brief and general. It contains no dates; our knowledge for the chronology of Germanus's visits derives from other sources. This is not to say that the text should be ignored, merely that its limitations must be understood and allowed for. It contains interesting material, but that material is presented within a well-defined context – that of the work of an active Gallic bishop. It thus says more about the activity of Germanus than the state of Gaul and Britain in his day.

A fifth century bishop can safely be expected to visit a major martyrial shrine, so that Germanus's attendance at the shrine of St Alban arouses no surprise. More surprising is the reception of Germanus and his entourage by a large gathering of Britons and the bishop's later assumption of the command of a British force which routed the invading Picts and Saxons. The latter achievement was exceptional, even for an energetic Gallic bishop. If a real victory was won over barbarian invaders under his leadership, the military incapacity of the Britons only twenty years after the end of Roman rule would be starkly revealed. Equally surprising is the fact that Germanus made no contact with military leaders of any kind who laid claim to territorial authority in southern Britain. Germanus arrived in Britain, according to Constantius, in response to a request for aid against heresy, was met by a large throng, made his way to the shrine of St Alban, and later led a British force to a major success in battle. Such an adventure is not wholly impossible, though it strains credulity at several points. Belief might be strengthened by detail which can be verified, but such detail is not forthcoming. In Constantius' *Life* Britain appears as a land without maps or any form of infrastructure. No cities are mentioned; even *places* are absent. Constantius does not use the customary terms for cities and other central places. All in all, there is a vagueness in his account of Britain which is in sharp contrast with what he has to say about Gaul and Italy. There are two possible explanations. Either the infrastructure of Britain had disappeared completely by the time that Constantius was writing, or the writer had no knowledge of the state of Britain in the second quarter of the fifth century. The two are, of course, not mutually exclusive.

Whatever Germanus achieved in Britain was not forgotten in the island. The saint was honoured in church dedications and in a variety of fabulous tales, in some of which he was involved with Vortigern. In the short term, however, his work is not likely to have borne much fruit. In the second half of the fifth century pagan barbarian groups began to settle in increasing numbers in eastern Britain, from Yorkshire to Kent. British Christianity maintained itself in the north and west, but how deeply founded it was is far from clear. Texts from the seventh century suggest that many Christian gatherings were seasonal affairs, occurring when a bishop or monk appeared in a particular locality. How profound an impression such activity had on a mainly rural society is open to question, but the impact is unlikely to have been high.

At one city there is testimony to a continuing Christian presence after the end of Roman rule, though it may have had little or no impact outside its own bounds. Canterbury was a centre of Christian cult by the late fourth century. Bede reports churches founded by Roman Christians here and we must accept his account. The dedication to St Martin of the church used by the Frankish queen Bertha in the late sixth century is obviously suggestive of an early date, perhaps early in the fifth century. Another church, Christ Church, was also built in late Roman Britain and 'recovered' by Augustine after 597, according to Bede. A third church, St Pancras, has been claimed as a Romano-British structure in its first phase, but the evidence is not conclusive. On what is known of these buildings at present, it is safest to follow Bede and take St Martin's to be the site of the church in use by Bertha and the mission of Augustine. It is, of course, possible that Bede's Canterbury sources were muddled or otherwise wrong, but this should not be assumed.

New settlers

A great deal of attention has recently been devoted to the earliest barbarian settlements in Britain, a subject of the greatest interest but one which should not be allowed to dominate or distort our view of the last age of the provinces. Rome had long been accustomed to the use of barbarian troops, in both regular and irregular formations, and there need be no surprise that items of equipment were brought by members of these groups from *Barbaricum*.[12] On the whole, it is strange that so little material introduced by barbarians has so far been recognized. The earliest Germanic cremation burials so far identified date from the early fifth century, a high proportion of them occurring outside the walls of several towns and cities in Eastern Britain: Ancaster, Caister-by-Norwich, York, Great Chesterford and possibly Cambridge. Other early urn-burials have come to light in the vicinity of cities, for instance Leicester, or on major routes, as at Newark, Sancton and Loveden Hill. The recent tendency has been to see these barbarian groups as settled by hard-pressed Romano-British authorities in areas from which they could ward off other, less amenable, barbarians much in the manner of the settlement of *laeti* in late third-century Gaul. The view has its attractions, though it would be misleading to pretend that all the pottery in the burials can be dated with perfect confidence to the earliest years of the fifth century, or that we can by any means distinguish between material associated with barbarians who settled on the land with Roman sanction, and that belonging to settlers who established themselves at their own volition. The question of date is of particular importance. Anglo-Saxon pottery and metalwork dating from the years 400–20, if such can be distinguished, will clearly be regarded in a different light from material of the mid-fifth century. Refinement of dating is work for the future. For the moment we can only record this early Anglo-

Saxon material and study it in relation to the faineant culture of Roman Britain. Seen as a whole, the earliest Germanic material is evident in East Anglia, Essex and north Lincolnshire, areas of obvious landfall for voyagers across the North Sea.[13] The dates of these objects fall in the first half of the fifth century, some of them not much later than AD 400/20 and their analogues are found mainly in northern Germany. After about AD 450, material from Frankish Gaul and the Rhineland occurs in small quantity in Kent and occasionally elsewhere, at York for example. There is a general tendency for this early Germanic material to be associated with late Romano-British sites, but rarely are the circumstances of discovery specific enough to clarify the relationship.

Commonly associated with the earliest barbarian settlers in Britain is a series of soldier-burials, of which the best known examples are those outside the walls of Dorchester-on-Thames (Dyke Hills) and Winchester (Lankhills).[14] The features which link these graves together are, above all, ornamented belt-sets with chip-carved designs – products in their original form of military supply workshops. The earliest examples of this equipment date from about the middle of the fourth century, though the British instances are mostly late, probably *c.* 370–400. There is no firm evidence for their prolonged use after 400. Interpretation of these graves requires great care. In the first place, the military equipment is to be seen as the property of the Roman army, not specifically of barbarian troops in Roman service. The more elaborate belt-sets were probably owned by high-ranking officers, as their occurrence in certain late fourth century hoards suggests. It may not safely be assumed, then, that all its wearers were barbarians. There are, however, several cases where an association with barbarians seems reasonably certain, for example at Dorchester-on-Thames and at Mucking (Essex). The likeliest explanation of their presence is as *gentiles*, irregular auxiliary troops, organized in units under regular Roman officers. There is no requirement to accept these barbarians as *foederati*. The offer of a *foedus* to barbarian groups was made very sparingly by Roman commanders in the later fourth century, the period to which most of these burials belong. On the evidence at present available, the bulk of this late military metalwork can be reasonably assigned to the Roman army proper and not to barbarian mercenaries.

The appearance of Romano-British versions of this metal-work at the end of the fourth century on villa sites and other rural settlements has aroused speculation that military units were widely used in the defence of the countryside at the end of the fourth century. Here, too, caution is necessary. Much of the material loosely described as

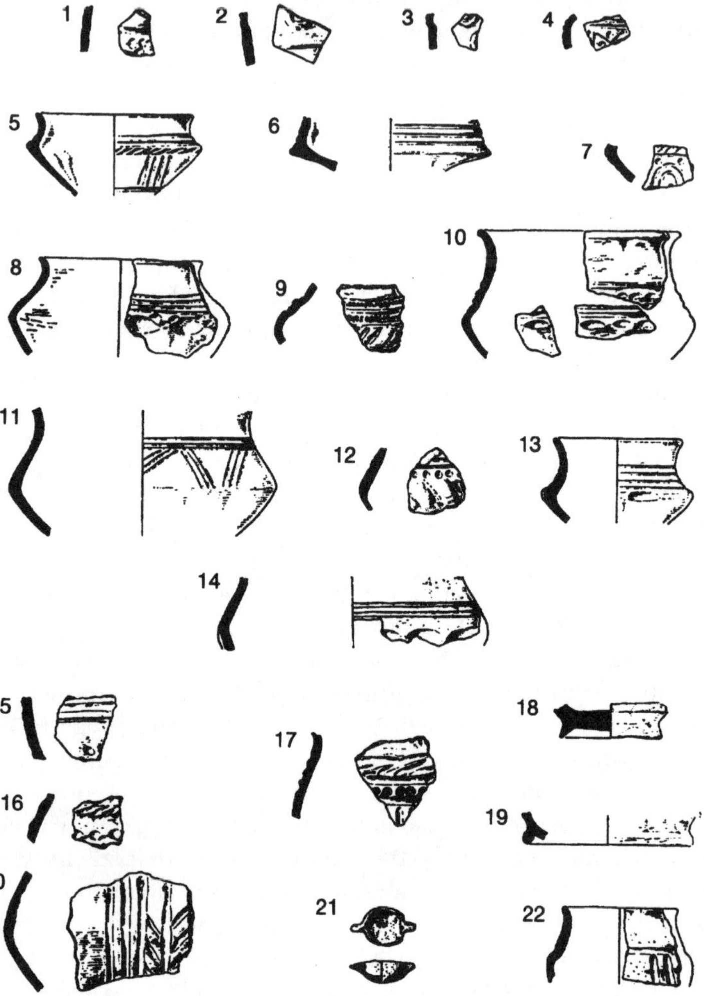

Figure 36 Fifth century Germanic pottery from Mucking (Essex).

'military equipment' – and this particularly applies to the British versions – may have no real link with the army. Rather it may reflect the spread of a fashion in paramilitary ornament to a wide sector of the civilian population, a phenomenon not unknown in our own day.

It seems most probable that the numbers of barbarians deliberately settled in Britain by the early fifth century were very small and their use in the defence of towns and cities very limited. In some cases, groups of them may have been located at strategic points. The community at Mucking would have been well placed to oversee the river approaches to London, that at Sancton to guard the road from the Humber towards York.[15] But the employment of barbarians as urban garrisons seems so unlikely as to be absurd. In any case, the defence of walled centres was not the most pressing task facing those responsible for the defence of Britain from 400 onwards.

Rural settlement

What happened to rural life and economy is of fundamental importance to our understanding of the final years of Roman Britain. Here considerable progress has been made recently, especially in the study of the latest phases of villas and of humbler rural settlements, and more significantly in the relationship between the earliest Anglo-Saxon settlement pattern and that of late Roman Britain. The great majority of rural sites, notably villas, have been so inadequately excavated that it is impossible to assess how frequently occupation of any kind continued into the fifth century and beyond. Recent excavation on a number of villas has revealed that a substantial number came to an end before 400 and in several cases in the middle decades of the fourth century. Several villas in the *Verulamium* region went out of use between 350 and 370, as did a number in the *civitas* of the Coritani. In the West several, including Kings Weston and Keynsham, were destroyed before 400, while others, such as Chew Park and Star, were abandoned to the elements. The abandonment of these houses need not imply that the estates themselves were no more, but archaeological evidence alone will not normally help us to define estate boundaries and what happened to them.[16]

The fate of villas was far from uniform. Several of the Cotswold villas, including Barnsley Park, Chedworth and Frocester Court, did continue into the fifth century – though how far has not been defined. In other regions much more exposed to barbarian raids villas also managed to survive, for instance in East Yorkshire, East Anglia and Lincolnshire. Some, indeed, were founded on new sites towards the end of the fourth century. But in no region have villas been shown to survive in recognizably Roman form for more than twenty or thirty years after the end of Roman rule, though individual buildings in some cases did remain in use for much longer.

Probably the most important recent contribution to the subject of continuity in the rural sphere has been the tracing of the survival of Roman estates in territorial organizations of Saxon and medieval date. The established tradition of the Romano-British estate was not, it seems, entirely swept away. In areas not affected by the earliest

Anglo-Saxon settlement there was no reason why it should be, and in such areas, especially in Wales and the north, impressive evidence for the continuation of ancient administrative units has been marshalled. From several parts of Northern England there are clear indications in medieval sources of institutions and territorial divisions which must long antedate the Anglian conquest. In South Wales there is abundant proof of the use of late Roman terminology (*ager, centuria, iugum, actus*) in early medieval charters. Some of the medieval estates mentioned there were evidently of some size and might be made up of multiple blocks of land with one recognizable centre. The analogy with the late Roman villa estate is thus remarkably close and, though direct descent from late Roman usage is not demonstrated, the broad similarity of social structure reinforced by the consistent use of Roman terms is striking.[17]

Another major demonstration of recent research has overturned the earlier belief that Germanic settlers avoided villa sites or found them inappropriate to the needs of their social order. Several villas are now known to have harboured Anglo-Saxon settlers early in the fifth century and earlier finds of Anglo-Saxon pottery and metalwork on villa sites – frequently dismissed as the relics of 'squatters' – probably point to other such cases. Further work on the latest phases of villas in areas of primary Anglo-Saxon settlement should be instructive on this point.

One of the most striking cases is that of Orton Longueville, near Peterborough, where Germanic material was in use within standing Romano-British buildings in the fifth century. At Shakenoak in Oxfordshire the picture is of discontinuity, the incoming Saxons settling within the ruins of the villa after a break, while at Barton Court Farm, near Abingdon, fifth century buildings were spread over the ditches of the farmstead, but avoided the old house; a century later that was used as the site of a cemetery. These single cases are instructive in that they illustrate the varied experience of rural sites after AD 400.[18]

It is highly likely that other villas and rural settlements received barbarian settlers in the decades after 400, without much archaeological trace being left behind. Several villas in eastern Britain have produced pottery and metalwork of the fifth century, usually unstratified and always in small quantity. These sites include Wingham (Kent), Southwell and Epperstone (Notts.), Market Overton (Leics.), Staxton and Elmswell (east Yorkshire), Ixworth (Suffolk) and Rivenhall and Gestingthorpe (Essex). Although the total yield of material is meagre, it must be recalled that the latest levels of villas are particularly vulnerable to natural erosion, ploughing and the depredations of early excavators. In any event, the material goods of incoming settlers will not have been extensive. Thus the number of rural settlements which received Germanic occupants after 400 may be significantly greater than appears at present.

Looking at the subject more widely, Romano-British rural settlement was not immediately supplanted by a stable, nucleated Germanic settlement, which in turn formed the basis for permanent medieval villages. An extended phase of shifting settlement, involving a series of short-lived steadings, is now known to have intervened in several areas of eastern England before a more stable pattern of Anglo-Saxon settlement emerged. There may, therefore, be a greater degree of rural continuity within areas of landscape than is presently suggested by the record of individual sites.

The general notion of rural continuity is supported by evidence from an increasing number of cemeteries. A large cemetery close to the Frilford temple complex in Berkshire seems to have continued from the fourth to the sixth centuries, the burial rite altering from late Roman inhumation to Germanic cremation. Not far away, at Dorchester, Roman and Germanic burials were apparently contemporary, implying a mixed and probably integrated population. Other cemeteries seem to point to the survival of British communities, which only later adopted Germanic burial rites. Such a case is the small late Roman cemetery at Wasperton, near Stratford on Avon, which received Anglo-Saxon burials late in the fifth century, beginning a sequence which extended to the seventh.

An equally firm indicator of rural continuity is the environmental record as expressed by the remains of plants and pollen. Although there are local variations, the prevailing pattern is one in which open landscapes were the norm and in which evidence for ecological change is slight. Change in the agrarian exploitation of the land introduced in the later Roman period appears to have established a pattern which was to continue for several centuries, possibly down to the creation of the major English kingdoms in the seventh century.

Some of the larger landowners went to considerable lengths to protect their estates. The linear earthwork of Bokerly Dyke on the north-eastern edge of Cranborne Chase in Dorset was gradually extended during the fourth century until by 400 it covered a broad gap between high ground. The estate thus protected could have continued until well into the fifth century.[19] There are other earthworks in the west which could date from this same period. The Bedwyn valley in Wiltshire is blocked by a dyke which faces north-eastwards, the direction from which danger might be expected. The great Wansdyke itself, or at least its eastern sector, is most convincingly explained as a boundary to a British territory which saw its northern flank as its most vulnerable border. There are other lesser earthworks in Wessex which may have similar origins. Further west still, some reflection of an altered social order may be seen in the occupation of numerous hill-top sites in the late fourth and early fifth centuries, recalling the contemporary construction or reconstruction of hill-top refuges in Gaul and Upper Germany.

No single indicator gives a more compelling picture of the collapse of Romano-British economic life than the coinage.[20] After 370 there was a considerable increase in the volume of gold coinage in circulation in Britain, notably of *solidi* from the Milan mint. Silver coinage, too, was abundant as numerous large hoards reveal. Britain's own wealth in silver clearly played its part here, the bullion being perhaps exchanged for new coins at the main western mints. The bronze coins in circulation at the end of the fourth century were a very mixed bag. They included large numbers of old pieces – some more than fifty years old – along with recent issues from the Gaulish and Italian mints. The new coins, however, circulated much more freely in the south and east than in the upland zones of the north and west. The incidence of the latest hoards in Britain also suggests that the volume of currency was proportionately much greater in the south and east. But by 400 coinage was still fulfilling a role in the economic system. Within a decade that role was significantly impaired. Shortly after 402, the flow of gold and silver coinage into the island was checked, and the later issues of the mints of Rome and Ravenna are only sparsely represented. From 406 – the year of Marcus' elevation by the army – the bronze issues too rapidly diminished in bulk and coins dating from after 408 are very rare finds. Small numbers of new silver coins continued to enter Britain in the second decade of the century, but the increasingly high proportion of clipped *siliquae* after Constantine's adventure tells its own story. Surprisingly, no local coinages appeared to fill the gap. No copies of the latest Roman issues emerged to continue the currency system in an attenuated form. The old coinage went on circulating for a time, but apparently only briefly. By about 425 at the latest, coinage had lost its function as a means of exchange, and there is no evidence either for circulation or for hoarding after this time.

For so small a part of the Empire, Britain has produced a strikingly large number of gold and silver hoards, nearly ninety in the period 350–420. It is difficult to believe that there is no connection with Britain's wealth in silver ore in particular. Major depositions made in the mid-fourth century, including the Mildenhall and *Durobrivae*

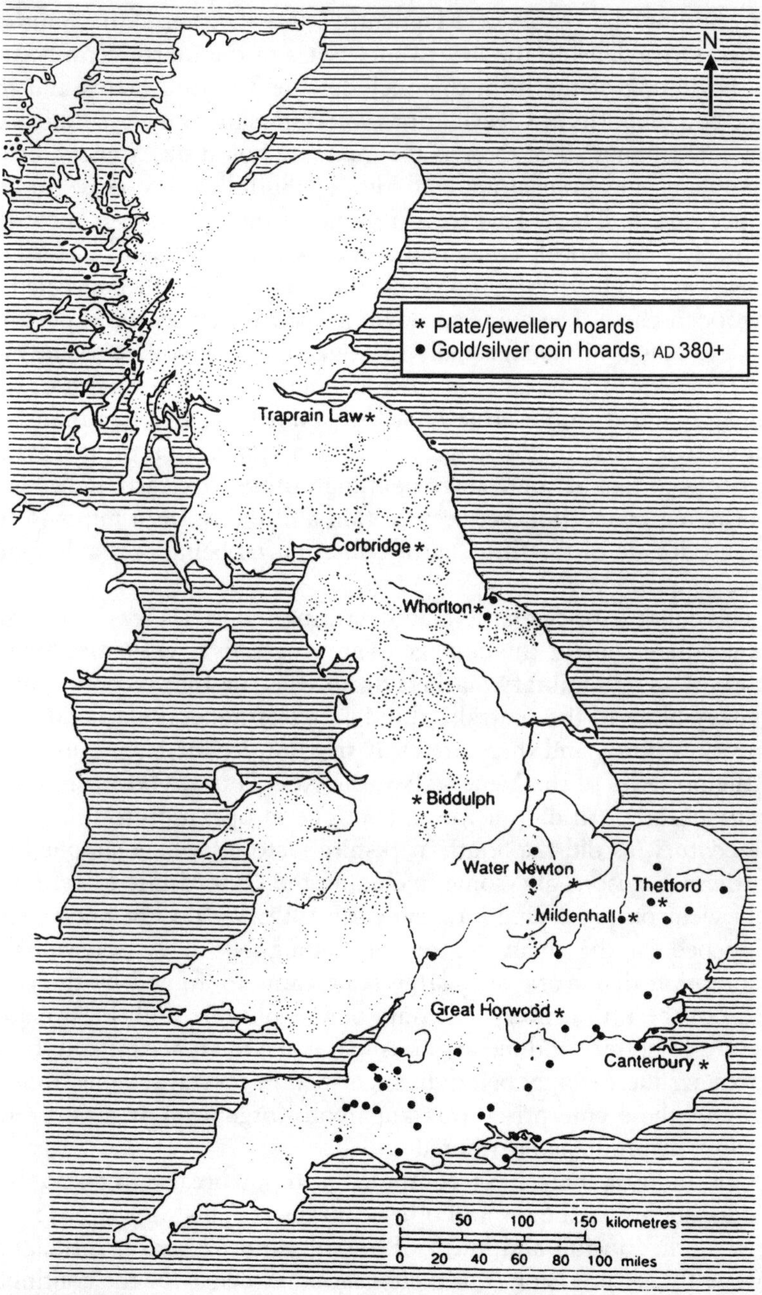

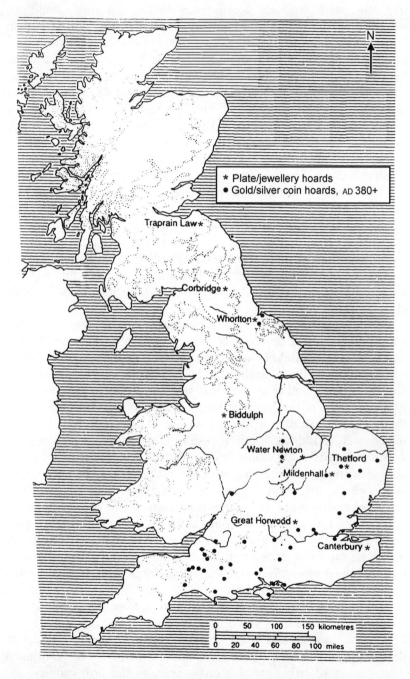

Figure 37 Precious metal hoards: fourth/fifth centuries.

treasures, were probably connected with the disturbed conditions surrounding the revolt of Magnentius and its aftermath. Another, larger, series dates to the last twenty years of the fourth century and the beginning of the fifth; this includes the Thetford hoard and the huge coin-deposits at Cleeve Prior (Worcestershire) and Eye (Suffolk). Far outstripping all of these is the immense hoard of jewellery, other ornaments and coins found at Hoxne (Suffolk) very close to the earlier find at Eye.[21] This treasure, one of the largest ever recorded in the Roman world, contained some two hundred gold and silver objects and well over 14,000 coins, the whole originally concealed in a wooden chest. The coins go down at least to AD 411 and possibly to 413. This is an unexpectedly massive hoard for so late a date and the context of its burial is of obvious interest. Such a wealth of late coinage (added to the large hoard of *solidi* from Eye less than two kilometres away) might suggest an official connection or at least an owner who had at some stage held high office. It clearly indicates a continuing connection between Britain and the western mints in the second decade of the fifth century, final burial being probably made close to 420.

The collapse of the large manufacturing industries was more prolonged than that of the coinage. The progressive weakening of the main urban and military markets during the late fourth century dealt a heavy blow to the centralized industries of mineral extraction and pottery-making, and there are clear signs of decline from about 350 in the potteries of the Nene Valley, the New Forest, Oxfordshire and Warwickshire. All did, however, continue in operation to the end of the century, as did the South Yorkshire factories which supplied the northern garrisons and some, including the Oxfordshire kilns, probably went on producing into the early fifth. We do not know what happened to the main centres of mining but it is a reasonable assumption that work on a large scale came to an end by the early years of the fifth century. It would be inexplicable if all local manufacture of pottery and metal goods had come to an abrupt end. Local wares are increasingly being distinguished in several regions, though none of these enterprises was apparently organized at a very high level or its products distributed widely.

One industry may have continued without break after 400, that producing bronze bowls and other containers. This subject has never been studied in full and much of the relevant material is difficult to date with any precision. But there is good evidence for the continued manufacture of lathe-turned bronzeware into the fifth century and later, providing models for the famed Anglo-Saxon hanging-bowls of the sixth and seventh centuries. The most impressive evidence comes from eastern Britain, from Yorkshire through Lincolnshire and Northants to Hertfordshire. The earliest vessels in the series may be the lathe-turned bowls from Finningley, near Doncaster, and Twyford (Leics.). The importance of the industry may have been enhanced by the sharp decline of pottery production from the end of the fourth century.

The year 409/410 marks the end of the Roman provinces of Britain, though not of all connection between Britain and the world of which Rome was still the symbol. In many respects, Britain was in the fifth century still a Roman island, though the unity given it by Rome was lost and was not re-established for many centuries. Ironically, it is only in the final years of Roman Britain that we hear of Britons who were significant figures in the history of their own time: Patrick above all, Pelagius, Ninian, Vortigern. Although fifth-century history, in so far as it can be written at all, is usually recorded as the first stage in the conquest of Britain by her Germanic invaders, it should in truth be regarded as a phase of British, not English, history. The prevailing culture of most of what had been Roman Britain was Romano-British, not Anglo-Saxon.

Among the material remains of Romanity which survived the end of Roman rule are inscriptions in Latin, most of them memorial stones to local leaders and their families in a Christian milieu. Almost all of these lie in the west and north, in Wales, Devon and Cornwall, and western Scotland beyond Hadrian's Wall. Most probably date from the sixth and seventh centuries, but some can be placed before AD 500 on the basis of their letter-forms and other similarities to late fourth and fifth century inscriptions in Gaul and Germany. The earliest of the British examples may fall in the early fifth century, close to AD 400. This is true of the Latinus inscription found at Whithorn, which is carefully arranged in horizontal lines of well-cut letters, neater than many late Roman texts. Several inscriptions found in Wales are incised to similar standards. One at Llanerfwl in Montgomeryshire follows a Roman format with considerable care and records a young girl in thoroughly late Roman terms. As the site lies within reach of the city of Wroxeter, there are possible links with a surviving community there.

These inscriptions, and others, underline the continuity between the latest inscriptions of Britain under Roman rule and those of the emerging 'Celtic' powers. The latest identifiable texts of Roman Britain have much in common with the early 'Christian' series. This is hardly surprising, as there must have been many visible Roman texts which might have served as models for memorial stones. The similarity in layout and letter-forms between late Roman milestones and inscriptions of the fifth and sixth centuries has often been noted. The possibility that the habit of inscribing stone monuments was not lost after AD 400 must be seriously entertained.

For Gildas in the mid-sixth century Latin was *nostra lingua*. In Ireland and Western Scotland, the Christian faith continued to gain vigour and an independent character. For a long period after the break with the Roman world, the Britons enjoyed a prosperity which was still remembered a century later, and at the very end of the fifth century they could still win a major victory against the invaders. The material remains of the fifth-century Britons are still difficult to identify, though our knowledge is steadily improving. Apart from the British enclaves which are recorded as surviving in the Chilterns in the sixth century the existence of British communities

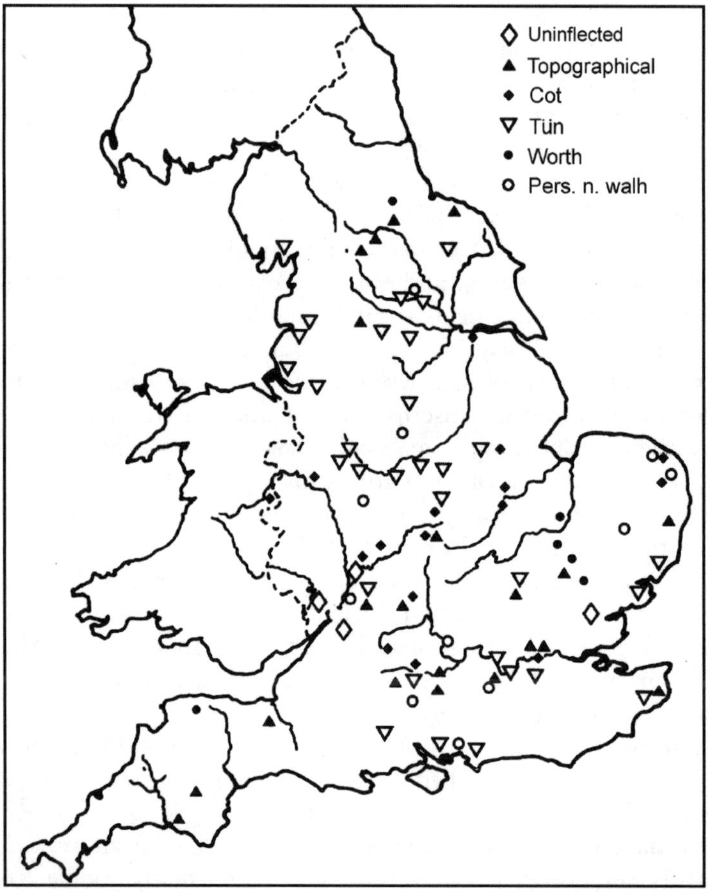

Figure 38 The place-names in *wealh*, after K. Cameron.

long after the wreck of the western Empire can still be glimpsed in certain place-names. Names containing the element *wealh*, meaning Briton or Celt, are recorded in most areas of England, and a high proportion of them seem to be directly linked with late Roman settlements.[22] Where these occur in the west, in Devon and the Welsh borders, these names can hardly have taken their form before the seventh or eighth century. Their very existence implies a far greater degree of British survival than is usually allowed for. These are the last distant echoes of Roman Britain.

Notes, Bibliographies and Ancient Sources

Chapter 1 Discovery and the First Invasions

1 C. F. C. Hawkes, *Pytheas: Europe and the Greek Explorers* (Oxford 1977); A. L. F. Rivet & C. Smith, *The Place-Names of Roman Britain* (London 1979), 37–49.
2 B. W. Cunliffe, *Hengisbury Head, Dorset I* (Oxford 1987); *idem, Greeks, Romans and Barbarians* (London 1988), 145–9.
3 J. G. Milne, *Finds of Greek Coins in the British Isles* (Oxford 1948) Numbers of Greek issues have been found in south-western Britain since Milne wrote, some in contexts which do not permit them to be dismissed as modern imports.
4 Polybius xxxiv, 10, 6; Strabo iv, 190; Strabo iii, 175–6.
5 *Numismatic Chronicle* i (1961), 91; B. Cunliffe, *Hengistbury Head, Dorset I* (Oxford 1987).
6 A. L. F. Rivet & C. Smith, *The Place-Names of Roman Britain* (London 1979), 37.
7 Julius Caesar: *The Battle for Gaul* (ed. A & P. Wiseman) (London 1980); S. S. Frere, *Britannia* (3rd. ed. London 1987).
8 R. E. M. Wheeler & T. V. Wheeler, *Verulamium. A Belgic and Two Roman Cities* (Oxford 1936), 16–23; C. F. C. Hawkes, 'Britain and Julius Caesar', *Proceedings of the British Academy* lxiii (1977), 125–92.
9 Ravensburgh has also been suggested; Hawkes, *op. cit.* 173.
10 Despite the ingenious arguments of C. E. Stevens in *Aspects of Archaeology in Britain and Beyond* ed. W. F. Grimes, London 1951), 332–44 there is no evidence that Caesar, or anyone else, regarded Britain as a Roman province after 54 BC, though the island may have been regarded as a potential sphere of operations by governors of Gaul.

Bibliography

T. Rice Holmes, *Ancient Britain and the Invasions of Julius Caesar* (Oxford 1907)
M. Cary & E. H. Warmington, *The Ancient Explorers* (London 1929)
B. Cunliffe, *Iron Age Communities in Britain* (3rd. ed. London 1990)
D. W. Harding, *The Iron Age in Lowland Britain* (London 1974)
S. Macready & F. H. Thompson, *Cross-Channel Trade between Gaul and Britain in the pre-Roman Iron Age* (London 1984)
M. Gelzer, *Caesar. Politician and Statesman* (Oxford 1968)

Ancient sources

Caesar, *Gallic War* iv, 20–38; v, 1–23.
Cicero, *Letters* iv, 15, 10; 16, 7; 18, 5.
Tacitus, *Agricola* 10–12.

Chapter 2 Britain and the Britons

1 Still important as a basic record are D. F. Allen, 'The Origins of Coinage in Britain: a Reappraisal', in S. S. Frere (ed.), *Problems of the Iron Age in Southern Britain* (London 1961), 97–308 and C. C. Haselgrove, *Supplementary Gazetteer of the Find-spots of Iron Age Coins* (London 1978). Fundamental is R. D. Van Arsdell, *Celtic Coinage in Britain* (London 1989).
2 S. Scheers, *British Numismatic Journal* xli (1972), 1–6.
3 D. W. Harding, *The Iron Age in Lowland Britain* (London 1974), 201–8; W. J. Rodwell in B. Cunliffe & T. Rowley (eds.), *Oppida in Barbarian Europe* (Oxford 1976), 243–79.
4 A. Birchall, *Procs. Prehistoric Society* xxxi (1965), 241–367.
5 Propertius, *Carmina* ii, 18, 1–4.
6 C. E. Stevens in *Aspects of Archaeology in Britain and Beyond* (ed. W. F. Grimes) (London 1951), 335. This is an interesting examination of the evidence, but it gives too much historical weight to the language of poets.
7 *Res Gestae* vi, 32.
8 D. F. Allen, 'Cunobelin's Gold', *Britannia* vi (1975), 1–19.
9 G. Bersu, *Procs. Prehistoric Society* vi (1940), 30–111. Its results must now be set alongside those of G. J. Wainwright, *Gussage All Saints* (London 1979).
10 On the general picture: B. Cunliffe, *Iron Age Communities in Britain* (3rd. ed. London 1991).
11 Diodorus v, 21, 5.

12 M. G. Fulford, *Procs. Prehistoric Society* liii (1987), 271–8.
13 D. F. Allen, *Archaeologia* xc (1944), Pls. I–III.
14 E. M. Clifford, *Bagendon. A Belgic Oppidum* (Cambridge 1961).
15 S. Piggott, in *Roman and Native in North Britain* (ed. I. A. Richmond, London 1958), 21–5.

Bibliography

T. G. E. Powell, *The Celts* (2nd. ed. London 1979)
B. Cunliffe, *Iron Age Communities in Britain* (3rd. ed. London 1991)
D. W. Harding, *The Iron Age in Lowland Britain* (London 1974)
R. Bradley, *Prehistoric Settlement in Britain* (London 1978)
R. Bradley, *The Social Foundations of Prehistoric Britain* (London 1984)
B. Cunliffe (ed.), *Coinage and Society in Britain and Gaul* (London 1981)
R. D. Van Arsdell, *Celtic Coinage in Britain* (London 1989)
J. Collis, *Oppida* (Sheffield 1984)

Ancient sources

Horace, *Odes* i, 35, 29–30
Catullus xi, 1–16
Tibullus iii, 7, 147–50
Propertius ii, 18, 1–4
Res Gestae vi, 32
Strabo, *Geography* ii, 5, 8; iv, 5, 1–3.
Frontinus, *Stratagems* 11, 13, 11.
Tacitus, *Annals* ii, 24
Suetonius, *Gaius* 44, 2; 46, 1.
Dio, *Roman History* xlix, 38, 2; liii, 22, 5; 25, 2; lix, 25, 1.

Chapter 3 The Claudian Triumph

1 J. P. V. D. Balsdon, *The Emperor Gaius* (Oxford 1934), 58–95; A. A. Barrett, *Caligula. The Corruption of Power* (London 1989)
2 The monument was later known as the Tour d'Odre: F. d'Ercé, *Revue Archéologique* 1966, 89–96.
3 R. W. Davies, *Historia* xv (1966), 124–8.
4 i.e. the flight of a native prince and indiscipline in the expeditionary force.
5 A. Momigliano, *Claudius* (Cambridge 1961); B. Levick, *Claudius* (London 1990)

6 Orosius later contrasted the failure of Caesar with the success of Claudius: vii, 6, 11.
7 His subsequent history is unknown.
8 R. Syme, *Classical Quarterly* xxvii (1933), 142–3.
9 B. Cunliffe, *Fifth Report on the Excavations of the Roman Fort at Richborough, Kent* (Oxford 1968), 3–21.
10 B. Philp, *The Excavation of the Roman Forts at Dover* (Dover 1981)
11 R. A. G. Carson, *Numismatic Chronicle* 6 xix (1959), 17–22.
12 The meaning of Dio's phrase is not clear. It should, however, mean 'the rest of the island', though some have argued that Claudian policy aimed at only the conquest of lowland Britain.
13 The quotation is from the inscription on one of Claudius' triumphal arches in Rome: *CIL* vi, 920.
14 *RIB* 91, with revised reading by J. E. Bogaers, *Britannia* x (1979), 243–54, rendering most earlier speculation about Cogidubnus' powers redundant.

Bibliography

B. Levick, *Claudius* (London 1990)
A. A. Barrett, *Caligula. The Corruption of Power* (London 1989)
G. Webster, *The Roman Invasion of Britain* (London 1980)
C. F. C. Hawkes & M. R. Hull, *Camulodunum* (Oxford 1947)

Ancient sources

Suetonius, *Claudius* 17, 1–2
Suetonius, *Vespasian* 4, 1
Tacitus, *Agricola* 14
Eutropius vii, 13, 2
Dio, *Roman History* lx, 19, 1–23

Chapter 4 The Conquest of Lowland Britain

1 The evidence of archaeology cannot, by its nature, illustrate in detail the ebb and flow of warfare. For that reason, when modern accounts present the Roman advance in Britain as a steady forward movement, reservations must be expressed. Tacitus' account of events in the fifties suggests strongly that the Roman advance was far from inexorable.
2 C. F. C. Hawkes & M. R. Hull, *Camulodunum* (Oxford 1947), 116–17; M. Todd, *Oxford Journal of Archaeology* iv (1985), 187–200
3 *Vespasian* 4, 1

4 I. A. Richmond, *Hod Hill, Vol. II* (London 1968), 31–3
5 R. E. M. Wheeler, *Maiden Castle, Dorset* (Oxford 1943), 118–20
6 B. Cunliffe, *Excavations at Fishbourne* (Oxford 1971), 37–76
7 *RIB* 2404.1; 2402.2
8 S. S. Frere & J. K. S. St. Joseph, *Britannia* v (1974), 1–129
9 M. Todd (ed.), *The Roman Fort at Great Casterton* (Oxford 1968)
10 *RIB* 254, 255 & 257
11 J. Wacher & A. McWhirr, *Early Roman Occupation at Cirencester* (Gloucester 1982)
12 H. Hurst, *Kingsholm* (Gloucester 1985)
13 Tacitus, *Annals* xii, 31
14 J. K. S. St. Joseph, *Journal of Roman Studies* lxiii (1973), 233–44
15 W. H. Manning, *The Fortress Excavations, 1968–71* (Cardiff 1981)
16 P. T. Bidwell, *The Legionary Fortress and Forum and Basilica at Exeter* (Exeter 1979)

Bibliography

C. F. C. Hawkes & M. R. Hull, *Camulodunum* (Oxford 1947)
I. A. Richmond, *Hod Hill, Volume II* (London 1968)
B. Cunliffe, *Excavations at Fishbourne* (Oxford 1971)
J. Wacher & A. McWhirr, *Early Roman Occupation at Cirencester* (Cirencester 1982)
V. E. Nash-Williams, *The Roman Frontier in Wales* (2nd. ed. (Cardiff 1969)
M. G. Jarrett, *Early Roman Campaigns in Wales* (Cardiff 1994)
RCHM (England), *Roman Camps in England* (London 1995)
M. Todd (ed.), *Research on Roman Britain, 1960–89* (London 1989)
S. S. Frere, *Verulamium Excavations, Volume I* (Oxford 1972)
M. Todd, *The Roman Fort at Great Casterton* (Oxford 1968)

Ancient sources

Tacitus, *Agricola* 14
Tacitus, *Annals* xii, 31–40
Dio, *Roman History* ix, 23, 1

Chapter 5 Revolt and Conquest Renewed

1 S. S. Frere, *Britannia* (3rd. ed. London 1987), 70–4; G. Webster, *Boudica* (London 1978); on the theme of revolt against Rome, S. L. Dyson, *Historia* xx (1971), 239–74
2 More usually the battlefield has been placed further to the north-west on the line of Watling Street, for no apparent reason.

3 A massacre at South Cadbury (Somerset) may date from this period: *Antiquity* liii (1979), 31–8

4 W. J. Rodwell, *Britannia* iii (1972), 290–2

5 A. Fox & W. Ravenhill, *Britannia* iii (1972), 56–111

6 W. H. Manning, *Usk. The Fortress Excavations, 1968–71* (Cardiff 1981)

7 B. Hobley, *Trans. Birmingham Arch. Soc.* lxxxiii (1966–7), 65–129; lxxxv (1973), 7–92; lxxxvii (1975), 1–56

8 Broxtowe is largely unpublished: Templeborough: T. May, *The Roman Forts of Templeborough near Rotherham* (Rotherham 1922)

9 Rossington Bridge: *Journal of Roman Studies* lix (1969), 103; Brough-on-Humber: J. S. Wacher, *Excavations at Brough-on-Humber, 1958–61* (Leeds 1969), 5–8

10 The foundation date of the York fortress remains uncertain. The early seventies is the most likely context, but a slightly earlier base cannot be excluded. B. R. Hartley & L. Fitts, *The Brigantes* (Stroud 1988), 19–21

11 W. Eck, *Senatoren von Vespasian bis Hadrian* (Munich 1970), 61; A. R. Birley, *Britannia* iv (1973), 186–7

12 I. A. Richmond, *Archaeological Journal* lxxxix (1932), 17–78

13 R. E. M. Wheeler, *The Stanwick Fortifications* (Oxford 1954)

14 V. E. Nash-Williams, *The Roman Frontier in Wales* (2nd. ed. Cardiff 1969); A. H. A. Hogg, *Archaeological Journal* cxxv (1968), 101–92; M. G. Jarrett, *Early Roman Campaigns in Wales* (Cardiff 1994)

Bibliography

G. Webster, *Boudica* (London 1978)
A. R. Birley, *The Fasti of Roman Britain* (Oxford 1981)
R. M. Butler (ed.), *Soldier and Civilian in Roman Yorkshire* (Leicester 1971)
H. Ramm, *The Parisi* (London 1978)
M. Todd, *The Coritani* (2nd. ed. Stroud 1991)
B. R. Hartley & L. Fitts, *The Brigantes* (Gloucester 1988)
RCHM (England), *Eboracum. Roman York* (London 1962)
V. E. Nash-Williams, *The Roman Frontier in Wales* (2nd. ed. Cardiff 1969)
G. Webster (ed.), *Fortress into City. The Consolidation of Roman Britain* (London 1988)
R. E. M. Wheeler, *The Stanwick Fortifications* (Oxford 1954)
S. S. Frere, *Verulamium Excavations I* (Oxford 1972)
RCHM (England), *Roman Camps in England* (London 1995)

Ancient sources

Tacitus, *Agricola* 15–17
Tacitus, *Annals* xiv, 29–39

Dio, *Roman History* lxii, 1, 1–12
Suetonius, *Nero* 18; 39, 1
Tacitus, *Histories* i, 9; i, 59–60; iii, 44–5

Chapter 6 *Britannia Perdomita*

1 This account accepts a start for Agricola's governorship in AD 77 rather than 78.
2 *Agricola* 23
3 N. J. Reed, *Britannia* ii (1971), 143–8
4 J. K. S. St. Joseph, *Journal of Roman Studies* lxiii (1973), 217–18; lxvii (1977), 135–42
5 J. K. S. St. Joseph, *Britannia* ix (1978), 271–87; G. Maxwell, *The Romans in Scotland* (Edinburgh 1989), 58
6 L. Pitts & J. K. S. St. Joseph, *Inchtuthil. The Roman Legionary Fortress* (London 1985)
7 A. S. Robertson, *Trans. Perthshire Society of Natural Science* Special Issue (1973), 14–29
8 G. Maxwell, *The Romans in Scotland* (Edinburgh 1989), 92. W. S. Hanson, *Agricola and the Conquest of the North* (London 1987)
9 I. A. Richmond, *Procs. Soc. Antiquaries Scotland* lxxxiv (1949–50), 1–37
10 R. S. O. Tomlin, *Britannia* xxiii (1992), 141–58
11 B. W. Jones, *The Emperor Domitian* (London 1992), 131–4
12 J. E. Bogaers in *Studien zu den Militärgrenzen Roms* (ed. H. von Petrikovits, Cologne 1967), 54; W. Eck, *Chiron* ii (1967), 459–62
13 D. Baatz, *Kastell Hesselbach* (Berlin 1973), 70–6
14 A. K. Bowman & J. D. Thomas, *The Vindolanda Writing Tablets* (London 1994); A. K. Bowman, *Life and Letters on the Roman Frontier* (London 1994)
15 A. L. F. Rivet in *Thèmes de recherches sur les villes antiques d'occident* (eds. P-M. Duval & E. Frézouls, Paris 1977), 161–72; J. S. Wacher, *The Towns of Roman Britain* (2nd. ed. London 1995)
16 R. Merrifield, *London. City of the Romans* (London 1983); G. Milne, *The Port of Roman London* (London 1983); P. Marsden, *The Roman Forum Site in London* (London 1987)
17 Tacitus, *Annals* xiv, 33 refers to *Verulamium* as a *municipium* and many modern commentators have accepted this as testimony to this status by AD 60. Tacitus may have been using the term anachronistically, the grant being made in the Flavian period. S. S. Frere, *Verulamium Excavations I* (Oxford 1972)
18 There may often have been a shortfall from 100, as was the case in certain North African cities.
19 M. Todd, *Studies in the Romano-British Villa* (Leicester 1978), 200–3

20 B. Cunliffe, *Excavations at Fishbourne* (London 1971); *idem, The Regni* (London 1973)

Bibliography

A. R. Birley, *The Fasti of Roman Britain* (Oxford 1981)
O. G. S. Crawford, *Scotland North of the Antonine Wall* (Cambridge 1949)
W. S. Hanson, *Agricola and the Conquest of the North* (London 1987)
J. Curle, *A Roman Frontier Post and its People* (Glasgow 1911)
G. Maxwell, *A Battle Lost* (Edinburgh 1990)
B. W. Jones, *The Emperor Domitian* (London 1992)
L. Pitts & J. K. S. St. Joseph, *Inchtuthil. The Roman Legionary Fortress* (London 1985)
A. K. Bowman & J. D. Thomas, *The Vindolanda Writing Tablets* (London 1994)
A. K. Bowman, *Life and Letters on the Roman Frontier* (London 1994)

Ancient sources

Tacitus, *Agricola* 8; 18–40
Suetonius, *Domitian* 10, 3

Chapter 7 The Frontier-builders

1 *RIC* 577 & *578* Britain was the only province singled out for reference at this time.
2 *RIB* 288
3 C. W. Phillips (ed.), *The Fenland in Roman Times* (London 1969); T. W. Potter in M. Todd (ed.), *Research on Roman Britain* (London 1989), 147–74
4 D. J. Breeze & B. Dobson, *Hadrian's Wall* (3rd. ed. London 1987); D. J. Breeze, *The Northern Frontiers of Roman Britain* (London 1982)
5 G. D. B. Jones, *Britannia* vii (1976), 236–43
6 In any case, Brigantian territory may not have extended so far.
7 The Wall itself was referred to as the *Vallum: RIB* 2034
8 *S. H. A. Hadrian* 5, 11, 2
9 G. Macdonald, *The Roman Wall in Scotland* (2nd. ed Oxford, 1934); G. S. Maxwell, *The Romans in Scotland* (Edinburgh 1989), 129–49; W. S. Hanson & G. S. Maxwell, *Rome's North-West Frontier* (Edinburgh 1986)
10 G. S. Maxwell, *The Romans in Scotland* (Edinburgh 1989), 148–9
11 J. P. Gillam, *Scottish Arch. Forum* vii (1975), 51–6

12 A further reason for their presence was the fact that this part of eastern Scotland contains some of the most productive land.
13 *RIB* 2034
14 *RIC* 930 & 934. These coins are common in Britain, very rare elsewhere.
15 B. R. Hartley, *Britannia* iii (1972), 15–42
16 M. Rostovtzeff, *Journal of Roman Studies* xiii (1923), 91–103

Bibliography

J. Collingwood Bruce, *Handbook to the Roman Wall* (13th. ed. rev. by C. M. Daniels Newcastle 1979)
D. J. Breeze & B. Dobson, *Hadrian's Wall* (London 1987)
D. J. Breeze, *The Northern Frontiers of Roman Britain* (London 1982)
E. Birley, *Research on Hadrian's Wall* (Kendal 1961)
I. A. Richmond (ed.), *Roman and Native in North Britain* (London 1958)
P. Holder, *The Army in Roman Britain* (London 1982)
Sir G. Macdonald, *The Roman Wall in Scotland* (2nd. ed. Oxford 1934)
W. S. Hanson & G. Maxwell, *Rome's North-West Frontier* (Edinburgh 1983)
G. Maxwell, *The Romans in Scotland* (Edinburgh 1989)
L. J. F. Keppie, 'The Antonine Wall, 1960–80', *Britannia* xiii (1982), 91–112
P. T. Bidwell, *Vindolanda* (London 1985)
J. Crow, *Housesteads* (London 1995)
M. Bishop & J. Dore, *Roman Corbridge. The Fort and Town* (London 1988)
J. S. Wacher, *The Towns of Roman Britain* (2nd. ed. London 1995)

Ancient sources

Ptolemy, *Geography* ii, 2–3
S. H. A. Hadrian 5, 11, 2
Fronto, *Letter to Marcus* 2
Dio, lxix, 13, 2; lxxi, 16, 2; lxxii, 8–9
S. H. A. Antoninus 5, 4
S. H. A. M. Antoninus 8, 4–8
S. H. A. Commodus 6, 1–2; 8, 4–5; 13, 5
S. H. A. Pertinax 3
S. H. A. Clodius Albinus 13

Chapter 8 *Propagator Imperii*

1 Dio lxxiii, 15, 1–2

2 A. R. Birley, *Septimius Severus. The African Emperor* (London 1971), 179–89
3 B. R. Hartley, *Northern History* i (1966), 18–20; D. J. Breeze & B. Dobson, *Hadrian's Wall* (3rd. ed. London, 1987), 133–8
4 *RIB* 637 (Ilkley); 730 (Bowes); 757 (Brough); 1163 (Corbridge)
5 Dio lxxv, 5, 4
6 D. J. Breeze & B. Dobson, *Hadrian's Wall* (3rd. ed. London 1987),
7 *Journal of Roman Studies* li (1961), 192
8 *RIB* 627
9 V. E. Nash-Williams, *The Roman Frontier in Wales* (2nd. ed. Cardiff, 1969), 22–7
10 Dio lxxvi, 10, 6
11 C. Iulius Septimius Castinus, possibly a kinsman of the emperor.
12 *ILS* 429 & 430
13 *RIB* 1234 & 1462
14 J. N. Dore & J. P. Gillam, *The Roman Fort at South Shields* (Newcastle 1979) 61–6
15 *Archaeologia Aeliana* 4 xxxvii (1959), 12–31; M. C. Bishop & J. N. Dore, *Corbridge. Excavations of the Roman Fort and Town* (London 1988) for plans.
16 Though not as high as the 50,000 quoted by Dio.
17 J. K. S. St. Joseph, *Journal of Roman Studies* lix (1969), 114–19; lxiii (1973), 230–3
18 J. D. Leach & J. J. Wilkes in *Limes* (Budapest 1978), 47–62
19 *Britannia* v (1974), 163–224
20 There is no evidence for a renewal of operations in or after 211.
21 J. C. Mann & M. G. Jarrett, *Journal of Roman Studies* lvii (1967), 61–4; S. S. Frere, *Britannia* (3rd. ed. London, 1987), 162–4

Bibliography

D. J. Breeze & B. Dobson, *Hadrian's Wall* (3rd. ed. London 1987)

A. R. Birley, *Septimius Severus. The African Emperor* (London 1971)

J. Casey, *Carausius and Allectus. The British Usurpers* (London 1994)

J. N. Dore & J. P. Gillam, *The Roman Fort at South Shields* (Newcastle 1979)

M. Bishop & J. Dore, *Roman Corbridge: the Fort and Town* (London 1988)

G. Maxwell, *The Romans in Scotland* (Edinburgh 1989)

N. J. Reed, 'The Scottish campaigns of Septimius Severus', *Procs. Soc. Antiquaries Scotland* cvii (1975–6), 92–102

J. K. S. St. Joseph, 'Air Reconnaissance in Roman Britain', *Journal of Roman Studies* lxiii (1973), 214–46

J. D. Leach & J. J. Wilkes, 'The Roman Military Base at Carpow', in J. Fitz, *Limes* (Budapest 1978), 47–62

R. P. Wright, 'Carpow and Caracalla', *Britannia* v (1974), 289–92

A. & V. Rae, 'The Roman Fort at Cramond', *Britannia* v (1974), 163–224
W. S. Hanson & G. Maxwell, *Rome's North-West Frontier* (Edinburgh 1983)

Ancient sources

S. H. A. Clodius Albinus 7–10
S. H. A. Septimius Severus 18, 2; 19, 1; 22, 4; 23, 3
Orosius vii, 17
Dio lxxiii, 15; lxxv, 4, 1; 5, 4; lxxvi, 10, 6; 11, 1; 12, 1–5; 13, 1–4; 15, 1–4; lxxvii, 1, 1
Herodian iii, 7, 1; 8, 2; 14, 1–10; 15, 1–6

Chapter 9 The Long Peace

1 *Procs. Soc. Antiquaries Scotland* lxviii (1933–4), 32–40; cxv (1985), 229–32
2 *CIL* xiii, 6592
3 *Archaeologia Aeliana* 5(1979), 127–43
4 *Antiquaries Journal* xli (1961), 224–8, but with revised reading.
5 B. Burnham & J. Wacher, *The Small Towns of Roman Britain* (London 1990)
6 *Journal of Roman Studies* xi (1921), 101; *CIL* xiii, 634
7 *Deae Nehalleniae* (Leiden 1971)
8 D. S. Neal, *The Excavation of the Roman Villa in Gadebridge Park* (London 1974); I. M. Stead, *Excavations at Winterton Roman Villa* (London 1976); D. S. Neal, A. Wardle & J. Hunn, *Excavation of the Iron Age, Roman and Medieval Settlement at Gorhambury, St. Albans* (London 1990)
9 A. L. F. Rivet, *The Roman Villa in Britain* (London 1969), 208–9; K. Branigan, *Trans. Bristol & Glos. Arch. Soc.* xcii (1973), 82–95
10 P. Salway, *The Frontier People of Roman Britain* (Cambridge 1965), 192–7
11 A. N. Sherwin-White, *The Roman Citizenship* (2nd. ed. Oxford 1973), 387–8
12 H-G. Pflaum, *Le Marbre de Thorigny* (Paris 1948); *CIL* xiii, 3162

Bibliography

P. Salway, *The Frontier People of Roman Britain* (Cambridge 1965)
H.-G. Pflaum, *Le Marbre de Thorigny* (Paris 1948)
R. Hingley, *Rural Settlement in Roman Britain* (London 1988)

B. Burnham & J. Wacher, *The Small Towns of Roman Britain* (London 1990)
M. Millett, *The Romanization of Roman Britain* (Cambridge 1990)
M. Henig, *Religion in Roman Britain* (London 1984)

Chapter 10 The Fourth-century Diocese

1 J. Casey, *Carausius and Allectus. The British Usurpers* (London 1994)
2 J. Casey, *Britannia* viii (1977), 283–301
3 S. Johnson, *The Roman Forts of the Saxon Shore* (London 1976), 23–33; V. Maxfield (ed.), *The Saxon Shore* (Exeter 1989).
4 M. W. C. Hassall in D. E. Johnston (ed.), *The Saxon Shore* (London 1977), 8–10 argues that some of the units listed in the *Notitia Dignitatum* may have been stationed in coastal forts from the late third century.
5 *RIB* 1912
6 D. J. Breeze & B. Dobson, *Hadrian's Wall* (3rd. ed. London, 1987), 214–16
7 J. Casey in J. Bird *et al* (eds.), *Collectanea Londiniensia* (London 1978), 181–93
8 C. Thomas, *Christianity in Roman Britain* (London 1981), 155–201 is a generous view.
9 S. S. Frere, *Archaeologia* cv (1975), 277–302
10 Unpublished in full. K. Painter, *The Water Newton Early Christian Silver* (London 1977)
11 G. W. Meates, *The Roman Villa at Lullingstone, Kent II* (Maidstone 1987), 11–39
12 J. M. C. Toynbee, *Journal of Roman Studies* liv (1964), 7–14
13 A. Woodward, *The Uley Shrines* (London 1993)
14 *RIB* 103 This may be a general reaction to new practices rather than against Christianity specifically
15 C. Johns & T. Potter, *The Thetford Treasure* (London 1983)
16 S. S. Frere, *Britannia* suggests that Constans' visit may have been connected with unrest in the island over the murder of Constantine II.
17 Ammianus Marcellinus xx, 1; xxvi, 4, 5
18 R. S. O. Tomlin, *Britannia* v (1974), 303–9 on the chronology of these operations.
19 K. Branigan in K. Branigan & P. J. Fowler (eds.), *The Roman West Country* (Newton Abbot 1976), 136–9
20 Ammianus Marcellinus xxviii, 3, 15

Bibliography

J. Casey, *Carausius and Allectus: the British Usurpers* (London 1994)
N. Shiel, *The Episode of Carausius and Allectus* (Oxford 1977)

S. Esmonde-Cleary, *The Ending of Roman Britain* (London 1989)
J. Matthews, *The Roman Empire of Ammianus* (London 1988)
C. Thomas, *Christianity in Roman Britain* (London 1981)
A. L. F. Rivet (ed.), *The Roman Villa in Britain* (London 1969)
M. Todd, *Studies in the Romano-British Villa* (Leicester 1978)
S. Johnson, *The Roman Forts of the Saxon Shore* (London 1976)
D. E. Johnston (ed.), *The Saxon Shore* (London 1977)
M. Henig, *The Art of Roman Britain* (London 1995)
J. S. Wacher, *The Towns of Roman Britain* (2nd. ed. London 1995)

Ancient sources

Eutropius, *Epitome* ix, 21–2
Eumenius, *Panegyric on Constantius Caesar* 12, 1–17; 19, 1
Anon, *Panegyric on Constantine* 5, 1; 7, 1
Ammianus Marcellinus xiv, 5, 6–9; xviii, 2, 3; xx, 1, 1–3; xxvi, 4, 5; xxvii, 8, 1–10; xxviii, 3, 1–9; xxix, 4, 7
Vegetius, *On Military Matters* iv, 37

Chapter 11 *Nostro Diducta Britannia Mundo*

1 J. Matthews, *Western Aristocracies and Imperial Court* AD 364–425 (Oxford 1975), 173–82
2 Claudian, *de laudibus Stilichonis* ii, 247–55; iii, 138–60. There must be serious doubt as to whether Stilicho pursued any military objectives in Britain.
3 J. N. L. Myres, *Journal of Roman Studies* 1 (1960), 21–36 gives a misleading account of Pelagianism in late Roman Britain. Better studies of the heresy are: P. Brown, *Journal of Theological Studies* xix (1968), 93–114; W. Liebeschuetz, *Latomus* xxvi (1967), 436–47 and *Historia* xii (1973), 227–41.
4 J. Matthews, *Western Aristocracies and Imperial Court*, AD 364–425 (Oxford 1975), 307–14; E. A. Thompson, *Britannia* viii (1977), 303–18. P. Bartholemew, *Britannia* xiii (1982), 261–70; I. Wood, *Britannia* xviii (1987), 251–62
5 Zosimus vi, 5, 2–4
6 Zosimus vi, 10, 2. There has been much discussion as to whether this passage refers to Bruttium or Britain. The latter is assumed here, but the point is debatable.
7 The notion of an appeal from the Britons to Rome was accepted by Mommsen, ignored by Bury (*History of the Later Roman Empire* [London, 1923]) and Haverfield (*The Roman Occupation of Britain* [Oxford 1924]) but given further currency by Collingwood (*Roman*

Britain and the English Settlements [Oxford 1937], 291–2), who also invented a 'protestation of loyalty'.

8 J. S. Wacher, *The Towns of Roman Britain* (2nd. ed. London 1995), 408–21; S. Esmonde-Cleary, *The Ending of Roman Britain* (London 1989), 144–55

9 Bede, *Ecclesiastical History* iv, 19

10 Bede, *Ecclesiastical History* ii, 16

11 E. A. Thompson, *St. Germanus of Auxerre and the End of Roman Britain* (Woodbridge 1984), 49–51; P. Barker, *Excavations in the Baths Basilica* (Wroxeter, 1996).

12 H. W. Böhme, 'Das Ende der Römerherrschaft in Britannien und die angelsächsische Besiedlung Englands im 5 Jahrhundert', *Jahrbuch Römisches Zentralmuseum Mainz* xxxiii (1986), 469–574

13 H. W. Böhme, *Germanische Grabfunde des 4 bis 5 Jahrhunderts* (Munich 1974)

14 S. C. Hawkes & G. C. Dunning, *Medieval Archaeology* v (1961), 1–70; G. C. Clarke, *The Roman Cemetery at Lankhills* (Oxford 1979)

15 H. Hamerow, *Excavations at Mucking. Volume 2. The Anglo-Saxon Settlement* (London 1993)

16 The attempt by H. P. R. Finberg, *Roman and Saxon Withington* (Leicester 1955), based on charter evidence and local topography was not wholly successful, but the approach was right in principle.

17 W. Davies, *An early Welsh Microcosm* (London 1978); *The Llandaff Charters* (Cardiff 1979)

18 Orton Longueville: D. F. Mackreth in M. Todd (ed.), *Studies in the Romano-British Villa* (Leicester 1978), 209–29; Shakenoak: A. C. C. Brodribb, A. R. Hands & D. R. Walker, *Excavations at Shakenoak Farm* I (1968); III (1972); IV (1973); V (1978); Barton Court Farm: D. Miles (ed.), *Archaeology at Barton Court Farm* (London 1986)

19 H. C. Bowen, *The Archaeology of Bokerly Dyke* (London 1990)

20 R. A. G. Carson, 'Gold and Silver Coin-hoards and the End of Roman Britain', in *The Classical Tradition* (London 1976), 67–82

21 C. Johns, *The Hoxne Treasure* (London 1994)

22 K. Cameron *et al.*, *Journal of English Place-Name Society* xii (1978–9), 1–53

Bibliography

S. Esmonde-Cleary, *The Ending of Roman Britain* (London 1989)

P. J. Casey (ed.), *The End of Roman Britain* (Oxford 1979)

L. Alcock, *Arthur's Britain* (London 1971)

C. Thomas, *Christianity in Roman Britain* (London 1981)

E. A. Thompson, *St. Germanus of Auxerre and the End of Roman Britain* (Woodbridge 1984)

J. Matthews, *Western Aristocracies and Imperial Court*, AD *364–425* (Oxford 1975)

H. W. Böhme, *Germanische Grabfunde des 4 bis 5 Jahrhunderts zwischen unterer Elbe und Loire* (Munich 1974)

D. Hoffmann, *Die Notitia Dignitatum und die spätrömische Bewegungsheer* (Düsseldorf 1969)

R. Goodburn & P. Bartholemew (eds.), *Aspects of the Notitia Dignitatum* (Oxford 1976)

Ancient sources

Orosius vii, 34, 9; 40, 4
Claudian, *On the Consulship of Stilicho* ii, 247–55
Claudian, *On the Gothic War* 404–18
Zosimus iv, 35, 2; vi, 2, 1; vi, 5, 2; vi, 10, 2
Procopius, *The Vandal War* 1, 2, 37
Gildas, *On the Ruin of Britain* 13–20
Bede, *Ecclesiastical History* 1, 11

General Bibliography

A select list of books

A. R. Birley, *Life in Roman Britain* (London 1964)
A. R. Birley, *The Fasti of Roman Britain* (Oxford 1981)
E. Birley, *Roman Britain and the Roman Army* (2nd ed. Kendal 1961)
E. Birley, *Research on Hadrian's Wall* (Kendal 1961)
A. K. Bowman, *Life and Letters on the Roman Frontier* (London 1994)
A. K. Bowman & J. D. Thomas, *The Vindolanda Writing Tablets* (London 1994)
D. J. Breeze, *The Northern Frontiers of Roman Britain* (London 1982)
D. J. Breeze & B. Dobson, *Hadrian's Wall* (3rd ed. London 1987)
R. G. Collingwood & I. A. Richmond, *The Archaeology of Roman Britain* (2nd ed. London 1969)
R. G. Collingwood & R. P. Wright, *The Roman Inscriptions of Britain I The Inscriptions on Stone* (Stroud 1995) *II* (eds. S. S. Frere *et al.*) (Stroud 1990–95)
J. Collis, *Oppida* (Sheffield 1984)
B. Cunliffe, *Greeks, Romans and Barbarians* (London 1988)
B. Cunliffe, *Iron Age Communities in Britain* (3rd ed. London 1991)
S. Esmonde-Cleary, *The Ending of Roman Britain* (London 1989)
S. S. Frere, *Britannia. A History of Roman Britain* (3rd ed. London 1987)
S. J. Greep (ed.), *Roman Towns: the Wheeler Inheritance* (London 1993)
W. S. Hanson, *Agricola and the Conquest of the North* (London 1987)
W. S. Hanson & G. S. Maxwell, *Rome's North-West Frontier* (Edinburgh 1982)
F. Haverfield, *The Romanization of Roman Britain* (4th ed. Oxford 1923)
M. Henig, *Religion in Roman Britain* (London 1984)
M. Henig, *The Art of Roman Britain* (London 1995)
K. Jackson, *Language and History in Early Britain* (Edinburgh 1953)
M. Jones, *England before Domesday* (London 1986)
J. C. Mann & R. G. Penman (eds.), *Literary Sources for Roman Britain* (London 1977)
G. Maxwell, *The Romans in Scotland* (Edinburgh 1989)
G. Maxwell, *A Battle Lost* (Edinburgh 1990)
M. Millett, *The Romanization of Roman Britain* (Cambridge 1990)
M. Millett, *Roman Britain* (London 1995)

R. M. Ogilvie & I. A. Richmond (eds.), *The Agricola of Tacitus* (Oxford 1967)
Ordnance Survey, *Map of Roman Britain* (4th ed. London 1979)
I. A. Richmond (ed.), *Roman and Native in North Britain* (London 1958)
I. A. Richmond, *Roman Britain* (3rd ed. London 1995)
RCHM (England), *Roman Camps in England* (London 1995)
A. L. F. Rivet, *Town and Country in Roman Britain* (2nd ed. London 1964)
A. L. F. Rivet (ed.), *The Roman Villa in Britain* (London 1969)
A. L. F. Rivet & C. Smith, *The Place-Names of Roman Britain* (London 1979)
P. Salway, *Roman Britain* (Oxford 1981)
P. Salway, *The Oxford Illustrated History of Roman Britain* (Oxford 1994)
C. Thomas, *Christianity in Roman Britain* (London 1981)
E. A. Thompson, *St. Germanus of Auxerre and the End of Roman Britain* (Woodbridge 1984)
M. Todd (ed.), *Research on Roman Britain, 1960–1989* (London 1989)
J. M. C. Toynbee, *Art in Britain under the Romans* (Oxford 1964)
J. S. Wâcher, *The Towns of Roman Britain* (2nd ed. London 1995)
G. Webster (ed.), *Fortress into City. The Consolidation of Roman Britain* (London 1988)

Index